Changing English Primary Schools?

The Impact of the Education Reform Act at Key Stage One

Andrew Pollard, Patricia Broadfoot, Paul Croll, Marilyn Osborn and Dorothy Abbott

CASSELL

Cassell
Villiers House
41/47 Strand
London WC2N 5JE

387 Park Avenue South
New York
NY 10016–8810

First published 1994

British Library Cataloguing-in-Publication Data
A catalogue record for this book is available from the British Library.

ISBN 0–304–32921–5 (hardback)
    0–304–32923–1 (paperback)

Typeset by Colset Private Limited, Singapore
Printed and bound in Great Britain by
Redwood Books, Trowbridge, Wiltshire

Contents

Preface

The manuscript of this book was completed in late June 1993, at a time when the education policies of the British government, as they related to England and Wales, had been under sustained critique from many teachers, parents and industrialists. Pressure for change had been steadily building when, in the early summer of 1993, the Secretary of State for Education commissioned Sir Ron Dearing to conduct a 'review' of the National Curriculum and the assessment procedures associated with it. Meanwhile, it was apparent that a teacher boycott of National Curriculum assessment procedures was holding and that teachers in England and Wales did have the support of many parents in their objections to many of the new curricular and assessment requirements. We concluded our book, sending key parts for Sir Ron's consideration, but not knowing how these issues would be resolved, nor how the associated political forces would play themselves out.

As we write this preface, in January 1994 and with the final proofs about to go to the printers, a new situation is beginning to unfold. Sir Ron Dearing's final report was published ten days ago and has been accepted by the Government. The report recognizes the extent and complexity of the National Curriculum and assessment procedures and accepts that they have resulted in teacher overload, curriculum fragmentation and unmanageable assessment requirements. The statutory curriculum and the assessment requirements are to be scaled down through a 'closely coordinated review' which will be guided, among other things, by the need to 'reduce prescription so as to give more scope for professional judgement'. In the light of the evidence we present in this book, this is a wise policy change.

As our data and analysis show very clearly, primary school teachers in England have enormous commitment to the quality of educational provision and they support the principle of a national curriculum. For these reasons, it is likely that they will respond constructively to the new spirit of partnership. In any event, we hope that future phases of the PACE project will be able to record whatever developments occur.

We have not attempted to revise our text in the light of the Dearing Report and the book thus remains as we prepared it in the summer of 1993, with a strong sense of the historical significance of the issues and of the period. We hope that, as the first major

report of what is probably the largest independent research project on primary education of the early 1990s, the book will act both as a faithful record of the classroom
impact of the 1988 Education Reform Act and as a sound analysis of the key issues and
dilemmas which it raised for teachers. As a case-study of national policy making and
its impact, it has lessons of relevance far beyond the shores of the UK.

Andrew Pollard, Patricia Broadfoot, Paul Croll, Marilyn Osborn and Dorothy Abbott
Bristol, January 1994

Acknowledgements

The research reported here was funded by a grant from the Economic and Social Research Council, R000231931. We are very grateful to the ESRC for its support and continued funding of the second phase of the study. We have also benefited from the comments and advice of the members of the ESRC panel who scrutinized the original proposal.

Crucial to the work of the project has been the cooperation of LEA officers, head-teachers, teachers and school pupils. The study has involved extensive interviews with heads, teachers and children, and substantial periods of time spent by members of the research team in classrooms and schools. We must express our gratitude for the cooperation of these schools and teachers and for the hospitable and open way in which we were made welcome. It is a tribute to the education service that, at a time of considerable pressure and increased workloads, so many headteachers and teachers were prepared to open their practice to scrutiny and give their time to answer our questions. The interest that was shown in the research, and the thoughtful and concerned way in which teachers and heads reflected on educational issues, made data collection both enjoyable and instructive.

A large number of colleagues at the University of the West of England, Bristol, and the University of Bristol, as well as members of our Federated Research Network and many others elsewhere, have provided advice and support. We thank Pat Abbott, Sandra Acker, Robin Alexander, Siamak Alimi, Angela Auset, Bridget Baines, Neville Bennett, Edie Black, Jill Bourne, Margaret Brown, Jim Campbell, Sue Cavendish, Sarah Delamont, Chan Kim Fook, Clive Carré, Farouk Chudry, Patsy Daniels, Sandra Daniels, Nona Dawson, Tony Edwards, Rita Egan, Susan Elliott, Ann Filer, Marion Gatrell, Caroline Gipps, John Gray, David Halpin, Linda Hargreaves, Cathie Holden, Martin Hughes, Pat Keele, Val Kitchen, Ann Lance, Jenny Lansdell, Martin Lawn, Ann Lewis, Bet McCallum, Ian Menter, Yolande Muschamp, Jennifer Nias, Jenny Noble, Oz Osborn, Cristabel Owens, Jenny Ozga, Angie Packwood, Clare Planel, Ian Plewis, Ros Pollard, Sally Power, Colin Richards, Pam Sammons, Diane Shorrocks, Christine Stone, Kathy Sylva, Mike Wallace, Rosemary Webb, Anne West, Penelope Weston, Geoff Whitty, Pearl Wilson and Ted Wragg for their interest in and support of the study.

Finally, we should like to thank the secretarial team who have facilitated the research since 1989 and so efficiently coped with the production of the typescript of this book. Jacquie Harrison, Viki Davies, Sarah Butler, Jenny Wills, Elspeth Gray, Maite Ridley and Sheila Taylor have all made important contributions to the research process and to this book, for which we want to express our appreciation.

Chapter 1

An Introduction to the Issues

When future historians seek to identify the English educational landmarks of the twentieth century, there can be little doubt that they will readily agree on the 1988 Education Reform Act as one of the most significant. It is likely to take its place alongside such educational milestones as the creation of local education authorities in 1902, the provision for universal secondary education under the Butler Act of 1944 and the institution of a policy of comprehensive secondary provision following Circular 7/63. What makes these particular pieces of legislation worthy of being regarded as landmarks in the educational landscape is their enduring influence on the shape and quality of educational provision in the years that followed.

That influence was only partly a function of the scale of the changes that were provided for in the legislation. It was also arguably just as much a function of how far the changes introduced were in keeping with the spirit of the times, embodying ideas and principles that had a wider contemporary currency. Thus, for example, the creation of a national system of educational provision based on local funding and control at the beginning of the century was entirely in keeping with more general ideas about government that had developed in England during the nineteenth century and with contemporary fears that a centrally run education system might be appropriated for ideological purposes (Silver, 1980).

By the same token, the 1944 Education Act was both a reflection of the demand for increased educational opportunity, which had been fuelled by the Second World War, and a recognition that more needed to be made of the available 'pool of ability'. It reflected a movement that was to result in the mass provision of secondary education in many countries of the world at that time. Twenty years later, against the growing volume of evidence attesting to the inaccuracies and wastage of the tripartite system, and in keeping with the widespread commitment to providing equality of opportunity, the momentous decision was finally taken to make a commitment to non-selective secondary educational provision.

Twenty-five years further on again, in the late 1980s, the dominant educational concerns were very different. Gone were the concerns with equality and social engineering that characterized the immediate post-war years. Gone was the easy trust in English education that underlay so many of the twentieth-century initiatives in educational provision. In its place, across Europe and the developed world, were attitudes born of the economic crises of the 1970s, of structural unemployment and declining international competitiveness. In Britain as in many other developed countries, the 1970s had seen the rapid rise of monetarist theories. The advent of the Thatcher administration in 1979, which brought with it a radical commitment to market ideologies and the power of competition, was to be felt in every area of state provision. The Government's need to make economies in national expenditure, which was translated into legislation to provide for increased central control of the education system, was also linked to its desire to determine educational goals in line with perceived national economic priorities. It found further expression in the explosion of accountability mechanisms to ensure value for money within state-funded services.

The 1988 Education Reform Act was a classic manifestation of the prevailing political climate in its explicit commitment to market forces and competition as a means of increasing educational productivity. In place of the broad consensus concerning education that had characterized the post-war decades, both the spirit of the changes provided for in the 1988 Act and the heavy-handed character of their implementation led inevitably to open hostility between government and educational professionals – a pattern mirrored in other countries, most notably New Zealand, where government sought to impose a market ideology on the educational system.

If it is easy for historians to account for major pieces of legislation in terms of the prevailing political *Zeitgeist*, the luxury of such dispassionate analyses is not available to those caught up with the effects of such changes: the teachers, pupils and administrators who must perforce adapt to the changes being imposed upon them. These are the people at the 'sharp end' – the people who, whether or not they are in sympathy with the avowed purpose of the legislation, find their working day the arena in which such policies will ultimately be realized. Change is never without pain. Even late-twentieth-century society, accustomed to increasingly rapid change as virtually the only constant of existence, does not easily throw off long-held ideals or the hard-won lessons of experience. Against the security of the known and the familiar, the education system finds itself obliged to engage with new, and in some cases alien, practices, their worth still untested, their essentially political provenance highly dubious from a professional perspective.

It is in this turbulent climate of conflicting perspectives and desires, prejudice and assumption that our study found its rationale. In the wake of the momentous and detailed changes that the 1988 Education Reform Act had set in motion, there was an urgent need for dispassionate enquiry into the process, the progress and the effects of change. For government there ought to be a pressing desire to learn in detail how the actual realization of its policies compares to their avowed purpose. For teachers and other education professionals there is a need to take stock, to interrogate evidence on which to base future judgements about support, adaptation or opposition to change. Ultimately, all such decisions should depend on the effect on pupils themselves: their perceived happiness, their enthusiasm for learning and, above all, the level and range of their achievements.

As if this were not in itself already a big enough research agenda, for researchers such as ourselves must be added the more general desire to understand how change takes place. We wished to learn more general insights from this particular innovation about how change can most effectively be managed and thus how best to develop the education system.

It was with all these ends in view that the Primary Assessment Curriculum and Experience (PACE) project was set up in late 1989. Funded by the Economic and Social Research Council, the project represents an independent enquiry into some of the momentous changes that were even then beginning to impact on the education system following the passing of the 1988 Act. We chose to study primary schools, partly to build on existing expertise and research data that members of the team already possessed, and partly because it was in Key Stage 1, the infant school, that the implementation of the National Curriculum and its assessment were scheduled to begin. We wanted to describe and analyse the responses of pupils and teachers in infant schools and departments to the National Curriculum, to collect views from headteachers and teachers concerning what was being proposed and what they thought its likely impact would be, and to explore the kinds of strategies schools were evolving to manage the changes impacting upon them. In particular, we wanted to discover how classroom life in infant schools might change or develop in terms of teaching method, time spent on different subjects and curriculum emphasis.

We still know relatively little about life in infant schools – particularly from the pupils' point of view. This is partly because of the difficulty of collecting data from five-, six- and seven-year-olds. Yet we felt that it was vital to examine how the requirements of the National Curriculum, expressed in terms of attainment targets, programmes of study and formal assessment, might be changing the nature of the educational experience that these young children encounter. In each of the core curriculum subjects of maths, science and English, five-year-olds started work on the programmes of study in September 1989, and we began to track the progress of these children. Thus our study has been able to monitor the impact of these new provisions from the outset, capturing the changes year by year as children move through the system.

The Education Reform Act provided for a range of changes that have affected schools directly. These included increasing the accountability of teachers through strengthening the powers of parents and governors, providing stronger management structures in schools, backed by procedures for teacher appraisal, and encouraging school-based decision-making through the introduction of devolved budgets. Coupled with this, the introduction of open enrolment further strengthened parents' potential power. All these changes were intended to lead to higher standards of pupil attainment coupled with more cost-effective and efficient schools. Whether this was in fact their effect, whether there were any associated unforeseen consequences, was one of the urgent and important questions that the PACE study set out to answer.

One of the issues we were particularly keen to explore was the effect of a climate of increased competitiveness on the pupils themselves. Supporters of the ideas behind the 1988 Act anticipated a positive impact of the changes it provided for. This, it was thought, would occur as a result of the provision of clearer targets for teachers to use as the basis for directing children's learning and the availability of assessment evidence concerning their progress. Critics of the Act feared that the climate of explicit assessment and school accountability, based on the published results of national assessment, would result in a narrowing of the curriculum and some pupils feeling a sense of failure and demoralization. We wanted to discover whether such pressures on teachers were being translated into a classroom environment in which children felt more constrained and were more conscious than before of their relative standing in terms of achievement. If so, we wondered if this in turn would be reflected in their approach to learning.

Teachers are clearly at the centre of all educational provision, and the implementation of any new and externally driven policy will inevitably be mediated by the enthusiasms, skills and practical constraints that characterize every teacher's daily practice. However, this process of translation was likely to be deeply problematic where, as in this case, much of the thinking behind the changes being put in place was rooted in a very different political ideology from that which had characterized educational policy-making and practice in England for many decades. Not only were teachers asked to change their daily practice in some quite fundamental ways, they were also being asked to change in ways that for many of them were in fundamental conflict with deeply held professional convictions concerning how best to provide for the learning of young children. Nowhere was this more obvious than in the issue of assessment and, in particular, the requirement to undertake Standard Assessment Tasks (SATs) to generate explicit, classificatory and detailed data on each child's achievements. Apart from the enormous extra workload for teachers that was inevitably associated with this new responsibility, the obligation to undertake the national assessments and the associated recording requirements arguably represented the most novel and potentially alien part of the 1988 Act's requirements. It was thus vital that the PACE project should include, as part of its overall consideration of changes in teachers' practice and pupils' classroom experience, an explicit concern with the effect of the new assessment and reporting requirements.

The PACE study set out to map these complex and interconnected aspects of the changes that have been taking place in infant schools since 1988. Its goal, however, goes beyond simply describing what is happening in a systematic and detached manner, important though this is. Although much of this volume is dedicated to reporting what we have discovered about the changes that have characterized life in English primary schools following the Education Reform Act, part of it is also concerned with a more theoretical attempt to understand and explain the changes taking place within a broader framework of social scientific enquiry. Thus we have sought to use appropriate theories and models generated from other research in other contexts and in other countries to help us understand the reactions we have documented and to explore their potential significance. A wide range of work has been drawn on, spanning fields as diverse as policy implementation, teacher professionalism and the management of change, theories of learning and pupil identity, curriculum codes and teaching strategies. We thus hope that the PACE project will make a contribution to our collective understanding of the nature of the complex web of social forces in which policy-makers, teachers, pupils and other educational professionals and consumers are inextricably enmeshed, and will highlight ways in which different aspects of this intricate reality ultimately impact on the quality of learning, which must remain its fundamental goal. Long after the ripples of the short-term reactions to change have been forgotten and the more enduring effects of the Act have become incorporated as unremarked features of the professional landscape, this book will remain as a case study of educational change, one of many stepping stones in the quest to understand the nature of the educational enterprise and, hence, how to provide for it most effectively.

The organization of the book reflects our dual commitment both to mapping the changes that have taken place in infant schools since the 1988 Act and to exploring their significance in terms of more gereral theoretical insights. Indeed, the structure of this volume is itself a manifestation of the central strategy of our research: that we should try to capture holistically the nature of the changes currently affecting infant schools in order that we may understand the interrelationship of different elements. The situation we are studying is certainly one of multiple innovation (Wallace, 1991), in which the effects of many different changes being implemented simultaneously are doubly unpredictable because of their potential interaction with each other. However, for the sake of presentational clarity, the major elements of change with which we are concerned have been separated out in the book in terms of school-level reactions to change, teachers' responses, curriculum, pedagogy and assessment.

Thus, following an historical chapter, Chapter 2, which describes the context leading up to the 1988 Act, Chapter 3 sets out an analytic framework. This provides a common interpretive structure for the separate analyses of various aspects of change that make up the main part of the book. Chapter 4 describes the details of how we collected our data, reconciling the rival demands of the need for both in-depth understanding of particular classrooms and a representative national sample.

Chapter 5 provides the first of our empirical chapters, describing the various strategies that schools used to implement the changes impacting upon them and the particular perspectives of headteachers in this respect. Chapter 6 explores various aspects of teachers' responses, detailing how teachers felt their practice had actually changed, and relating this to teachers' professional ideology and personal priorities.

Chapters 7 to 10 are all concerned with describing what our classroom studies data can tell us about the changes that have actually taken place, based as they are on a combination of detailed observation and interviews with pupils and teachers. In this respect they complement the data reported in earlier chapters, documenting what teachers perceived to have been the main changes. The first two of the chapters in this section concern curriculum changes, such as the amount of time given to different subjects. They document the way in which National Curriculum requirements were realized by teachers and experienced by pupils. Chapters 9 and 10 explore the related issue of teaching method, of pedagogy, again both in terms of changes in teachers' practice and regarding what this may have meant for pupils, in terms of, for example, their degree of engagement in learning, their classroom relationships and experiences.

Chapters 11 and 12 address the closely related topic of assessment. Chapter 11 documents how teachers and pupils in infant classrooms felt about continuous, formative assessment and the ways in which national assessment requirements have brought about changes in teachers' perspectives and practice. Chapter 12, by contrast, explores issues for both teachers and pupils in the controversial implementation of Standard Assessment Tasks for seven-year-olds at the end of Key Stage 1.

No study of this kind would be complete without some attempt to understand the historical, political and educational significance of the data reported. Chapter 13 revisits the theoretical framework introduced in Chapter 3 to summarize and interpret the complex picture of stasis and change, excitement and anxiety, success and failure that our data depict.

If, in conclusion, we can only say that 'the jury is still out', our readers will not be surprised. Indeed, many of those in schools will be only too aware of the continuing pace of educational changes as successive waves of amendments to the original provisions of the 1988 Education Reform Act are made.

It is partly for this reason that we have sought to continue our study and will continue to track our cohort of children through their junior schools at least to the age of nine in the second phase of the PACE research, while also continuing to monitor more general changes in infant schools. However, it is also probable that it is still too early to capture many of the more profound and long-term effects of the changes that have taken place. We hope, therefore, that a third stage of funding will allow us to follow these children until the end of their primary school education, thus yielding the unique insights of a longitudinal study of the first group of pupils to experience fully the effects of the 1988 Act.

Meanwhile, we hope that those reading this book will find data and analyses that are of interest. Our greatest aspiration is that it will help to focus attention on the questions that need to be asked, concerning how best to provide for the education of young children into the next century.

Chapter 2

Echoes of the Past

2.1 INTRODUCTION

In this chapter we set the scene for the rest of the book by highlighting some origins and key features of the major beliefs and practices that influence modern primary education. In an eclectic foray through the educational history of England, we will show how recent debates revisit those of the past and how enduring dilemmas have been re-solved and new priorities set by the decisions of different generations of policy-makers. In so doing, we will trace how changes in national circumstances and in the balance of power and influence between central government, local government, schools and teachers are reflected in educational policies for primary school teaching and in the role of the teaching profession.

The chapter is in five main sections. Sections 2.2 and 2.3 trace the influence of two of the major traditions in primary education (Blyth, 1965): the elementary and the developmental. We see echoes of the former in many recent government initiatives and legislation, and developmentalism, in its 'child-centred' manifestation, retains its place as a focus for much recent critique. Perhaps aspects of the preparatory school tradition are also gaining ground, and we will discuss this possibility in the conclusion to the book. Section 2.4 is concerned with the emergent form of teacher professionalism, which, we believe, has been developing from the late 1970s and which, though offering a great deal for the development of educational quality, is very much challenged by recent innovations. Section 2.5 reviews the nature and sources of the critique of primary education since the late 1960s, while section 2.6 elaborates the main features of the Education Reform Act 1988 and some succeeding legislation.

2.2 REVISITING ELEMENTARY EDUCATION?

The 1988 Education Reform Act is often referred to as the most radical restructuring of British education since R. A. Butler's 1944 Education Act. However, its effects on the subjective experience of those who work in schools have arguably been far more drastic than those of the 1944 Act. The latter was planned in a spirit of optimism and cross-party cooperation towards the end of the Second World War. In contrast, the debate that preceded Kenneth Baker's 1988 Act resonates not with the post-war climate of optimism and consensus but with the anxieties about Britain's place in the world that were expressed in the nineteenth century during the slow and hesitant shaping of universal elementary education.

Should children in British schools be taught a curriculum prescribed by central government? How often should children's learning be tested? Does the country get value for money from education? Will the skills and knowledge imparted to pupils in our schools equip them for their future roles at work? Will the country fall further behind its main industrial competitors because of the superior training of foreign workforces? How far should the curriculum reflect traditional culture? Such questions could be dated within the past two decades or a century or so earlier. Thus W. E. Forster, introducing the 1870 Education Bill, spoke in the House of Commons of 'covering the country with good schools', because 'Upon the speedy provision of elementary education depends our industrial prosperity . . . uneducated labourers – and many of our labourers are utterly uneducated – are for the most part unskilled . . . [and] will become over-matched in the competition of the world (Forster, 1869). One hundred and twenty years later, John Banham, of the Confederation of British Industry, called for an extension of education in the UK, with a heavy emphasis on training:

> There is no shortage of challenges . . . Even the Japanese are looking anxiously at the economics of South East Asia – South Korea, Taiwan, Singapore and Hong Kong . . . we have a very serious and a continuing skills gap. A gap that because of the inadequacies of our education and training system over decades will need to be grappled with in the period ahead.
>
> (Banham, 1990)

And when Stuart Sexton, of the Institute of Economic Affairs, discussed the 'inefficient use of the already large sum spent' (Sexton, 1987, p. 6), his was one of many recent statements that echoed earlier concerns, such as those of the 1858 Newcastle Commission into the extension of 'sound and cheap elementary education'.

In contrast to this long-running concern for value for money, there was no talk of teacher autonomy in the 1850s. Indeed, the views of elementary school teachers were not likely to be thought worthy of consideration; such teachers were, according to Evans (1975, p. 122), usually recruited from the working classes. Hurt (1979, p. 179) shows that teachers in small rural schools were often paid less than manual workers; village school teachers' posts were sometimes advertised together with work for a brother as an outdoor or indoor servant.

Distinction between social classes and the unequal distribution of power and resources

Table 2.1 *Requirements for annual examination, Revised Code of 1862: by standards*

Reading
I Narrative monosyllables.
II One of the narratives next in order after monosyllables in a reading book used in the school.
III Short paragraph from a reading book used in the school.
IV Short paragraph from a more advanced reading book used in the school.
V A few lines of poetry from a reading book used in the first class of the school.
VI Short ordinary paragraph in a newspaper or other modern narrative.

Writing
I Form on blackboard or slate, from dictation, capital, small, and manuscript letters.
II Copy in manuscript character a line of print.
III A sentence from the same paragraph slowly read once and then dictated in single words.
IV A sentence slowly dictated once by a few words at a time, from the same book, but not from the paragraph read.
V A sentence slowly dictated once, by a few words at a time, from a reading book used in the first class of the school.
VI Another short ordinary paragraph in a newspaper, or other modern narrative, slowly dictated once by a few words at a time.

Arithmetic
I Form on blackboard or slate, from dictation, figures up to 20: name at sight figures up to 20: add and subtract figures up to 10, orally, from examples on blackboard.
II A sum in simple addition or subtraction, and the multiplication table.
III A sum in any simple rule as far as short division inclusive.
IV A sum in compound rules (money).
V A sum in compound rules (common weights and measures).
VI A sum in practice or bills of parcels.

were to be rigorously maintained. Thus the radical recommendation of the 1868 Taunton Commission for a universally available, national system of education, free to those who could not afford to pay, was thrown out, having enraged the headmasters of the privately run 'public schools', which would have been integrated into the system. 'For a moment the heart leaps', wrote Gathorne-Hardy (1977, p. 109), speculating on the difference such sweeping away of privilege and differentiation might have made to the country. However, social differentiation was built into the system from its beginning, and has, of course, remained.

The job of the elementary school teacher for most of the nineteenth century was to deliver the curriculum specified by Parliament. The Newcastle Commissioners were not ambitious, agreeing with one of their number, James Fraser: 'We must make up our minds to see the last of [the peasant boy] at 10 or 11 . . . it is quite possible to teach [him] all that is necessary . . . by the time that he is ten years old' (Fraser, 1861, p. 243). The curriculum was structured by 'standards' and concentrated narrowly on 'the basics' (see Table 2.1).

Robert Lowe's 1862 Revised Code managed to combine central control of what was taught with strict economy. Children over the age of six would be tested annually on this basic curriculum. Grants to schools, and thereby teachers' already small salaries, would be cut if standards were not deemed satisfactory by the school inspectors. Lowe's boast to the House of Commons that the system would be efficient if not cheap and cheap if not efficient has resounded through the years. The stultifying and stress-inducing effects of the Revised Code's notorious system of 'payment by results' were persistently documented, most influentially perhaps by Matthew Arnold (1889). Its grip was gradually loosened, although there is little evidence of much subsequent liberalization of the curriculum (Dent, 1970, p. 18).

Looking back from a hundred years later, it is noticeable that never since the mid-1800s had the idea of nationally planned testing of seven-year-olds been advocated, until the debate over the Education Reform Bill began in 1987. Arguments of the 1950s and 1960s about the 11 plus exam centred on the benefits that abolition of such testing would bring in the shape of broader and more exciting teaching. It would be difficult to exaggerate the incredulity that would have followed any suggestion of returning to testing at seven.

Significantly, the 1944 Education Act emphasized pupils' age, abilities and aptitudes as the relevant factors in determining their education. It omitted any mention of what children were to be taught, apart from religious education and the specification of a daily act of communal worship. However, in the post-war years, just as the existence of the School Certificate examination exerted control over the grammar school curriculum, so in the newly named 'primary schools' the 11 plus selection system had its own effect. Whatever the rhetoric about parity of esteem of secondary modern, technical and grammar school education, primary schools were largely judged by parents on their success rate in achieving grammar school 'passes' for their pupils. Although the type of examination varied in different LEAs, it resulted in a heavy concentration on the teaching of maths and English, not to mention coaching for the 'verbal reasoning' paper, which was taken as an indicator of innate 'intelligence'. To these were added other traditional elements of earlier curricula: history, geography, some music, art and religious instruction.

Thus, although the primary school class-teacher and the individual school had considerably less autonomy than is sometimes assumed, scope for independent judgement grew enormously with the gradual phasing out of the 11 plus and the broadening of expectations that accompanied the spread of comprehensive secondary education.

2.3 EXCURSIONS INTO CHILD-CENTRED EDUCATION?

The late 1960s and the 1970s saw the end of consensus on the curriculum. Oversimplifying, it could be said that the argument polarized on the debate about child-centred education and a perceived over-compensating trend away from the rigid and narrow legacy of the elementary system.

The values attached to child-centred perspectives have a history far longer than that of universal education in this country. Although a detailed examination would be out of place here, we can note that they are exemplified in the Romantic poets' view of childhood, 'trailing clouds of glory', and in the ideas of the Enlightenment philosopher Rousseau. Developed in the actual practice of Froebel and Pestalozzi, theories of child spontaneity, exploratory discovery and natural development entered the mainstream of education discourse.

Even in the nineteenth century, advocates of forms of child-centredness usually concentrated on highlighting the achievements of star practitioners. Thus the school started at King's Somborne by the local vicar and Cambridge graduate, Richard Dawes, was praised enthusiastically and in convincingly concrete terms by Matthew Arnold in his evidence to the Newcastle Commission and in his 1853 report. Here, pupils began their study of history by visiting historical sites, and nature study was linked to direct observation. What the unusually gifted individual can accomplish, however, can rarely become common practice, and when Edmond Holmes published his influential *What Is and What Might Be* in 1911, he made clear his view that the experience of most young children at school was closer to that of their Revised Code predecessors than to the pupils at King's Somborne:

> The excessive regard that has always been paid in our elementary schools to neat hand-writing and correct spelling is characteristic of the whole Western attitude towards education. No 'results' are more easily or more accurately appraised than these, and it follows that no 'results' are more highly esteemed by the unenlightened teacher . . . And in proportion, as we tend to value the results of education for their measurableness, so we tend to undervalue and at last to ignore those results which are too intrinsically valuable to be measured.

(Holmes, 1911, pp. 128–9)

Holmes compared the children in the average elementary school – listening, for example, 'with ill-concealed yawns, to *lectures* on history, geography, nature study and the rest' – to those in 'Utopia', the village school led by Harriet Finlay-Johnson. Naming her 'Egeria', Holmes held up this teacher for admiration. In her care the utopian child was

> alive, alert, active, full of latent energy, ready to act, to do things, to turn his mind to things, to turn his hand to things, to turn his desire to things, to turn his whole being to things . . . In Utopia the training which the child receives may be said to be based upon the doctrine of original goodness.

(Holmes, 1911, p. 155)

Others were less impressed by Egeria's achievements and, following a hauntingly familiar public outcry, Holmes was driven to publish a further volume, *In Defence of What Might Be* (Holmes, 1914). As he put it, 'The glowing account that I gave of Egeria and her school was bound to expose her and it to denigration' (Holmes, 1914, p. 333).

The 1931 Hadow Report demonstrated the hold that enlightened humanism had gained over discussions of the education of young children. In addition to its much quoted dictum that 'the curriculum of the primary school is to be thought of in terms of activity and experience, rather than of knowledge to be acquired and facts to be stored' (Board of Education, 1931, p. 93), the report discussed the importance of developing aesthetic sensibility, oral expression and manual skills, and the possibility of teaching by topics rather than by separate subjects.

What is noticeable, from a 1990s viewpoint, is the apparent absence at the time of contrary arguments. Selleck's (1972) close study of the growth of progressivism argued that reaction against the harsh control and narrow and depressing curriculum of the elementary system was so strong that any contrary ideology was virtually bound to be accepted in its place. Thus no rational defence of child-centred education was thought necessary. Selleck analysed the spread of progressive discourse into colleges of education and the inspectorate to the point where for a time it became the orthodoxy – an influence that continued and spread into LEAs, as more recent work by Alexander (1984, 1992) affirms.

The 1944 Act left primary school teachers in control of what was increasingly assumed to be a relatively child-centred, individualistic curriculum, however greatly this may later have been shown to be at odds with actual classroom practice (Galton *et al.*, 1980). Thus, gradually evolving as direct forms of national control weakened (Lawn, 1987), there was general support for teacher autonomy right through the 1950s and 1960s. We should note, though, the surprise expressed to the House of Commons on 21 March 1960 by the Conservative Minister of Education, Sir David Eccles: 'We hardly ever discuss what is taught . . . we treat the curriculum as though it were a subject . . . about which it is "not done" for us to make remarks . . . This reticence has been overdone. We could with advantage express views on what is taught' (Eccles, 1960). Thirty years on, however, one's eye is caught by his assurance that, 'of course, Parliament would never attempt to dictate the curriculum'. Times change. Nevertheless, Eccles did establish a Curriculum Study Group, and this was in turn replaced by the Schools Council. This body engaged in much curriculum development work but 'never succeeded in outlining a systematic approach to the whole curriculum' (Lawton, 1989, p. 2).

Perhaps the post-war initiative that had most influence on primary education prior to the 1980s was the Plowden Report (CACE, 1967). Thousands of words have been expended in discussion of this report, *Children and Their Primary Schools*. It is generally described as marking the apogee of the acceptance of child-centred doctrine in this country. Indeed, committee members seemed to move through the schools they visited in a happy glow, accepting that 'dismal corners' existed, but assuring readers that 'the gloomy forebodings of the decline of knowledge which would follow progressive methods have been discredited. We have, for the most part, described English primary education at its best. That, in our belief, is very good indeed' (para. 1233/4). Endorsement of child-centred principles was strong: ' "Finding out" has proved to be better for children than "being told" ' (para. 1233). However, here, as Richards (1984, p. 37) put it, a 'questionable assertion is paraded as an unchallengeable truth'. Indeed, finding the most effective ways in which children may learn and teachers teach has proved to be a more complex business than either the elementary or child-centred approaches implied. We therefore need to trace the gradual development of more sophisticated forms of teacher expertise.

2.4 AN EMERGENT PROFESSIONALISM?

We begin this account by returning to the early 1800s, when educational provision was at a very embryonic stage, and was mainly provided by churches, charities and other voluntary bodies. Teachers at that time were selected in a relatively *ad hoc* manner by drawing upon people 'of the right standing and experience'. This source was gradually supplemented by the practice of using senior pupils as 'monitors' to assist the 'masters' with the large numbers of children in their care. Not until 1846 was the issue of the quality of teachers themselves seriously considered. By then the monitorial system had been discredited and a case for some form of training had been made by inspectors and others, in the interests of 'rendering more efficient the education of people'. In December 1846 the Committee of the Council on Education passed a set of regulations that set up structures for the 'instruction and training of school apprentices'. The apprentice teacher was to work for five years under the instruction of a 'competent master or mistress' in a 'well furnished and well supplied' school where 'discipline is mild and firm, and conducive to good order' (Council on Education, 1846, pp. 2–9).

As we saw earlier, Forster's Education Act was passed in 1870, and more systematic provision of elementary education, and of School Boards to manage it, was established across England. The major evaluation of this expansion came in 1888 with the report of the Cross Commission. This report recommended the avoidance of high entry qualifications for teachers so that those 'with a natural aptitude and love of learning' would not be excluded. However, it was suggested both that more 'women of superior social position and general culture' should be recruited and that apprenticed teachers should be retained. It was also agreed that the training of such apprentices needed to be 'improved' (Ministry of Education, 1888).

Gradually, over these years, there had been a steady expansion and development of teacher training colleges. The first were established early in the nineteenth century (Dent, 1970).

In this period we can see many of the issues that still concern the Government today: the problem of supply, the concern with efficiency, competence and costs. In addition we see some of the types of thinking that endure in the way teaching is conceptualized as a profession: suitable for 'caring middle class women' of 'average intellectual ability', a necessary mass system, an enterprise in which engendering morality and ensuring social control seems almost as important as intellectual and skill development *per se*.

The history of such thinking is a long and continuous one but it has, perhaps not surprisingly, been contested by members of the teaching profession with equal and continuing commitment. One way of approaching this is by considering the gradual evolution of the relationship between the 'practice of education', which reflects the emphasis of the apprenticeship system, and the 'academic study of education', which had its heyday in the post-James Report Bachelor of Education courses of the early 1970s.

The initial 'pre-academic' stage was that of the nineteenth-century apprenticeship, the weaknesses of which were temporarily and partially addressed in the early 1900s through the generation and study of 'principles of education'. As academic disciplines and further professional awareness developed, the importance attached to study of academically defined 'subjects' grew and the four contributing 'disciplines of education' became established, particularly in the post-war years: psychology, history, philosophy and sociology. After the James Report of 1972, a decision that all new teachers were to be graduates was taken and new Bachelor of Education courses were developed. Such courses redefined academic education by synthesizing, linking and applying the disciplines to classroom concerns. The model of school application for students became that of 'teaching practice': students went to schools to practise what they had learnt in college.

In reaction to such academically inspired approaches, efforts were made to recognize and develop the craft and practical knowledge of teachers. This movement gradually emerged in the 1960s and 1970s under the particular influence of Lawrence Stenhouse (Stenhouse, 1975). Stenhouse argued that teachers could develop their own professional insight and expertise through systematic processes of 'action research'. Rigorous classroom-based self-evaluation, drawing on evidence and critiques from other teachers, could increase the quality of teaching. The influence of such action research approaches developed at the end of the 1970s, when deficiencies of the academic disciplines/teaching practice approach were becoming apparent. On the other hand, it was also clear that some classroom-based action research could be parochial and introverted (Barton and Lawn, 1980/1).

Alexander (1984) identified an emergent *practical theorizing* of the 1980s as a possible reconciliation of the tension between professional insight gained by academic study and the necessity of practical experience in developing classroom competence. Practical theorizing thus conceptualizes a modern synthesis of previous experience and a recognition of the importance for professional teachers of understanding, knowledge, competence and the capacity for continuous reflection and development. In many teacher education courses a variant of this approach has been described in terms of 'reflective teaching' (Pollard and Tann, 1987) and we would suggest that practical theorizing contributed to the strengthened professionalism of primary school teachers.

Through the 1980s there was also a growing influence of subject associations and of curriculum development projects that fed teachers' subject expertise. Similarly, the disposition to draw eclectically on a range of teaching approaches was maintained and enhanced by the development of groupwork skills. Many of these curricular and pedagogic developments were underpinned by new understandings about children's learning and the active role of teachers in that process, which moved well beyond naive developmentalism. Partnership with parents, particularly regarding reading, was developed in many LEAs, and school management began to become more coherent and purposeful as more became known about school effectiveness. Many teachers also became more aware of wider social responsibilities, of equal opportunities issues and of the role of education in society. Practical theorizing was one key feature of these developments. It was the process by which teachers analysed and learned from their actions.

This emergent professionalism, though clearly identifiable, was not consistent across all schools. Thus, while it demonstrated the very high quality of what was possible, it did not provide a structure for ensuring pupil entitlements or for monitoring school practices and achievements nationally. HMI were still critical of much classroom practice, referring to 'examples of poor discipline coupled with low motivation where the tasks allotted are inappropriate, where the curricular material is seen as irrelevant or undemanding, or where the teaching style is over-didactic and rigid' (DES, 1985b, p. 6). Many teachers, recognizing that deficiencies existed, supported the introduction of the National Curriculum as a structure within which more consistent and effective provision could be made in all schools.

Interestingly, the National Curriculum and assessment procedures that emerged following the 1988 Act were also partly a reflection of the new professionalism. Its achievements were reflected in the various working parties on curriculum subjects and in the support for formative assessment – despite the lack of provision of a whole-curriculum framework or of reconciliation of the tensions that were inherent in the formative and summative elements of the government's assessment policy. Indeed, it is somewhat curious, as we shall see, that these contributions were made within a legislative structure that had essentially anti-professional intentions. Gradually, of course, these tensions have become apparent and, for that reason, we will return to the issue later in the chapter.

We posit 'competent professionalism' as a further stage of development in teacher education. This reflects very recent moves towards school and competency-based teacher education, which, though informally developing through school and college partnership schemes, were formally made legal requirements in 1993 (DFE, 1993). Of course, these developments could easily degenerate into a modern version of the nineteenth-century apprenticeship system and, with the government proposal that non-graduates should be allowed to become teachers of children under the age of eight, the danger of reversion has been made particularly clear.

The specification of competencies for beginning teachers is, in one sense, merely a particular manifestation of the almost continuous critique to which education has been subject in the past two decades. Indeed, prior to further discussion of teacher professionalism, we now need to be more explicit about the nature of this critique.

2.5 CRITIQUE AND PUBLIC POLICY

The Plowden Report of 1967 was the focus of much criticism in the early 1970s because of its elements of pastoralism and utopianism. It seemed to reflect a romantic poets' view of childhood as a Golden Age that, given the right sort of teaching skills, could be re-created for every child in primary schools. Symbols of organic growth and gentle nurture were prevalent but were criticized. For instance, Alexander (1984) considered Plowden's well-known rubric, 'at the heart of the educational process lies the child', and wrote: 'Plowden's use of the words "heart", rather than the more neutral "centre", and "lies", with the image of the child recumbent, dormant and maternally cradled, seems hardly accidental' (Alexander, 1984, p. 18). Child-centred discourse, Alexander continued, is too ready to assume that concern for the curriculum is in opposition to concern for the child. However, Alexander, both in this and in his later work (Alexander, 1990; Alexander *et al.*, 1992), has not sought a return to the elementary school style, but has wanted more attention to be paid to how teachers actually teach and to what children actually learn.

Publication of the Black Papers criticizing 'progressive' ideas began in 1969 (Cox and Dyson, 1969) and received a great deal of debate and media attention. They continued to appear until the mid-1970s (Cox and Boyson, 1975, 1977), by which time dissatisfaction with primary education was being voiced ever more loudly and often.

While some attacks were virulent, contemptuous and ill-informed, not all educational conservatism, even in the Black Papers, was expressed with a disregard for direct educational experience. Writing elsewhere, Froome, one Black Paper author, drew on his experience as a primary school headteacher to suggest that Dewey's 'dogmas', such as making children the agents of their own learning, while attractive in theory, were impossible to reconcile with large classes and with children who might be 'unwilling participators in the educational struggle' (Froome, 1974, p. 14) This judgement was, of course, uncomfortably confirmed by much of the research of the later 1970s (Bennett, 1976; DES, 1978; Galton *et al.*, 1980).

During the 1970s, concerns about 'progressivism' intermingled with concern about the degree of teacher autonomy. Indeed, calls for teachers to be made more accountable were already growing when, in 1974, parental concern regarding the William Tyndale Junior School reached the press. In the ensuing media sensationalism, the school was fallen upon with delight. Taking the school as a demonstration of all that was wrong, with accounts of disorganization, teacher and child autonomy and an imbalanced curriculum, the subsequent inquiry (Auld, 1976) provided an impetus towards the reforms of the 1980s, including the move towards greater accountability through community and parental control of schools. Despite poor evidence concerning the other 20,000 or so primary schools in England and Wales, the Tyndale 'radicals' were characterized as typical of their contemporaries. They were thus taken to demonstrate that teachers were not to be trusted.

Dale's analysis of the period (Dale *et al.*, 1981) points out that teacher autonomy had always been constrained by teacher–pupil ratios, resources and public expectations that children would be taught to read and write. Such guidelines were implicit and internalized, but the result of their perceived abuse by the William Tyndale teachers was 'a recognition of the political nature of teachers' classroom autonomy in a period when there was no clear consensus on educational goals, and a consequent attempt both to specify the aims and objectives of the education system more explicitly and to routinise teachers' accountability' (Dale *et al.*, 1981, p. 313). Other questions brought to the forefront by the situation at the school concerned the role of LEAs, HMI and the DES. If teachers at this or any other primary school were failing to meet the needs of their pupils in providing a balanced curriculum, whose was the responsibility for putting things right?

It would be easy to exaggerate the role played by the Tyndale affair in the change of climate – it has already been demonstrated that concerns were widespread well before the events of 1974 – but it would also be a mistake to regard it as a trivial episode. What the affair proved was the power of anecdotal evidence; the name of the school entered educational debate as a powerful symbol of all that was seen to be wrong. In a way it became a negative and reverse image of Holmes's Utopia.

Into this mid-1970s context of growing doubt and concern about the nature and direction of educational provision, the Labour Prime Minister, James Callaghan, initiated a 'Great Debate' with a speech at Ruskin College, Oxford, in October 1976. During his speech Callaghan paid brief tribute to 'the enthusiasm and dedication of the teaching profession' (Callaghan, 1976, p. 332), before going on to express his disquiet about low standards of numeracy, the lack of basic skills among school-leavers, informal teaching methods, the lack of a 'so-called "core curriculum" of basic knowledge', the examination system and the preference among students for the humanities over science and engineering. The emphasis was again, although not exclusively, on Britain's ability to earn its living in the world:

> There is no virtue in producing socially well-adjusted members of society who are unemployed because they do not have the skills, nor at the other extreme must they be technically efficient robots. Both of the basic purposes of education require the same essential tools. These are basic literacy, basic numeracy, the understanding of how to live and work together, respect for others, respect for the individual.
>
> (Callaghan, 1976, p. 332)

In the 1970s and 1980s HMI were active in promoting discussion of the curriculum in a series of documents: *Curriculum 11–16* (DES, 1977), the primary education survey (DES, 1978), *Education 5–9* (DES, 1982) and the Curriculum Matters series (e.g. DES, 1984, 1985a). Thus, when Margaret Thatcher's Conservative Government was elected in 1979, moves towards strengthening central control of the curriculum and weakening class teacher autonomy were well under way. Her first Secretary of State for Education, Mark Carlisle, was succeeded by Sir Keith Joseph, a devout Thatcherite, who was as dedicated as his leader to being seen as a benefactor of the education service – particularly, he said, for the lower end of the ability range – while cutting public expenditure. He disbanded the Schools Council, with its teacher representatives, and set up, and made direct appointments to, the Secondary Examinations Council and the School Curriculum Development Committee. Teachers' control of the curriculum, says Lawton (1989, p. 39), was virtually over.

Innovations appeared with gathering rapidity and variety throughout the 1980s. For instance, on the management of schools, the 1980 Education Act ensured that each school would have its own governing body, on which there would be at least two teacher and two parent representatives. In 1986 parents were given equal representation with LEAs. Governors were now required to oversee the curriculum of their school, to make copies of curriculum policy documents available to parents and to issue an annual report on the past year's activities. A meeting of governors and parents was to be held each year. In 1988 provision was made for the 'local management' of schools in most financial and educational matters and for schools to opt out of local authority control by becoming 'grant maintained'. This movement was given a further impetus for primary schools by the Education Act of 1993, which increased the eligibility of schools to opt out.

Such innovations of the Conservative Governments of the 1980s and early 1990s show the influence of small but active pressure groups, such as the Parental Alliance for Choice in Education, the Centre for Policy Studies, the Hillgate Group and the Institute of Economic Affairs. The members of such groups, including Roger Scruton, the philosopher and editor of the right-wing *Salisbury Review*, Caroline Cox, Stuart Sexton and Lawrence Norcross, often overlapped with one another and with Black Paper authors. Generally known as the 'New Right', these groups in many ways set the agenda for political debate throughout the period. They specialized in saying the unsayable, but there was an uncanny pattern in the ways in which their ideas were converted into legislation and became taken for granted.

For instance, the Hillgate Group's *Whose Schools? A Radical Manifesto* (1986) preceded the 1988 Act in suggesting the establishment of independent self-governing trusts for schools. Government grants would be linked to the number of pupils on the roll and this would produce a strong consumer influence on educational policies.

Similar free market policies were advocated by Sexton, a former adviser to Keith Joseph, in *Our Schools: A Radical Policy* (1987). He argued for devolved financial management to schools, the expansion of the assisted places scheme, an 'apprenticeship' or 'articled' system of training new teachers and the opportunity for schools to opt for direct grant status. Parental choice would be increased by issuing 'education credits', leading to 'a consumer-led system rather than, as at present, a provider-led one, greater and more effective pressure for higher standards and move away from State bureaucratic dependence' (Sexton, 1987, p. 28). As he put it, 'A large enough number of well informed and motivated parents is sufficient to influence what is provided for all' (Sexton, 1987, p. 28). No one comparing the recommendations of these publications with the innovations of the 1988 Act, or later legislation, could doubt the growth in influence of the educational right.

However, there were important differences among members of the New Right concerning the extent to which central government needed to exert control over the curriculum and education system. Some believed this to be necessary in order to control 'left-wing' local education authorities and to maintain traditional values and national culture. Others believed that market forces should simply be left to operate with minimal control. However, as Whitty suggested,

> the contrast between apparent centralisation in one sphere and apparent decentralisation in the other may not be the paradox it at first appears. Schools which are responsive to choices made by parents in the market are believed to be more likely than those administered by state bureaucrats to produce high levels of scholastic achievement, to the benefit of both individuals and the nation. It then becomes imperative to police the curriculum to

ensure that the pervasive collectivist and universalistic welfare ideology of the post-war era is restrained. In this way, support for the market, self-help, enterprise and the concept of the 'responsible' family and a common 'national identity' can be constructed.

(Whitty, 1989, p. 331)

Whatever the nature of such differences of view, the influence of the New Right has been very considerable and this was clearly seen in the 1988 Education Reform Act.

2.6 THE EDUCATION REFORM ACT AND AFTER

Perhaps the most radical reform of state education since its inception, the Education Reform Act 1988 (ERA) was passed under Joseph's successor as Secretary of State for Education, Kenneth Baker. The Act specified educational aims for the first time in the history of education in England and Wales. Children were to be offered

a balanced and broadly based curriculum which –
(a) promotes the spiritual, moral, cultural, mental and physical development of pupils at the school and of society; and
(b) prepares such pupils for the opportunities, responsibilities and experiences of adult life.

A National Curriculum, with associated assessment procedures, was to be introduced. Central control of what was taught and the measurement of pupil achievements thus became a reality once again – the first time that such control had been exercised in such a way since the nineteenth century. While the legislation brought the primary school curriculum of England and Wales closer to international norms in terms of content (Meyer *et al.*, 1992), it was noticeable that in terms of the degree of localized teacher judgement that was allowed for, the move was against the trend of countries such as France, Sweden and the USA. In any event, all primary schools were to teach a core curriculum of maths, English and science, and other foundation subjects of history, geography, technology, music, art and physical education. Religious education, while compulsory, was not a foundation subject. Core and foundation subjects, it was estimated, would take up about 70 per cent of the time available. Special arrangements were to be made for children with official statements of special educational needs. Interestingly, independent schools were not covered by the legislation.

The Secretary of State set up a National Curriculum Council (NCC), with its Welsh equivalent, and a School Examinations and Assessment Council (SEAC). Their role was to advise the Secretary of State, who would make final decisions on curricular, assessment and many other educational matters.

One of the most controversial elements of the Act, and the greatest source of dissatisfaction (within the Conservative Party and Government, as well as elsewhere), were its arrangements for testing. A Task Group on Assessment and Testing (TGAT), chaired by Professor Paul Black, had devised a system combining teachers' own formative assessment (teacher assessment, TA) with Standard Assessment Tasks (SATs) (DES, 1987). The latter would, it was hoped, be perceived by pupils not as tests but as normal classroom tasks, perhaps carried out in groups, and they would be closely supervised by teachers for gathering assessment evidence.

From teacher assessment and SAT results, pupils would be judged to have achieved certain 'levels' in each subject and regular progression was anticipated (see Figure 2.1).

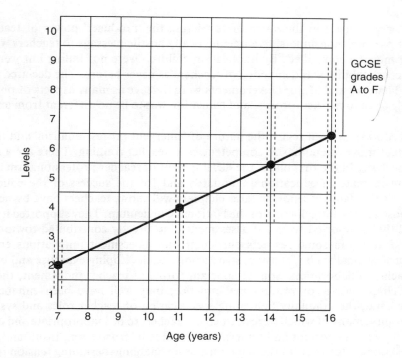

Figure 2.1 *Sequence of pupil achievement of levels between ages 7 and 16 (TGAT, 1987).*

As can be seen in Figure 2.1, 80 per cent of seven-year-olds were expected to reach levels 1, 2 or 3. All pupils would thus be able to show progress and SATs would allow for a wide spread of achievement. Assessment was intended to be criterion-referenced (linked to specific tasks) rather than norm-referenced (measured by the performance of others of the same age).

The years after 1988 saw further legislation and circulars as the principles of the ERA were extended, implemented and reviewed. For instance, the Education Act 1992 was incisive in removing many powers of local education authorities, in extending encouragement of grant-maintained schools and city technology colleges and in restructuring the work of Her Majesty's Inspectors in favour of new inspection teams registered by the Office for Standards in Education (OFSTED). There was also a constant programme of implementation as the National Curriculum and assessment procedures were introduced. On this there were both successes and problems, as this book will document in some detail. Of the problems, the manageability of assessment procedures and the overload of the primary curriculum were recognized by the Government and are, as we write, the subject of a review by Sir Ron Dearing. Assessment policy provided a focus for much continuing argument. Teachers supported formative teacher assessment and reporting of this to parents to support pupil learning directly. However, the Government insisted on the need for published league tables of aggregated school performance to provide public accountability of schools and teachers.

Overall, teachers did not feel that their professional concerns were recognized and respected. This was not surprising, bearing in mind the Government's basic strategy of

taking power to itself in the name of restricting the 'producer' power of teachers in favour of parental 'consumers'. An unequivocally hostile message to teachers was spelt out: they must be controlled. By implication children were not failing but were being failed. Accountability was demanded of teachers as never before. The declared aims of both the Thatcher and Major Governments were to leave as many aspects of public life as possible open to market forces – and education was to be no different from any other service.

In this context, we can revisit the nature of 'emergent professionalism' and the 1993 Government move to emphasize competencies in teacher training. There are a number of tensions here. In the first place, the development of teacher professionalism is essential for an increase in educational standards and for the success of the educational reforms. As the data we report in later chapters will show, teachers have by no means been opposed to the introduction of the National Curriculum. They supported it in principle and they supported forms of assessment that directly contributed towards pupil learning. Indeed, in some respects curricular and assessment innovations enhanced teacher professionalism by focusing, structuring and developing expertise and by developing teacher collaboration. Some important forms of teacher judgement, the quintessential characteristic of professional practice, may well have been enhanced. On the other hand, the gradually tightening specification of teacher roles and systems of accountability, many of which were deemed by teachers to be inappropriate and counterproductive, were a constant and undermining source of frustration, insult and, potentially, deskilling. However, at the same time as an enabling–deskilling tension is played out, we have to recognize that teacher professionalism has also proved to be a source of mediation and of direct resistance to government reforms. This tension was vividly illustrated during 1993, when teachers boycotted assessment procedures and prevented league tables being drawn up in any meaningful way.

Teachers' skill and professional judgement are thus essential in the fulfilment of government aims. They have been both enhanced and threatened by developments since the Education Reform Act, but they remain a source of knowledge, commitment and independence in mediating and, if necessary, resisting change. It may be that the new emphasis on classroom competencies that was imposed on all primary teacher education courses in 1993 was an attempt to exercise some control over these tensions.

2.7 CONCLUSION

In this chapter we have traced the influence of the elementary and developmental traditions in primary education, the latter in its child-centred form. We have also seen how, despite the gradual emergence of increasingly sophisticated forms of practical theorizing and professional practice by teachers, critiques of 'progressivism' developed and were then superseded by market models of educational provision. Specification of the National Curriculum and of assessment procedures were two policies among many that were introduced to define educational purposes and to increase the accountability of teachers and schools through market mechanisms.

We have also argued that a new form of teacher professionalism was emerging over the period. This built on practical theorizing and, at various times, both contributed to and was developed by government policy – but it has also been a source of mediation and resistance. Competency models of teacher education may be an attempt to stabilize this tension, and they will take their place alongside the specified contracts of employment and appraisal systems for teachers that were also developed over the period as a means of controlling teachers' work.

Most of the rest of this book does not range so widely until our concluding chapter. It simply reports our empirical findings on the impact of the National Curriculum and assessment innovations on schools and classrooms, teachers and pupils. Thus, while the present chapter was intended to set the scene for that account and establish its significance in terms of themes and issues, the bulk of the book describes and analyses patterns of action and response more directly.

However, before beginning such an exposition, we offer two further forms of overview of the study. The first is essentially conceptual, for Chapter 3 provides an analysis of various 'dimensions' of educational practice, and of the themes of power, values and understanding, that we have used in monitoring change. The second is methodological: in Chapter 4 we detail the research design and methods on which our research has been based.

Chapter 3

Dimensions of Change: An Analytical Framework

3.1 INTRODUCTION

The passing of the Education Reform Act in 1988 is widely acknowledged to have been one of the most significant milestones in the shaping of the form and content of English state educational provision. In terms of primary schools in particular, as we saw in Chapter 2, it represented an almost unprecedented attempt by government to control the content and balance of the curriculum. Furthermore, it required teachers and schools to undertake assessment and reporting on pupils' progress and achievement with a degree of formality that was equally new. Associated with these requirements were new types of accountability, through governors, parents, inspection and new types of performance indicator. However, the criteria to be applied were centrally generated. Encompassing as they did the subjects to be taught, the outcomes to be achieved and the mechanisms for reporting these to potential consumers, the criteria formed an explicit set of obligations against which schools were to be judged.

In short, the requirements of the 1988 Act implied a shift from a professionalism characterized by very personal, often intuitive and informal judgements on the part of individual teachers and schools concerning curriculum, pedagogy and assessment. The new condition of teachers' work was to be characterized by the pursuit of more specific and externally imposed learning targets, in which the various elements of professional activity associated with achieving these targets, especially curriculum planning, assessment and reporting of achievement, were to be made increasingly explicit.

As we write, in 1993, teachers are being required to fulfil their professional role in a legislative context that is characterized by three main features. First, their autonomy has been severely curtailed. Second, legislation has shaped a working context in which educational priorities are to be determined by some combination of political dictate and consumer demand – but certainly not by teachers themselves. Third, and most fundamentally, concepts concerning what education is and should be for are now no longer the primary preserve of teachers, but have become the subject of continuing public controversy.

Thus the changes currently taking place centre on issues of power and ideology. They are about the nature of educational priorities, different ways of conceiving the task of achieving those priorities and the power to impose that conception. These three central themes of *values*, *understanding* and *power* permeate the analyses of this book. We have had a baseline against which to compare the very different assumptions of the post-ERA policy climate by drawing on pre-ERA studies of English primary schools, teachers and classrooms, such as those of Barker-Lunn (1970), Bennett (1976), Bassey (1978), Galton *et al.* (1980), Alexander (1984), Bennett *et al.* (1984), Pollard (1985), Mortimore *et al.* (1988) and Tizard *et al.* (1988). Such work provides rich, descriptive pictures and analyses of both the prevailing ideologies and the characteristic practices of English primary schooling before 1988. The content of the legislation itself, together with documents that were issued by government concerning the National Curriculum and its implementation, and the public debate that these provoked, provided a stark contrast with the prevailing pre-ERA assumptions in terms of our three underlying themes of values, understanding and power.

To crystallize the issues involved we want, for the moment, to focus more specifically on the issue of ideologies and their relationship to social values.

3.2 IDEOLOGIES AND SOCIAL VALUES

Educational ideologies and social values are perhaps the most fundamental issue this book addresses, for their consideration engages directly with global conceptions of what education is for and how, broadly, it should be delivered.

Bernstein's work over many years (e.g. Bernstein, 1975, 1990) has provided a comprehensive analytic framework both for locating differences in overarching educational ideologies and for understanding variations in the dimensions through which they may be characterized. We are unable to encompass the full breadth of Bernstein's conceptualization here, but we do want to revisit his identification of two types of educational code: 'collection' and 'integration'. As he put it,

> The collection type of curriculum tends to be rigid, differentiating and hierarchical in character. How much so depends upon the general culture of the society . . . Where we have curricula of the integrated type, we will find a shift in emphasis from education in depth to education in breadth or, in less evaluative terms, from content closure to content openness. In order to accomplish integration, the relational idea, the supra content concept, must focus much more upon general principles. This in turn is likely to affect the pedagogy:

it will tend to emphasise ways of knowing rather than states of knowledge. If the underlying theory of pedagogy under collection is didactic, then under integration the underlying pedagogic theory is likely to be self-regulatory. Such a change in emphasis and pedagogy is likely to transform the teacher–pupil–lecturer–student authority relationships, and in particular increase the status and thus the rights of the pupil or student. We might also expect the organisation of teaching groups to undergo a change and exhibit considerable flexibility compared with the rigidity of collection. Given all these changes, a pressure will be set up towards introducing forms of evaluation, forms of examining, which is appropriate to the curriculum and pedagogy.

(Bernstein, 1975, pp. 82–3)

Table 3.1 shows the main points of contrast from this account, with implied features in parentheses.

At first sight, this could simply be taken as a neat categorization and mapping of the main features of the commonplace, but not very helpful, distinction between 'traditional' and 'progressive' views of the curriculum and practice in primary schools. Yet there is a good deal more to it, for Bernstein (1975, p. 81) goes on to argue that 'The selective organisation, transmission and evaluation of knowledge is intimately bound up with patterns of authority and control . . . The battle over curricula is also a conflict between different conceptions of social order and is therefore fundamentally moral.' This takes the debate to a quite different plane, the plane of ideologies, power and influence over social policy and practice.

As we saw in Chapter 2, the developmental tradition, drawing on deep-rooted integration education codes, has ebbed and flowed over time, but faced strong attack since the high-point of its endorsement in the Plowden Report. The pre-eminent values and ideologies of the 1980s, those of the New Right, were suffused with assumptions derived from collection codes and, of course, these were manifested in the 1988 legislation. Confirming Bernstein's analysis, public statements of the time repeatedly made explicit links between education and the social, moral and economic order of the nation. Recent changes in primary education may thus have focused on issues such as curriculum, classroom practice or teacher accountability, but they also articulate with much more wide-ranging social, economic and political movements, trends and struggles (Simon, 1989).

We shall return to these themes more discursively and holistically in Chapter 13. For the moment, however, we move on to trace their specific impact in terms of more particular substantive issues. As we do so, we shall identify a number of analytic dimensions, which in due course will be used to highlight the main features of our empirical findings.

Table 3.1   *Education codes*

Collection code	Integration code
Rigid	(More flexible)
Differentiated	(Less differentiated)
Hierarchical	(Less hierarchical)
Depth in education	Breadth in education
Content closure	Content openness
States of knowing	Ways of knowing
Didactic pedagogy	Self-regulatory pedagogy
Rigid organization of teaching groups	Flexible organization of teaching groups
(Categoric evaluation)	(Formative evaluation)

It is important to be clear about the status of these analytic dimensions and our use of them. We use dimensions to represent variations in policies, practices, beliefs or actions as they relate to the educational issues that have assumed particular importance for this study. In some respects they articulate with Berlak and Berlak's (1981) conceptualization of 'dilemma', a concept they used to focus attention on the tensions teachers face in trying to resolve competing priorities in the complex environments of school and classroom. In a sense, then, the concept of 'dimension' expresses the range in the ways in which such dilemmas are typically resolved. Thus, dimensions should not be misunderstood as polarities, but they do provide an analytical means of mapping patterns of change as teachers and others respond to evolving circumstances and competing priorities.

We now turn to our discussion of more substantive issues and we begin this by focusing on school change.

3.3 SCHOOL CHANGE

As we have seen, educational initiatives over the recent past have almost all originated from the government. Moreover, the policy changes that have taken place have been unusual in the thoroughness, tightness and overtness with which aims, accountability structures and reporting procedures have been specified. This aspect of change emphasizes the centrality of the concept of *power* in understanding the new context in which schools find themselves. While many previous educational reforms had been essentially 'permissive' (Kogan, 1978), in that they allowed LEAs and schools, the actual deliverers of education, to make or negotiate new developments, the current reforms were imposed upon schools and LEAs. As we have seen, mechanisms were also set in place to make schools accountable for the appropriate implementation of change.

We can thus identify a dimension for understanding the mode of current changes at school level, in terms of

school-based development – negotiated change – imposed change

However, although the reform associated with the National Curriculum involved an unusual degree of central direction and explicit mechanisms for accountability, it would be over-simplistic to represent them entirely in terms of top-down policy directives straightforwardly implemented at local level. Indeed, in many other places in this book we will identify the role of educational practitioners in responding to and mediating educational policy, so that the impact may differ from that originally intended. We shall argue below that in professions such as education such mediation is not only possible but inevitable. We must also remember that, in principle at least, schools and teachers may choose to resist centrally directed reform. Consequently, we can identify a further dimension in relation to responses to power relationships in educational change:

compliance – mediation – resistance

The dimensions considered so far relate to the relationship between the school, teachers and external forces. Of course, there are also internal questions to be addressed in relation to educational change and school development. In particular, the ways in which changes are implemented will depend upon, and may also reveal, managerial structures and power relationships within the school. They may range, for example, from the explicit and autocratic use of headteacher power to impose change to more democratic, collegial approaches that promote more gradual developments. We can therefore identify a dimension relating to the degree of participation in school decision-making, in terms of

top-down management – managed participation – collegial management

The nature and effect of *values* at school level are clearly related to the culture of each school, which, in turn, is a reflection of the beliefs and actions of the head and individual teachers (Pollard, 1987; Nias *et al.*, 1989).

In the past it has been said that primary schools have been based on relatively individualized ways of working, with each teacher maintaining his or her classroom privacy and curriculum autonomy (Lortie, 1975). However, there has been considerable discussion recently of 'whole-school' collegial approaches as models for educational development (e.g. Nias *et al.*, 1992), and such approaches have been encouraged by both external requirements for greater coordination and teacher responses to imposition. There is thus a basic values-related dimension that underlies school practices and that we identify as

individualism – collegiality

Finally, we can characterize schools in terms of the *understandings* of educational knowledge, which are represented either implicitly or explicitly in their structures and curricula. Particularly relevant for recent debates and policy initiatives is the way in which the curriculum is described and organized. The question of curriculum integration, through topics or projects, has been criticized in favour of consideration of more subject-based teaching (Alexander *et al.*, 1992), and this has considerable implications for school organization, staff roles and deployment. It is therefore appropriate to identify an analytic dimension that is related to the staffing implications of different forms of curricular understanding. We do so in terms of

subject specialist staffing – subject generalist staffing

We shall draw on our empirical findings to illuminate these issues both in Chapter 5, on headteachers' perspectives and strategies for change, and elsewhere in the book. For now, though, we move on to consider some of the major issues associated with teacher professionalism.

3.4 TEACHER PROFESSIONALISM

Consideration of teacher professionalism in the context of the many challenges of the past decade requires discussion of many issues, but we will focus on aspects of professional values, perceptions of role, teaching as an activity and teachers' working situations.

Central to notions of professionalism are the *values* that define and underpin them and, related to these, the self-identity of teachers as professionals. A distinctive feature of English primary school teachers' professionalism has been the emphasis put by many teachers on the expressive aspects of their roles in terms of personal fulfilment and self-identity (Nias, 1989). Teaching is seen in these terms as having powerful intrinsic rewards and is associated with a considerable degree of self-motivation and commitment. This is distinct from a more instrumental motivation in which the self is more detached from the role, as has been found in some comparative research. However, if the moral basis of teacher commitment is undermined and aims, structures or practices are imposed, teachers are likely to feel alienated from their work (Etzioni, 1966; Poppleton and Riseborough, 1990; Broadfoot and Osborn, 1993). We can express these distinctions and consider shifts in response to current changes in terms of the value dimension:

expressive commitment – instrumentalism – alienation

This dimension encompasses teachers' feelings about the nature of their personal commitment and also the extent to which teachers feel personally at ease with the aims of primary education as articulated in prevailing government policy.

Other values can be related more specifically to the content of the educational aims of teachers or to what is often broadly described as their ideology. Particularly important in the English context is the extent to which notions of competition between children and explicit differentiation in terms of achievement are endorsed or rejected.

Similarly, there are different teacher priorities regarding educational aims in the broadest sense. These have been characterized in 'individualistic' and 'societal' terms (Ashton *et al.*, 1975): the former affirm differentiated responses to specific pupil needs and interests; the latter assert the case for ensuring basic competencies, skills and knowledge for all pupils.

Closely related to the values of teachers are the *understandings* they have of their professional role. Hoyle's (1974) analysis of restricted and extended professionalism is useful here. The distinction draws attention to the way in which teachers may focus on their immediate responsibilities and classroom concerns (restricted professionalism) or engage with educational issues, structures and practices beyond their own classroom (extended professionalism). Of course, a teacher who sees professionality in restricted terms may be just as committed to children and their education as an extended professional, for the distinction is essentially related to different conceptions of the range of appropriate teacher roles rather than to depth of commitment (Broadfoot and Osborn, 1993).

Many of the concerns over the introduction of the National Curriculum and its impact on teachers can be related to the notion of restricted and extended professionalism. For instance, it has been feared that a more directive approach to curriculum and assessment is inherently restricting professionally. On the other hand, developments in the direction of whole school and collegial responses, and of greater awareness of public policy issues, also suggest the development of extended professionalism. Following Hoyle, and Broadfoot and Osborn, we will thus use this dimension to explore the impact of the National Curriculum on teachers' conceptions of their professional roles and responsibilities:

restricted professionalism – extended professionalism

Teacher professionalism also needs to be considered in terms of the extent to which teachers-as-professionals have control over their working situation, as against the extent to which they are controlled through directing it. This is essentially an issue of *power*. We can therefore identify the dimension

autonomy – constraint

along which we can consider changes in the power context of teachers' work.

We can also identify aspects of the operation of power that relate more generally to teachers' capacity to achieve goals. There has been much recent debate on this: are recent educational changes empowering for teachers or do they deskill them? Certainly both cases can be argued and in Chapter 6 we will bring some empirical evidence to bear on the issue.

Having considered school change and teacher professionalism, we now develop our argument to focus on classroom practice and pupil experience.

3.5 CLASSROOM PRACTICE AND PUPIL EXPERIENCE

Curriculum, pedagogy and assessment are three aspects of classroom practice that were central to the provisions of the Education Reform Act and thus to the PACE project. They were also identified as the basic 'message systems' in Bernstein's notion of integrated and collection codes. Bernstein's model is thus a particularly appropriate framework with which to model and integrate our analysis of the impact of current changes in classrooms.

Curriculum

Bernstein developed the concept of *curriculum classification* to express ways of representing educational knowledge. Classification is concerned with the relationships between the contents of the curriculum rather than the content of the curriculum itself. As Bernstein wrote:

> Where classification is strong, contents are well insulated from each other by strong boundaries. Where classification is weak, there is reduced insulation between contents, for the boundaries between contents are weak or blurred. Classification thus refers to the degree of boundary maintenance between content.
>
> (Bernstein, 1975, p. 89)

In the context of primary classrooms this distinction is particularly significant in respect of topic-based and subject-based forms of curriculum organization, and many studies of primary education have also used the extent of curriculum integration as an important indicator of types of classroom practice (e.g. Barker-Lunn, 1970; Bennett, 1976; Mortimore *et al.*, 1988). A particular feature of this evidence has been its demonstration of how common it has been for the subjects associated with the 'basics', of literacy and mathematics, to be taught in separate, highly classified, ways, while most other aspects of curriculum provision are merged into various forms of topic-work (Alexander, 1984).

The National Curriculum, with its distinct subject-based structure, clearly asserted the primacy of 'subjects' as a planning, delivery and assessment medium for teachers. The influence went further too, as the practical requirements of implementation, support and evaluation required the creation of subject-based roles and bureaucracies within NCC, SEAC, LEAs and schools.

In a variety of ways, then, the highly classified way in which the National Curriculum was structured impacted on the forms of knowledge that were in use in schools. As part of the PACE research, we wanted to monitor the extent to which this might be reflected in a move from integrated curricular provision towards more subject-based collection codes. Explicit encouragement of this was somewhat muted in the immediate aftermath of the 1988 Act and some parts of the Non-statutory Guidelines that accompanied the National Curriculum Orders did endorse the use of topic work within whole-curriculum planning. However, the National Curriculum Council was remarkably slow to respond to the concern, regularly expressed by teachers at the turn of the decade, for help in providing a coherent, cross-subject curriculum as a *whole*. An initial government position was to attack integrated curricula as 'dogmatic orthodoxy' (Clarke, 1991). This strategy was also reflected in the report of the so-called 'Three Wise Men', which strongly advocated the greater use of subjects and asserted that 'Over the last few decades, the progress of primary pupils has been hampered by the influence of highly questionable dogmas which have led to excessively complex classroom practices and devalued the place of subjects in the curriculum' (Alexander *et al.*, 1992, para. 3.2). However, by 1993 there was official recognition of the overloading of the curriculum (NCC, 1993; OFSTED, 1993) and a major review under Sir Ron Dearing was set up.

The extent to which teachers actually responded to these new curricular structures, injunctions and revisions remains to be seen and is an empirical issue that the PACE research has monitored closely. In analytical terms, we can express them as a dimension:

strong classification of curricular – weak classification of curricular
knowledge   knowledge

Our results regarding curriculum organization and practice will be reported in Chapter 7 of this book.

We shall also consider the issue of curriculum balance in terms of content. This must be viewed in the context of many earlier studies of primary education, which have described the disproportionate amount of curriculum time spent on a relatively narrow curriculum of the 'basics' of literacy and numeracy (e.g. Bennett, 1976; Galton *et al.*, 1980; Alexander *et al.*, 1989). Other recent studies have also documented the relative neglect of science and technology and the lack of confidence many teachers feel in these areas (e.g. Croll and Moses, 1990; Bennett *et al.*, 1992). Yet the expressive curriculum – art, music, drama – has been of great importance in primary schools and has been linked to the social integration of children with the overall life of the school (Broadfoot *et al.*, 1993), to pupil motivation and to cognitive as well as affective development (Armstrong, 1981).

There was thus a tension between different aspects of National Curriculum thinking as it related to curriculum balance. On the one hand the nine subjects of the National Curriculum were intended to *extend* the curriculum and give all children access to a wide range of curriculum content, including expressive subjects. On the other hand, both the general approach to educational reform, which had characterized the previous few years, and the highest priority of many teachers had been to emphasize the *basic skills*. The curriculum, in these terms, was seen as being 'overloaded'. We can express this tension using the dimension

broad curriculum content – narrow curriculum content

As a final curricular dimension we wish to draw attention to the significance of the perceptions of policy-makers, teachers and others concerning sources of knowledge and modes of learning. This is a fundamental issue and, in its simplest terms, can be crystallized in a contrast between those who believe that knowledge is 'established' and those who believe that it must be 'constructed'.

Established knowledge is, one could argue, that which has been discovered and built up in the past – and, for educational purposes, is now reflected in National Curriculum documentation. It reflects the products of our history, culture and science, and tends to be associated with a concern that pupils should be required to be inducted into and thus should 'learn' such knowledge. It may be associated with a concern for the integrity of subjects, as, for instance, in the call by Alexander *et al.* (1992, para. 64) for consideration of subjects as 'some of the most powerful tools for making sense of the world which human beings have ever devised'. Of course, in England, such views have always been stronger in secondary education and in independent preparatory schools than in primary schools, whereas in France and much of continental Europe they provide the dominant convention throughout their education systems. In pedagogic terms, perceptions of knowledge as established tend to be associated with more didactic, or transmission, forms of teaching, in which knowledgeable adults instruct pupils. Whole-class teaching thus seems to be an appropriate and cost-effective method.

Constructed knowledge is seen as understandings or skills that are gradually developed by learners through their experiences. Those who see knowledge in this way thus tend to place more emphasis on teaching–learning processes and on the quality of learning experiences. There have been two distinct educational variants of this 'constructivist' view since the 1970s. Initially teachers were influenced by Piagetian research (1926, 1950), which was interpreted as emphasizing the importance of individual pupils interacting with a rich and intellectually stimulating curriculum and classroom environment. Such ideas also contributed to integrated models of curriculum provision. However, since the early 1980s constructivist views of knowledge and of learning have been influenced more by Vygotsky's ideas (1962, 1978). These emphasize the importance of the cultural context, of social interaction and of teachers, and others with expertise, in guiding and supporting learning through discussion and appropriate instruction. Those who hold constructivist views of the development of knowledge tend to favour teaching of individuals and groups so that carefully matched support of pupils' developing understanding can be provided. In this more recent 'social constructivist' variant, teachers have also begun to see their key role as mediating between pupils' understandings and culturally derived established knowledge, which may be reflected in subjects. This, of course, is a form of *rapprochement* between those who emphasize established knowledge and those who emphasize constructed knowledge alone.

We can thus identify a further analytic dimension in terms of perceptions of knowledge and learning:

established knowledge – constructed knowledge

Pedagogy

Bernstein analysed the underlying structure of pedagogy using the concept of 'frame' and we too have found it extremely useful. Frame does not refer to the content of pedagogy, but to the *form of the context* in which teaching and learning take place and to the 'specific pedagogical relationship of teacher and taught'. As Bernstein put it,

Frame refers to the *strength of the boundary* between what may be transmitted and what may not be transmitted in the pedagogical relationship. Where framing is strong, there is a sharp boundary, where framing is weak, a blurred boundary, between what may and may not be transmitted. Frame refers us to the range of options available to teacher and taught in the *control* of what is transmitted and received in the context of the pedagogical relationship. Strong framing entails reduced options; weak framing entails a range of options. Thus frame refers to the degree of control teacher and pupil possess over the selection, organisation, pacing and timing of the knowledge transmitted and received in the pedagogical relationship.

(Bernstein, 1975, p. 89)

At first sight, this is a rather abstract concept to grasp, but issues of control in classroom and school situations are at its centre. A wide range of issues are involved: the selection of work and tasks in classrooms; the organization of the groups, space and resources in which classroom activities take place; the ways in which teaching takes place, its timing and the nature of support offered. In a more overarching way, frame also relates to the taken-for-granted rules that normally exist in classrooms and structure the behaviour of both teachers and pupils.

Weak frame implies low levels of constraint and a considerable degree of self-determined control. Strong framing reverses this so that constraints are great and choices are reduced. Clearly this concept relates to the operation of power within the classroom and is incorporated as a dimension:

strong pedagogic frame – weak pedagogic frame

The concept of frame is particularly helpful in relation to the question of the scope that pupils should have to determine their own activity. Some teachers take the view that children need considerable opportunity to select, organize, pace and time their work. Excellent examples of this argument and of the quality of the practice that is possible have been provided by Armstrong (1981) and Rowland (1984). On the other hand, some research work has shown that, where pupils have a high degree of autonomy, there tends to be less 'on-task' behaviour by pupils and less 'teaching' by teachers (Galton, 1987).

As we saw above, frame is also important regarding classroom order and, in a way, describes the extent to which teachers and children are successful in establishing and maintaining a consistent structure of rules and understandings about classroom behaviour. This, of course, provides a means by which the challenges of relatively large class sizes are met. It provides a framework for discipline and for the development of interpersonal relationships. The structure of classroom rules and understandings thus underpins both the order and morality of classroom life (Pollard, 1985, 1988). In these respects, the concept of 'frame' is a very real one to teachers, and one that is monitored continuously and almost instinctively in teaching sessions. Frame is also an important determinant of the nature of pupil experiences and, in this sense, can be seen to describe the extent to which choice and control of activities is given to pupils. Of course, the question of the relative influence of teachers and pupils over classroom activities is a complex one and research evidence has generally shown that even where teachers are strongly committed to pupil choice and autonomy in the classroom, they nevertheless establish a clear framework of rules and expectations. For this reason, a consideration of the relative influence of teachers and pupils is probably not best put in terms of the balance of control, but rather in terms of the extent to which pupils are empowered within their classroom.

As we saw in our earlier discussion, views of knowledge and of learning have a direct relationship to pedagogy. Perhaps this is reflected most directly in terms of teaching contexts and the instructional roles that teachers adopt. Chapter 9 focuses on such issues (for instance, considering the extent of whole-class, group and individual teaching and the use of teacher time), while Chapter 10 considers many of the same issues from the perspective of pupils.

Assessment

Bernstein identifies a third message system in the realization of educational knowledge codes, which he terms 'evaluation'. It is this message system, embodied in the assessment arrangements of the National Curriculum, that has been one of the most controversial aspects of the reforms introduced by the 1988 Education Reform Act, and it has received a great deal of public attention. Perhaps this is so because, on the one hand, it was central to the Government's attempt to increase school accountability and to provide comparative information on which to base parental choice in an educational market, while, on the other hand, the proposed procedures for standardized assessment threatened almost all the commitments to the quality of child experiences in school that primary school teachers so valued. Assessment was thus a site of direct confrontation.

This reminds us of the theme of *power* in our consideration of responses to the National Curriculum and there is no doubt that assessment arrangements, both formative and summative, were initially imposed upon teachers. Standardized National Curriculum assessment, through SATs, proved a time-consuming and curriculum-disturbing activity, and led to a teacher boycott in 1993. However, other, more formative, aspects of assessment, through teacher assessment, were incorporated into classroom practice, with teachers recognizing their value in supporting pupil learning (MacCallum *et al.*, 1993). Assessment thus provides yet another example of the range of teacher responses, through implementation and mediation to resistance.

Perhaps the key factor in this has been teacher judgement of the purposes to which assessment was to be put. Assessment policy is thus a direct reflection of educational *values*. This applies at a number of levels, and does not just involve the use of assessment data to produce inter-school league tables. For instance, at a classroom level assessment can be used in summative ways to record pupil attainment after programmes of work have been completed. On the other hand, it can also be used in a more formative manner to provide more precise support for the learning of all children at their particular levels of achievement. The distinction between assessment as a means of measuring pupil attainment and its use to support the learning processes of children can be expressed in the dimension

formative assessment – summative assessment

This, of course, is a dimension that articulates with teachers' affective concerns for the quality of pupil learning experiences, and, as we shall report in Chapters 11 and 12, we found much evidence of teachers striving to develop constructive forms of assessment while protecting children from what were perceived as threatening experiences.

Assessment practices also reflect educational *understandings* and, in particular, the extent to which outcomes can be identified with categoric certainty compared with outcomes being seen as tentative, provisional and continually constructed by teachers and pupils. While these perceptions clearly relate to characteristics of summative and formative assessment, they also relate to the extent to which assessments are made explicit or remain implicit. Once again, as we saw above, views of knowledge underlie such perceptions. Thus explicit and categoric assessment tends to be associated with views of knowledge as established, while implicit, provisional assessment tends to be used with constructivist approaches to learning. These ideas can be expressed in the dimension

weak categorization – strong categorization

3.6 INTEGRATING DIMENSIONS OF CHANGE

We have now reviewed a wide range of analytic dimensions associated with the substantive themes involved in our research on educational change: school change, teacher professionalism, curriculum, pedagogy and assessment and their impact on pupils. In this section we provide two brief illustrations of their analytic power: first, with regard to teacher professionalism; and second, with regard to classroom practice.

As we have seen, teacher professionalism is multifaceted. However, for the analytical purposes of this research we can identify three particularly important dimensions of teacher thought, context and perception. Regarding teacher views of knowledge and learning we can use the established–constructed dimension. For context, we distinguish between external constraint and classroom autonomy, while for perceptions of the professional role we can recall the distinction between restricted and extended professionalism. Figure 3.1 represents these dimensions together.

An analytic device of this sort has weaknesses, but is useful. For instance, we might compare the traditional, centralized primary schools of France with primary schools in England (Broadfoot *et al.*, 1993). French schools are characterized by highly constrained structures, restricted professionalism among teachers and a view of knowledge as strictly established and codified. Yet much primary school practice in England in the post-war years has been based on teacher autonomy, extended professionalism and teacher commitment to an underlying constructivist view of how children learn and make sense of knowledge. This is an application of the model in Figure 3.1, for international comparison.

It is possible to use such models for making comparisons in the same country over time and this, of course, is what we intend to do regarding the data from the longitudinal PACE research that are reported in this book. In principle, then, we should be able to map the trends of change regarding each key dimension and to produce an integrated analytical summary of them. This is attempted in Chapter 13.

Our second attempt to analyse the interrelationships of key dimensions of change concerns classroom practice. Here we revisit Bernstein's identification of curriculum, pedagogy and assessment as three message systems indicating underlying educational codes. In our discussion in section 3.5, we particularly focused on the relative strengths of curriculum classification, of pedagogic frame and of assessment categorization as distinguishing features of classroom practices. As an analytic device we are again able to represent these factors together (see Figure 3.2). Once again, we can use such a model for both comparative and longitudinal purposes.

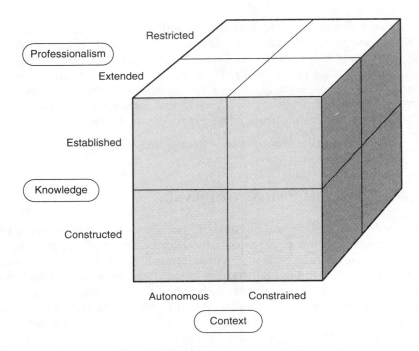

Figure 3.1   *Dimensions of teacher professionalism.*

French primary school education is based on a clearly defined curriculum, tight class-room organization with considerable proportions of whole-class teaching, and strong, categorical assessment of pupil attainment. English primary school classrooms before the 1988 Act revealed a great deal of diversity, but tended to provide more flexible curriculum activities and considerable negotiation of individual work, movement and activity but, in the main, relatively unstructured and tentative assessment.

During the 1980s and since the Education Reform Act of 1988 English primary educa-tion seems, at first sight, to have strengthened and to have become more overt in terms of each of our three dimensions. Thus the National Curriculum has explicitly asserted what must be provided in schools and teachers have been urged to reconsider their classroom teaching practices and to take up more whole-class teaching. They have also been required to implement annual standardized assessment procedures for all seven-year-olds. Of course, the truth, or otherwise, of these rather generalized impressions regarding curriculum, pedagogy and assessment is exactly what this research has been designed to illuminate, and the following chapters do consider these issues in consider-able detail. Again, we will return to this overall analysis in Chapter 13.

In the chapter as a whole, we have seen how our underlying themes of values, under-standing and power relate to various dimensions associated with the school and class-room lives of teachers and pupils. Our discussion has, of necessity, been somewhat abstract and analytical, and in writing the chapter we have been concerned that the holistic realities of the issues we have been discussing should not be lost. With this in mind, we conclude the chapter with a case study of one teacher – a case that underlines

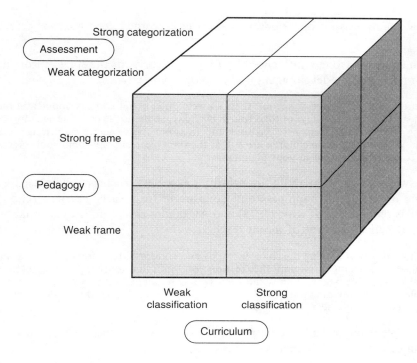

Figure 3.2 *Dimensions of curriculum, pedagogy and assessment.*

the danger of oversimplifying issues that are of great complexity and also demonstrate the cumulative power and personal impact of the multiple innovations that have taken place since the Education Reform Act of 1988.

3.7 INTO PRACTICE

We begin this case study with brief extracts from a teacher interview conducted during the PACE study. We will call the teacher Sally Jones. She has been selected because she provides a particularly lucid example of views, complexities and dilemmas that very many of the teachers in this study expressed. She was not exceptional in her views.

Sally's attitude to children's learning seemed to place her firmly in the developmental tradition of children exploring and learning naturally, the teacher being present simply to respond to their expressed needs for resources and support. There are echoes here of the tone of the Plowden Report of the 1960s, with its confident, constructivist assertion that ' "Finding out" has proved better than being told.' As she put it:

> I think that throughout the primary years, throughout all years in education, there should be time to think, to explore, to do, to find out for yourself. If we're not careful, we'll be going back to Victorian days of a didactic teaching style: this is what we're doing, this

is how you do it, you copy it down from the blackboard. I *don't* want to go back to that!

She seemed to be strongly influenced by Piaget's theories of the stages through which children pass, and by developmental psychology generally:

> When the children arrive at school, there's a very wide social and developmental range. Some start within a few days of their fourth birthday, so there's a very wide age range even among reception children, between four and five, but the developmental range is even wider. Within that, some children are still at the three-year-old developmental stage; you have to be aware of that in your planning.

In answer to a question about her priorities as a class teacher, Sally placed a strong emphasis on children's happiness and comfort in their early years at school. This response is reminiscent of King (1978) and Alexander (1984) on the maternal role and holistic, affective concerns of infant teachers:

> My first priority is making the children happy and comfortable, I don't think you can do any form of teaching at all until they're *with* you, until they're listening and feel at ease. If they're worrying where Mum is and what's going to happen next. . .you're not going to be able to teach anything until they're made to feel 'This is home, this is a good place to be, I'm comfortable here.' What I do after that is a bonus.

However, elements in Sally's own personal biography had also influenced her in the direction of a modified emphasis on basic skills:

> I think it's necessary to have freedom within structure. I like to structure what the children are learning so that there's a natural progression, but to give the children some freedom within that. I was trained in the 1960s – the complete integrated day, do as you will – and it didn't work; I was taught that way myself. I was taught at a progressive school myself; I didn't read until I was eleven or twelve. Now I've got two Open University degrees, and when I look back, I think it was all very well. I was a very good artist and I played the recorder beautifully, but it didn't give me the basic skills I needed. At eleven I thought, 'This is silly; I know what I want to do. I want to teach children, and not in this way.'

The different facets of the perspectives of this one teacher, deputy head of a small village school, are notable. She was concerned for the whole child and for basic skills, she believed that children need happiness and freedom to learn but she also asserted the value of classroom structure and of direct teaching.

The complicated pattern of this teacher's ideology demonstrates the impossibility of trying to fit most teachers into neat compartments: progressive/formal, didactic/exploratory. As many ethnographic studies of schools and teachers (e.g. King, 1978; Pollard, 1985; Nias, 1989) have shown, the behaviour and beliefs of teachers are part of a complex structure of macro and micro factors: personal biography, views of freedom and justice, coping strategies, interests at hand and experience.

Figure 3.3 illustrates in more detail the range of factors that to a greater or lesser extent are likely to influence any one teacher's classroom practice. Starting with the teacher's own professional ideology – itself a construct resulting from a blend of personal biography, training, professional experience and national professional traditions (Broadfoot and Osborn, 1993) – Figure 3.3 illustrates the way in which this ideology is translated into the kind of professional discourse that Sally Jones provides in the above

Figure 3.3 *Factors in classroom practice.*

extract. It is a discourse that embodies the teacher's fundamental ideas about how education should be conducted, but that is mediated by the experienced reality of a sometimes conflicting network of obligations and practical constraints. For this teacher, the influence of both obligation and constraint was very real.

In addition to her duties as deputy head, heavier in a small school where the head teaches a class on four days of the week, Sally was also in charge of ordering stock, was curriculum leader for information technology and science, and ran the school football club, organizing practice sessions and matches with the help of parents. She was interested in her own professional development and had taken an Open University degree and an external BEd, mostly in her own time. She had hoped to go on to an MEd course, but in both 1990 and 1992 had found it impossible to integrate this with the extra paperwork – detailed curriculum planning around attainment targets, recorded assessment, etc. – that the National Curriculum entailed.

Many of Sally's responses to interview questions and comments made in informal conversations revealed clear links between her life experience and her ideology, though the pattern was complicated. Further factors were the type of school where she worked and her experience within it. As the school was situated in a small village, links between it and the community were strong; parents, governors and retired people were seen in the school every day, working with groups of readers, helping with craft activities, coaching football.

This was a twofold process. Sally Jones had a detailed knowledge of the families and backgrounds of her pupils, which supported her practice; at the same time she and her colleagues were open to scrutiny in a way that made establishing relationships of trust essential. Community knowledge influenced her interaction with her pupils and was used to enhance the educational process: parents were always invited into school to discuss any problems that arose, whether the initiative came from them or from the school. Again and again, during her interaction with her pupils, there was evidence not only of Sally's knowledge of her pupils' backgrounds, but also of her readiness to share with them her own.

The reactions of Sally Jones to the introduction of the National Curriculum and other ERA innovations were not easy to categorize as positive or negative. Like many other PACE interviewees, she welcomed the structure of the new curriculum, and felt that it reflected much of her previous practice:

> I'm pleased, because I've been doing these things with children for years, and I've had heads who've said, 'Are you sure you ought to be doing these things with them?' And I've smiled quietly to myself and . . . yes, I have been doing these things because they were at that developmental stage, and I'm a great believer that children at four or five are at their fastest learning phase.

These positive reactions, however, were probably outweighed by the teacher's concerns about what she saw as the disadvantages of the new procedures. These centred chiefly on paperwork, recording and, particularly, constraint:

> I've studied the National Curriculum now, and the Programmes of Study. I've not been worried by them at all, because I've been saying we've been doing that for years. It's the recording of it, that in my head I've had a sort of computer with all this information in, and I've handed it on perhaps once or twice a year to the next teacher, and perhaps the head, so I don't feel I'm going to do any different *work*; it's the recording . . .

In spite of Sally's reservations about what she saw as an over-emphasis on creativity in her own schooldays, she greatly valued the expressive side of the curriculum and was worried by what she saw as the growing imbalance in the opposite direction:

> Have you noticed that the paint has not been out at all this week? I mean, my ancillary would have taken up the whole morning, she would have been drawing children out and doing painting or craft work with them. Now in that area where the sand is now, I used to have a table, it was permanently ready for children painting and doing craft work. She would draw children out in twos, threes or fours daily, so they would have their expressive arts time . . . but I cannot give up my ancillary's time now, it's needed for reading and for maths groups. I *have* to have the ancillary there. Music – I would like to sing more with the children, because singing is a very pleasurable activity; you're all together, sharing a pleasure. *That's* cut down.
>
> With creative writing . . . there's less chance for it to *flow* about what *they* wish to flow. I try to make it interesting, but some of the best writing I have ever had from children has been when they have done something or been somewhere and I really feel I must say, when a child has done this, 'Would you like to write about it?', and I *let* them.

It was clear from many of Sally's comments that she was in a position where she had constantly to try to resolve tensions between what she was required to do, not all of which was unwelcome, as we have seen, and what she judged to be in the best interests of her pupils. Her chief strategy in dealing with these difficulties was to impose an enormous burden of work on herself, and to allow the planning and recording she now felt to be more necessary than ever to make ever greater inroads into her personal time. She had always planned in great detail and had always given freely of her time outside school hours, but she now found that she had to synthesize programmes of study and attainment targets with what she considered to be the appropriate – in fact, an integrated – curriculum for the three age groups within her class. The extra demands meant that she had given up many recreational, pleasurable activities and now found time for one of her favourite pastimes, reading novels, only during holidays.

> What I do is, I make my long-term plan and then on Friday evenings I take all the children's work home and I look through their books, pick up points that are non-topic-related and need to be worked on – could be maths, could be handwriting, could be a maths concept that they haven't got . . . I realize I'd better put that right . . . then I look at my week's plan, and anything I've missed out from the week before I fit in here. I usually look at all the maths that I'm going to do and I work through the Year 2 plots, then Year 1 and then reception and I plan all their maths then. On this plan I've worked out for a month what work I'm going to cover for each group . . . Then I have another one for science and another for language.
>
> It takes me four hours on Friday evening to look through their work, to look through these plans, to get their work in their books and any worksheets ready, it takes another hour on Saturday to write this up, and maybe another two hours of either mounting or other work.

Of more concern to Sally was the difficulty of fitting a prescribed curriculum into her teaching time without allowing this to erode what she valued in her pedagogy:

> The only thing is, I allocate more of my own time now to planning, because I have to literally make sure that my freedom within the structure is the whole teaching time, as opposed to the greater chat time that we had with the children – the freedom within the structure to *talk* to the children about what they're doing, and that's so interesting . . . that's gone, a little bit. You are now very much aware that you're timetabled.
> I have to do a lot of planning prior to teaching to make sure that I fit in that valuable talking time, so I have to be very time-conscious, that I've heard three children read, now I must circulate, or I've heard three children read, now I must go and discuss this topic with them, this maths topic – there is no time to think, 'Oh, I've just seen that they're doing so-and-so, I'll just pop over and ask them about that.' I've thought in my head, I've noted what the children are doing, and probably in the evening I'll think, I must make sure I'll get around to discussing that with them. There's more time taken now; you see things happening and perhaps a year ago I'd have left what I was doing and gone over and chatted, but there are certain things that perhaps don't get picked up.

Perhaps a useful way of examining Sally's efforts to reconcile the contradictory pressures within her practice – the needs of different age groups, curriculum balance, open-ended or prescriptive work, instruction, direction and control – may be to consider some of the defining characteristics of Sally's practice. Table 3.2 lists some of the more typical features of her pedagogy exhibited during a week in which she was closely observed.

The list could be far more detailed, but is probably long enough to make the point. Sally's values were generally child-centred: she found the National Curriculum too prescriptive and felt that it left too little room for the creative, expressive side of education. Yet of the twenty features of her practice listed, allowing that the last two have no particular relevance to any one pedagogic style, only half of the others are possible to relate even roughly to what might usually be expected of a 'progressive' teacher. These features are asterisked; those not so marked are perhaps more generally associated with a 'formal' traditional style.

Table 3.2 *Typical features of the pedagogy of Sally Jones*

Teaches basic maths – sums?	Yes
Uses exploratory maths tasks?	Yes*
Teaches basic English, e.g. phonics?	Yes
Uses reading schemes?	Yes
Uses 'real' books?	Yes*
Gives pupils closed writing tasks?	Yes
Gives pupils open-ended writing tasks?	Yes*
Gives pupils creative writing?	Yes*
Insists on moderate quiet in classroom?	Yes
Refuses to allow children to tease others?	Yes
Tries to develop speaking and listening skills?	Yes*
Uses whole-class teaching?	Yes
Teaches groups?	Yes*
Teaches individuals?	Yes*
Organizes cooperative group work?	Yes*
Differentiates by age?	Yes*
Assesses and marks written work?	Yes
Approves of a broad curriculum?	Yes
Works far longer than designated hours?	Yes
Organizes out-of-school hours activities?	Yes

*Progressive features.

It seems, then, that like many other teachers, our case study teacher has evolved a complex pattern of professional behaviour and beliefs, an eclectic mixture that draws on multiple sources of influence and demonstrates the difficulties involved in simplistic attempts to categorize (or caricature) teachers. It also illustrates the range of factors that are likely to determine the realization of any particular policy directive in practice. It explains why we have chosen to use a range of analytic dimensions as the basis for examining the complex and interrelated changes that have been brought about in primary schools as a result of the 1988 Act.

3.8 CONCLUSION

In this wide-ranging chapter we have considered aspects of educational ideologies, values, policies and practices. We have related debates concerning these to the substantive questions of school change, professionalism, curriculum, pedagogy, assessment and pupil experience. We have also tried to suggest where such educational debates may reflect wider social issues.

In delineating analytical 'dimensions of change' we have aimed to build on a simple idea and use it to provide an integrative conceptual framework. We hope that this will enable readers to interpret the considerable depth and detail of empirical findings that are reported in subsequent chapters of this book.

The underlying themes we have discussed – values, understanding and power – will recur as constant themes in our analysis, leading us finally to the concluding chapter of the book. There we provide an overview of the changes we have documented and make some final judgements of the significance of what is now happening in English primary schools.

Chapter 4

Research Design and Data-Gathering Methods

4.1 INTRODUCTION

The PACE project was designed to monitor the impact of the curricular and assessment structures introduced by the Education Reform Act 1988 for primary schools, teachers and pupils. It identified, for particular study, a sample of infant children from the first group of pupils who would experience the new National Curriculum in full. As we discussed in the introduction to this book, the project was wide-ranging from the start, and it has become no less complex as the phenomenon of almost continuous educational change in the past few years has evolved. From the point of view of the research design, there were two related problems.

First, there was the issue of multiple innovation (Wallace, 1991). As we saw in Chapter 2, while the phenomenon we set out to study – change in primary school classrooms following the introduction of the National Curriculum and assessment – has, itself, several dimensions, these were set in an even wider context of other changes, such as local management of schools, the roles of local education authorities, school inspection requirements, school accountability structures, teacher appraisal systems and the introduction of the market philosophy to education through open enrolment, opting out and publication of league tables of assessment performance. The project team could not address the ramifications of all these issues, nor could we ignore them. Our solution to this dilemma was to attempt to liaise with other research teams and to maintain awareness of the wider social, political and historic context in which our study was set, while maintaining our prime focus at the classroom level. The study can thus contribute to a holistic understanding of the many facets of change in the early 1990s but its contribution, while necessary and perhaps unique, is not sufficient to embrace the full complexity of the system-wide innovation that has occurred.

The second major challenge to our research design concerned when, how and from whom to gather data that would be as nationally representative as possible and would provide valid indications of trends in perspectives, classroom practices and provision. Of course, research resources are always limited and judgements are always required to identify the most worthwhile data-gathering strategies and scheduling. However, in this case these routine decisions were complicated further by the continuing process of change. Even as we write in mid-1993, a major review of the structure of the National Curriculum and assessment procedures is in process. Our approach to this issue, building on ethnographic work (Pollard, 1990; Pollard with Filer, forthcoming), was to identify as a major priority a mapping of the educational experiences of a pupil cohort as they developed within the new structures. The core of the PACE study is thus a longitudinal study of 54 children from nine schools drawn from across England as they move through their schools. The children are among the first pupils who will experience the impact of the National Curriculum and assessment in full and our plan to monitor their experiences is illustrated in Table 4.1.

As Table 4.1 shows, the PACE project has been planned in three parts. This book reports the first phase (PACE 1), the second phase (PACE 2) will be completed in 1994 and the final phase (PACE 3), if funded, is scheduled to finish in 1997.

While this longitudinal strategy monitors pupil experience effectively, it does not yield comparative data on which to base an analysis of change at particular points in the education system. With that in mind, our core, longitudinal, research design was complemented by the collection of a number of cross-sectional data sets from matched samples of teachers and pupils. We have used this strategy both in advance of our cohort study (for example, with regard to the implementation of assessment for seven-year-olds) and to compare how perspectives or practices have developed since our cohort moved on (particularly through the use of interviews with teachers).

Table 4.1   *Phases of the PACE study*

School year	Pupil year	PACE
1988/9	Reception	
1989/90	Year 1	↓ PACE 1
1990/1	Year 2	
1991/2	Year 3	↓ PACE 2
1992/3	Year 4	
1993/4	Year 5	↓ PACE 3
1994/5	Year 6	

Regarding the tracking of change over a longer period, we designed many of our research instruments so that our new, post-ERA data on classroom practice in primary schools would be broadly comparable with earlier studies, such as the ORACLE research (Galton *et al.*, 1980), the Junior Schools Project (Mortimore *et al.*, 1988) and the Bristaix project (Broadfoot and Osborn, 1993). The last project was based on comparisons between teachers in France and England regarding their views of professional responsibilities in the mid-1980s, and this is being partially replicated for the 1990s so that some international comparisons will also be possible (Broadfoot *et al.*, 1993).

The PACE project was thus designed to track pupil experiences and monitor change on a very wide front, though not least among the project aims was the concern to analyse and theorize the new developments. While we take the view that all social science is, inevitably, somewhat inexact, our task has nevertheless been to gather data as carefully as we can and to analyse them to provide a meaningful interpretation of recent developments. This will, we hope, have as much policy relevance for government as it does for teachers.

In the sections of this chapter which follow, we provide more details on data-gathering methods, beginning with an outline of the data-gathering schedule and an explanation of how our national sample of schools was drawn.

4.2 THE DATA-GATHERING SCHEDULE

The first phase of the project was organized around nine main elements of enquiry, each with different aims and data collection methods. There were two rounds of both interviews and questionnaires to a large sample of teachers, two rounds of both classroom and assessment observational studies, using multiple data-gathering methods, and several meetings of a 'federated network' of related research projects. The scheduling of these elements is set out in Figure 4.1, with this phase of the project scheduled from the autumn of 1989 until the end of 1992. Figure 4.1 provides an overview of the different phases of data-gathering and illustrates both the longitudinal and cross-sectional features of the research design.

4.3 THE NATIONAL SAMPLE OF SCHOOLS

Sampling issues are vital in a study of this sort, where an attempt is being made to provide data that are broadly representative of schools, teachers and pupils across a whole country. At its most general level our analysis is derived from 150 teachers and headteachers in 48 schools in eight English local education authorities. At its more specific level, it is based on the perspectives and practices of nine teachers for each year of the study (18 classrooms and teachers being reported here) and six children in each school moving through their primary school careers in those classrooms (a total of 54 pupils). Given the enormous national significance of the innovation being studied and, not least, its cost, it is unfortunate that the sample could not have been bigger. However, given this impossibility and the scarcity of funding for educational research, we took steps to attempt to ensure that our sample represented a full range of primary school practices and circumstances.

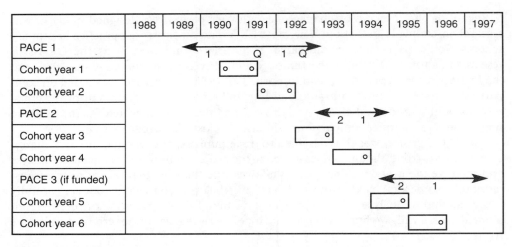

	1988	1989	1990	1991	1992	1993	1994	1995	1996	1997
PACE 1										
Cohort year 1										
Cohort year 2										
PACE 2										
Cohort year 3										
Cohort year 4										
PACE 3 (if funded)										
Cohort year 5										
Cohort year 6										

Key: o Classroom or assessment studies
       1 Key stage 1 teacher interviews and headteacher interviews
       2 Key stage 2 teacher interviews and headteacher interviews
       Q Questionnaire on assessment to teachers and headteachers
Note: PACE 3 is not yet funded and the research design may be developed further.

Figure 4.1   *Phases of data gathering in the PACE project.*

The main sample

An initial strategy, following Economic and Social Research Council advice, was to sample in local education authorities that were regarded as having 'positive support structures' for the implementation of the National Curriculum. A comparison of different types of support at LEA level was not one of the project's aims, and it was felt that this strategy could reduce some extraneous variables from our data-gathering. After consultation with HMI and others, we identified eight such LEAs, aiming for a balance in terms of socio-economic factors, urban/rural areas and a geographical spread in the north, midlands, south-east and south-west of England, as well as making some allowances for ease of access. The chief education officer in each LEA was approached in the first instance for permission to carry out the research in the authority and, with permission obtained, local primary inspectors were designated as liaison officers.

   To identify schools within each local education authority a random sample of 20 infant schools or departments was drawn from a sector of the LEA that had been nominated by local advisers as being broadly representative of the LEA as a whole. From each of these lists, six schools were then selected to reflect different socio-economic locations and distinctive features, such as religious denomination or styles of internal organization. Overall, in producing the final selection of 48 schools, the aim was to obtain a sample that encompassed the considerable variety of educational approaches that currently exist within primary schools. Schools with separate infant departments and schools where infant and junior sections were integrated were both chosen in order to explore any differences that these organizational variations might

Table 4.2 *Sample schools by location and predominant social class of local communities*

	Number	Percentage
Rural, mixed social class	9	19
Urban, settled working/lower middle class	13	27
Inner city, deprived working class	15	31
Urban/suburban middle class	7	15
Urban, mixed social class	4	8
Total	48	100

Table 4.3 *Sample schools by size*

No. on roll	Number of schools	Percentage
Under 150	12	25
151 to 350	29	60
351 to 650	7	15
Total	48	100

have produced. Infant schools that were not attached to any one junior school were excluded in order to ensure the capacity for longitudinal study.

The sample schools were classified broadly in terms of location and social class, and this is shown in Table 4.2. The spread of the sample in terms of school size is shown in Table 4.3.

The sub-sample

In the light of analysis of data collected from the advance questionnaire and first round of interviews, a sub-sample of nine schools was selected for more detailed and observational study in our 'classroom studies' and 'assessment studies'.

Two of these schools were in a relatively accessible area and one was in each of the other LEAs. We attempted to achieve a school sub-sample reflecting the range of socio-economic circumstances, school size and responses to change that we had found, but it cannot be claimed to be strictly representative. Negotiations regarding access moderated our initial selection to avoid problems such as major building works and staff illness. The result was that our final sub-sample was not quite as well balanced as had been hoped. For example, both small rural schools and Roman Catholic schools were over-represented in terms of their occurrence nationally. Nevertheless, the sub-sample schools did, we feel, reflect many of the common characteristics and circumstances of English primary schools. Brief details of the sub-sample schools are as follows.

St Bede's was a Roman Catholic primary school, built in the 1960s, in an established suburb of a medium-sized city in the south of England. Caring and fairly traditional in its approach, although open-plan in design, it was popular with Roman Catholic parents and attracted pupils from across the city. Routines and values were clearly established and the ethos was cohesive.

Kenwood Infant School was situated in very similar surroundings. It was built early this century and was set in a concrete playground, relieved by a new nature area. It had a well-stocked library and resource rooms. There was an emphasis on good behaviour and on making progress, and considerable effort was made to involve children in planning their own work. Children transferred to the nearby junior school at age seven.

Meadway was an open-plan single-storey primary school built in the 1970s. It was set in an inner-city housing estate and was surrounded by high-rise blocks of flats. The area suffered from high unemployment, significant crime rates and considerable vandalism. The school was light, airy and attractively decorated with children's work and other displays, and its pupils and staff reflected the multi-ethnic character of the local community. Among the teachers there was a high degree of joint planning, but their efforts often had to be directed towards the behavioural needs of the children. Ancillary support staff were provided to help with this.

Greenmantle Primary School was located in a market town, in central southern England, where traditional agricultural occupations coexisted with modern light industry. Its buildings were a mixture of Victorian and newer architecture. It was a traditional school, popular locally, where a high proportion of the pupils had prosperous, professional family backgrounds. Teaching methods were fairly traditional, with a good deal of positive reinforcement.

St Anne's was a Roman Catholic primary school in one of the country's least affluent LEAs in the north of England. The school population was drawn from a large council estate of very disadvantaged families. Many parents were unemployed and some children were on the 'at risk' register. The Roman Catholic ethos provided a stabilizing influence. Teaching, which was topic-centred, was normally fairly structured, while allowing for pupil choice of activities for part of each day.

Orchard was a small rural primary school in central England, surrounded by trees and fields, and drawing pupils from other nearby villages. It served a mixture of professional, business and farming families. Parental expectations were high and pupils were well motivated. Because of the school's small size all the children were in mixed age classes. Class teachers had considerable classroom autonomy.

Lawnside Primary School was set in a village near a large Midlands conurbation. The population consisted of a mixture of commuters and local families with agricultural connections. Conditions were cramped but the school was welcoming and provided for a number of travellers' children from a nearby site. The ethos was caring and structured. School uniform was almost universally worn and most parents were supportive.

Valley was another rural school, set in a traditional village in the south-west of England. The core of the school was Victorian but there were modern extensions and good facilities. The population was a socio-economic mixture including local farming families and professional people who worked in nearby small towns. There was a fairly high proportion of the latter and the school attracted pupils from the surrounding area. The level of support was high, both from parents and from other local residents, and the children were generally enthusiastic. All the classes were of mixed age and teaching methods were eclectic.

Audley Infant School was built between the wars. It was somewhat over-crowded but busy and well resourced. The location was an industrial village in the North-West where there was little unemployment compared with the surrounding area. Nevertheless, few local people were particularly affluent. There was a fairly high degree of teacher control, but children were allowed a degree of freedom within tasks. Children transferred to the neighbouring junior school at age seven.

All schools and LEAs were provided with outlines of the project's aims, design and ethical guidelines. As the project has progressed they have received project newsletters and occasional papers and we have been grateful for the very high degree of support and cooperation they have offered. Pseudonyms are, of course, used in this book for all LEAs, schools, teachers and pupils.

In the following sections we discuss sampling methods in more detail with regard to each method of data-gathering.

4.4 THE ADVANCE QUESTIONNAIRE TO TEACHERS

An initial 'advance questionnaire' was distributed by post to the main sample of 48 schools. This was designed to gather evidence of headteacher and class teacher perceptions on topics such as accountability, professional responsibility and educational aims, as well as to provide background information on age, gender, length of teaching experience, etc. In the first instance, questionnaires were completed by headteachers and by teachers of reception and Year 1 classes, since the children who would later form the cohort to be studied were at that time in reception classes. For cross-sectional comparative purposes, identical questionnaires were again distributed and completed two years later, in the summer term 1992, when heads and teachers of Year 1 and Year 2 classes took part.

The response rate from schools was 100 per cent in the first round when the researchers collected the questionnaires personally, but slightly less good in the second round (85 per cent), when we relied upon schools returning questionnaires by post with follow-up letters and telephone reminders. Apart from one open-ended question, the questionnaires used pre-coded scaling techniques in order to ensure rapid completion. Questions about gender and age group, for example, were answered by means of ticking boxes, while the importance teachers attributed to various educational objectives was indicated by a five-point scale. Teachers' views of their relative accountability to such categories as colleagues, parents, pupils, the Government and society in general were similarly graded on a five-point scale. However, the final question was open-ended: respondents were asked, 'What does professional responsibility mean to you?' These questions and procedures were modelled on the Bristol–Aix (Bristaix) study (Broadfoot and Osborn, 1993) and enabled comparisons to be made with a sample of English teachers questioned before the introduction of the National Curriculum, and with teachers in France.

The pre-coded questions were processed for statistical analysis using the SPSS statistical package. Responses to the open-ended question on professional responsibility were analysed for themes and categories and subsequently coded along four dimensions: responsibility to whom, responsibility for what, responsibility for areas of teaching and reflections on the role of 'being a teacher'.

The resulting analysis was tabulated, where appropriate, and circulated among team members using data analysis record sheets. These recorded data codes, sources, descriptions, dates and modes of analysis, summaries of findings and introductory comments on significance. This system of sharing and disseminating analysis was used for all strands of the research.

4.5 STRUCTURED INTERVIEWS WITH TEACHERS

In the same 48 primary schools, a first round of interviews was conducted in the summer term 1990. In each school, the headteacher or the head of the infant department, the teacher of the reception class and a Year 1 infant teacher took part. The interviews were based on a structured schedule, but many questions were open-ended and exploratory. They aimed to explore staff perceptions of the impact of National Curriculum requirements on their own work and on the life of the school as a whole.

The main areas of discussion were:

1. Headteachers' perceptions of the changes needed and their strategies for providing for these. In addition to the more obvious obligations enshrined in the curriculum and assessment arrangements, issues here also included perceived changes in the school ethos, in the head's role, in staff relationships and in relations between staff, parents and other outside bodies.
2. Teachers' perceptions of the impact of National Curriculum and assessment arrangements on the curriculum and pedagogy of the school as a whole and of their own individual classrooms. Topics here included changes in curriculum content or in time allocation to different subjects, in teaching style, in assessment and record-keeping, in the quantity and quality of extra-curricular activities and in relations with parents.
3. Perceived changes in pupils' responses to schooling, both in their attitudes and in their learning.
4. Teachers' responses to the preparation they had been given to help them meet the novel requirements being placed upon them. During the initial stages of the project such discussion focused on the in-service training itself, whereas later on it was possible to gather some data on teachers' actual experiences of implementing new procedures, especially the standard assessment tasks (SATs).

Interviewers made detailed notes of the interviews, marking particularly illuminating responses for later transcription from tape-recordings, which were used for subsequent extension or cross-referencing as necessary.

Similar interviews and questionnaires were again completed two years later, in the summer term 1992, when headteachers and teachers of Year 1 and Year 2 classes took part. The core of the interviews was unchanged to make it possible to trace changes taking place in teachers' perceptions during the study period. However, in view of the multiple changes in government policy during the intervening period, schedules were adjusted to take account of such innovations as 'league tables' of schools' assessment performance and the strengthened role of governors.

A coding schedule and coding sheets were constructed after pilot analysis of a few interviews, with the schedule being developed to allow for diversity as well as for typicality. Most coding categories allowed for 'other' responses, which were included in the subsequent analysis when they occurred in significant numbers. Statistical analysis of the coded data was carried out using SPSS and evaluated by all members of the research team. Methods of analysis included comparisons of frequency distributions of variables for the 1990 and 1992 sweeps. Tests of statistical significance (chi squared) were used to assess the significance of the changes. Cross-tabulation and factor analysis were also used for investigative analysis.

4.6 CLASSROOM STUDIES

Detailed case studies of individual Year 1 classrooms in 1990 and Year 2 classrooms in 1991 provided the next element of data collection.

All the sub-sample classrooms selected for closer study were visited for a full week during each of the autumn terms of 1990 and 1991. This phase of the research included qualitative observation, systematic observation and interviews with pupils and teachers. The research focused primarily on curriculum and pedagogy, while assessment processes, although observed and recorded, were the prime focus for a separate element of the study. This is discussed in section 4.7.

Six children from each classroom were sampled by means of random selection from the class list. This procedure was extended in subsequent rounds if one of the original sample of children was absent or had left the class. When the sample school had been identified according to the criteria discussed in section 4.3, and cooperation had been agreed, the headteacher and class teacher were sent an overview of the week's data collection plan (see Table 4.4). The classroom study data collection plan set up a

Table 4.4 *The classroom studies timetable*

In advance	*Ask for*:	Class list	
		Curriculum plan	
		Sociometry	
	Give:	Overview of research intentions for week	

During week	a.m.	p.m.	Other
Monday	Field notes	Teacher interview	In evening: analyse sociometric data, consider friendships in relation to pen sketches
		Field notes	
Tuesday	Teacher audio-recording	Two child interviews (A + B)	
	Systematic observation of two children and teacher (child A + B + teacher)	Systematic observation of two children and teacher (child C + D + teacher)	
Wednesday	Recording and observation as Tuesday (child C + D + teacher)	Interviews with child C + D	Over lunch, etc. on Tuesday, Wednesday and Thursday: hold general discussions with teacher
		Observation as Tuesday	
Thursday	Recording and observation as Tuesday (child E + F + teacher)	Interviews with child E + F	
		Observation as Tuesday (child A + B + teacher)	
Friday	Field notes Contingency time	Teacher interview	

schedule for each day, which provided blocks of time for particular types of data-gathering and ensured efficient sequencing of the process.

Before the visit by a member of the research team, each teacher was asked to provide copies of the class list, a curriculum plan and sociometric data collected from all the children in the class. The last of these, and each of the other major data-gathering methods used in the classroom studies, are described in more detail below.

Sociometry

Each child was asked to write the names of three friends within her or his own class on a sheet specially designed for this purpose. These were later used to complete a sociometric grid showing children's friendship patterns and group membership, with a view to examining possible differentiation and polarization.

Field notes

Field notes were relatively open-ended. The aims were to provide a rich and detailed account of the various routine procedures and phases of a school day and, at other times in the week, to record any particularly interesting or theoretically significant events, statements or activities.

Systematic observation

Systematic observation was carried out during the mornings and afternoons of the three central days of the week of classroom study, so that a wide spread of activities could be observed. Break-times were not observed. Each of the six 'target children' in each class was observed during both a morning and an afternoon, and a rotational system was used to focus successive periods of observation on target children and the teacher.

Observations were recorded on coding forms relating to a ten-minute period (see Figure 4.2, pp. 52–3). Six minutes of systematic observation, using a ten-second interval, were followed by four minutes of contextualizing notes. When focusing on the teacher, the observer coded 'interaction' and 'teacher activity' simultaneously at ten-second intervals. When a pupil was being observed, the observer coded 'child activity' and 'interaction' at all ten-second intervals. 'Teacher activity' was recorded only when the target child was directly interacting with the teacher or with another adult.

The sheet also carried a list of 'curriculum context' categories – English, maths, etc. – and another of 'pedagogic context', including class interaction and individual and group work. These were recorded, at the end of each six-minute observation period, in terms of the 'main' or 'part' aspects of the curriculum and pedagogic context. Where more than one curriculum context or pedagogic context had been observed, both 'main' and 'part' were used. More qualitative contextualizing notes were also completed immediately after the timed recording and these were structured by the headings of curriculum, pedagogy, interactions/relationships, assessment, other/general.

Reliability of the systematic observation schedule was established by means of pairs of observers coding simultaneously in classrooms that were not part of the research sample. Reliability coefficients are based on the occasions on which the observers agreed as a proportion of the total of observations made. Percentage reliability figures for all the variables presented here were above 80 per cent as follows: pupil activity 89.4, pupil interaction 94.0, teacher activity 90.4, teacher interaction 82.5, curriculum content 86.1, pedagogic context 83.0. (In some cases, satisfactory reliability figures were obtained by merging categories where agreement was low; for example, different types of group context and the distinction between pupil interaction with one or more than one other child. In these cases it is the merged categories that are used in the analysis.) See the Appendix for definition of each category used in the systematic observations.

Child interviews

Each target child was interviewed, individually, following the period during which he or she had been a focus for classroom observation. The aim here was to complement observational data with material on pupil perspective, so that explanatory analyses could be attempted.

Child interview questions were structured and covered the following areas:

- discussion of an observed curriculum task;
- views of curriculum subjects;
- child culture and friendships;
- views of curricular activities;
- views on pupil control;
- views on hierarchy in achievement;
- views on teacher assessment and responses;
- views on relationships with the teacher.

In the early stages of the project the children interviewed were very young, i.e. aged six and seven. It was particularly important to establish and maintain rapport and interest. If necessary, interviewers would rephrase questions and, if the child appeared to lose concentration, break off and complete the interview later. Most children appeared to enjoy the interviews and many requests for interview were received from children not in the sub-sample.

An attempt was made to embed the interviews in pupils' experiences. Thus, for the first questions the researcher and child discussed some work produced during a classroom activity that had been observed earlier. Children were then asked whether they felt the activity was enjoyable and the reasons for their judgement, what they saw as the teacher's reasons for giving them the activity and their views of their own achievement in this and in other curriculum areas.

The next set of questions referred to child culture, polarization, stigma and views of self. For orientation purposes, children were shown the illustration of a playground scene on the cover of the Puffin book *Please, Mrs Butler*, by Allan Ahlberg (1984). This shows clearly discernible friendship groups and typical playground activities. Children were then asked to confirm their friendships, to describe activities in their playground and explain more about their peer relationships.

Further questions were based around a picture book that the PACE team had

PACE CHILD OBSERVATION

Observer	Teacher		Pupil year	LEA
. . . .	. . . .		. . . .	. . . .

Target child	Pupil code	Time	Date
. . . .	. . . .	. . . . :	. . . . / . . . . / . . . .

Child activity

Child interaction

Teacher activity

Child activity

Child interaction

Teacher activity

CHILD ACTIVITY

TE	Task engagement (apparent)
TM	Task management
D	Distracted
B	Both distracted and TM
A	Assessment (explicit)
W	Waiting for teacher
X	Waiting (other)
O	Out of room/sight
R	Reading to teacher

CHILD INTERACTION

O	Alone
TC	With teacher in whole class
TO	With teacher one-to-one
TG	With teacher in group
AO	With other adult one-to-one
G	With individual girl
B	With individual boy
X	With a group of boys
Y	With a group of girls
M	With a mixed group

TEACHER ACTIVITY

I	Instruction (curriculum)
C	Control (behaviour)
D	Direction (task management)
A	Assessment (explicit)
E	Encouragement (support, facilitating)
N	Negative (discouragement, criticism)
R	Hearing children read
O	Other

PEDAGOGIC CONTEXT

	Main	Part
Class teaching		
Individual work		
Cooperative group work		
Group with teacher		
Other (specify)		

CURRICULUM CONTEXT

	Main	Part
RE		
English		
Maths		
Science		
History		
Geography		
Music		
Art		
Physical education		
Technology		
Per. & soc.		
Non-curric.		

Figure 4.2 *(this page and opposite) The child observation schedule (note: teacher observation sheets contained no 'child activity' categories and listed 'teacher interaction' rather than 'child int . . . . . .*

Observer	Teacher	Class	LEA	Date	Target Child	Time

NOTES:

Notes to yourself
where necessary

Curriculum
Classification
(strength of subject boundaries)

Pedagogy
Framing
(control over pacing and organization of tasks)

Interactions/Relationships

Assessment

Other/General

produced. Again this was an attempt to embed the interview in contexts that would be familiar to the children – in this case discussion of a picture book. The book began with a double-page collage of bright illustrations of children engaged in twelve different classroom activities, derived from the Ahlbergs' Picture Puffin *Starting School* (Ahlberg and Ahlberg, 1988). The activities shown varied from core curriculum subjects to expressive areas, and children were asked about their curricular likes and dislikes and the reasons for these. These questions were followed by others on pupil and teacher control of classroom activities.

Other illustrations, some commissioned for the study, were used to stimulate pupils' responses to questions on differences in attainment at school and to elicit views on hierarchy in achievement. To examine children's views on aspects of teacher assessment, an illustration was used of a teacher talking to a child about his work. The feelings of the child in the picture were discussed. Children were then asked about their own feelings when the teacher looked at their work and about teachers' responses to their work.

The last questions in the child interview dealt with children's views on their teacher and relationships with her or him. Another picture from *Starting School* was used, showing a whole class sitting with a teacher, and children were asked how they got on with, and what they liked best about, their teacher.

The interviews were recorded in longhand and then typed. Analysis was initially undertaken using the Ethnograph, a computer program for processing qualitative data. However, this was later abandoned in favour of a relational database capable of integrating qualitative interview data, data on pupil sex, attainment, social class and sociometric status, and the quantitative results of the systematic observations.

Teacher interviews

Structured interviews with the class teachers took place on the first and last afternoons of the observation week. Notes were made on a schedule during the interview, but the whole conversation was also tape-recorded for transcription.

The first day's interview was aimed at obtaining:

- pen sketches of target children;
- brief descriptions of attainment, behaviour and social relationships of each child in the class;
- curriculum plans;
- details of the procedure for the allocation of work to children;
- normal routines of the teacher's morning.

The last day's interview covered:

- teacher assessment;
- the teacher's views of work and changing role;
- the teacher's views of pupil control of learning;
- the teacher's views of relationships with children.

Unstructured discussions, throughout the week, supplemented these pre-specified interviews. Observers took whatever opportunities arose to seek clarification or ask questions suggested by observation or field notes, and teachers' views were written up in full as soon as possible afterwards.

Tape-recorded interaction

In some classes, teachers agreed to carry small cassette recorders fitted with throat microphones for some teaching sessions. Tapes were not transcribed in full, but extracts were used for analytical purposes in conjunction with field notes to provide a more detailed picture of pedagogy and of teacher–child interaction.

Analysis of classroom studies data

As with all other elements of data-gathering in the PACE study, responsibility for data analysis was shared and data analysis sheets were produced to record and summarize results for circulation among the team. Sociometric diagrams were completed for each class, revealing sociometric status and the membership of friendship groups. Systematic observation data were entered and analysed using SPSS. Questions from both child interviews and teacher interviews were distributed among team members for initial analysis and tabulation.

From this point in each round of data-gathering, the analyses from the various empirical aspects of the classroom studies were compared and integrated together where possible. This provided for a degree of methodological triangulation and multifaceted analysis. For instance, teachers' views of children's achievement levels could be compared with pupil perceptions on both their own and their classmates' attainments, related to other data from the pupil interviews and then linked to patterns that had been produced from the systematic observation of teacher or pupil classroom behaviour. Field notes and transcripts of tape-recorded teacher–pupil interaction were also available for further augmentation of any emerging analysis.

4.7 ASSESSMENT STUDIES

During the early part of the summer term 1991, Year 2 classes in the nine schools of our sub-sample were visited for two days each while Standard Assessment Tasks (SATs) were in progress. This meant that pupils who were one year older than our longitudinal pupil sample, and their teachers, were observed and interviewed while the first round of SATs took place. This was our first use of an anticipatory cross-sectional strategy (see section 4.1) and was designed to enable us to make comparisons of change as our main pupil cohort experienced the SATs in the following year and to monitor the piloting of SATs.

Observers watched whichever SATs teachers had chosen to carry out in the data-gathering period and the unit of analysis was taken to be the SAT as a complete classroom episode. An attempt was thus made to observe each SAT in operation from beginning to end and to record, using field notes, as much detail of the interaction and process as possible. Following SAT observation, interviews were conducted, on an individual basis, with as many as possible of the pupils who had experienced the observed SAT.

During the 1992 assessment study the process was similar, but this time the cohort of pupils on which we focused *was* that of our continuing study. This was, in other words, our third major period of sustained observation and interviews with these children. This time data were gathered for three days in each classroom and qualitative observations were more focused. Again, as many pupils as possible were interviewed: observers made sure that these included the six target pupils in each class.

Further details of the data-collection processes follow.

Classroom observation during the SATs

Observers used open-ended observation methods, making field notes and written records of teacher–child and child–child conversation and other interaction, while recording at intervals brief notes on such pre-selected categories as preparations for the SAT, arrangements for the rest of the class, extra help, if any, provided for the teacher and post-SAT events. Various SATs were observed in use. However, when the same SAT was observed in different classrooms it was possible to examine the effect of different styles of teacher presentation and of physical circumstances on the perceptions and performance of pupils.

In the 1992 assessment studies there were some adjustments to the data-gathering programme to increase standardization of data. Schools were also asked if observers could be present when one specific SAT, Maths 3, was carried out. It was thus possible to record, for an apparently 'standardized' test situation, the effects of different contexts and interaction.

Interviews with teachers about assessment

Teacher interviews were structured in both rounds and covered such areas as their perceptions of the role assessment should have in infant classrooms, the relative degree of value they found in SATs and in teacher assessment, and the support they were given in carrying out the process. Further topics covered included their perceptions of their pupils' experience, including the question of whether National Curriculum assessment procedures reinforced a sense of academic hierarchy among the children and whether they took steps to address this issue. Interviews conducted one year later during the second SAT period differed only slightly from the first set, so that changes in perceptions could be tracked.

Interviews with pupils about assessment

Children were asked about whether they had enjoyed the tasks observed, how they rated their own performances and those of their classmates, whether they discussed the work at home and how they saw the purpose of the tasks carried out. These data were coded and entered on our database for analysis.

4.8 ASSESSMENT QUESTIONNAIRES

The final strand of data-gathering on assessment took place after completion of SAT procedures, in both 1991 and 1992. All 48 schools in the main PACE sample received questionnaires for all teachers involved in carrying out SATs. The response rate was 92 per cent of schools in 1991 and 81 per cent in 1992. Teachers were asked to note, using five-point scales, their views of the degree of difficulty in organizing the tasks, the degree of value they attached to the results, the support they received within their schools and the reactions of their pupils. Headteachers were asked an open-ended question about the experience of the process in their schools. Both quantitative and qualitative material was therefore available for analysis on this major innovation.

4.9 THE FEDERATED RESEARCH NETWORK

The final layer of research activity concerned 'federated research', through which the project aimed to facilitate the sharing of concerns and findings with other researchers. This provided an opportunity for coordinated research, development and dissemination, through seminars, the exchange of papers and the organization of conferences. Five specific PACE meetings, of various sorts, were convened during this first stage of the project and members of the project team liaised with researchers in many other universities and, occasionally, with officials of NCC and SEAC.

Through such liaison, it was also intended that the relatively wide-ranging PACE data set could articulate with and contextualize qualitative studies, such as Nias *et al.* (1989, 1992), Acker (1990), Muschamp (1993), Stone (1993), Filer (1994) and Pollard with Filer (forthcoming). In this, we were conscious of the strengths and weaknesses of different research approaches and believed that there could be a reciprocal exchange of insights.

4.10 A NOTE ON THE PRESENTATION OF THE QUANTITATIVE DATA

Tests of statistical significance have been used in connection with our teacher interview and questionnaire data. For the tables of findings, the convention has been adopted of indicating levels of statistical significance by means of asterisks alongside the tables. Probabilities from chi squared tests are shown as follows:

$$p \geqslant 0.05 \qquad \text{not significant}$$
$$0.05 > p \geqslant 0.005 \qquad *$$
$$0.005 > p \geqslant 0.0005 \qquad **$$
$$0.0005 > p \qquad ***$$

Where tables are based on data derived from systematic observation, the figures are percentages of observations rather than percentages of individuals. Tests of statistical significance are therefore not appropriate.

Tests of significance have not been used in the case of the pupil interview data because the overall samples of children in Year 1 and Year 2 are not independent of one another. In most cases figures for Year 1 and Year 2 refer to the same children, but, as there was some natural drop-out and replacement of children from Year 1 to Year 2 (see section 4.6), the groups are neither identical nor totally independent of one another. It is therefore not appropriate to use tests of statistical significance.

4.11 CONCLUSION

The procedures outlined above provided large quantities of varied data allowing for analysis on several levels. The range and richness of the data set was an excellent resource. However, there was a potential risk that the scale of empirical work would steer the project towards description of change, rather than providing the foundation for analysis and theorization. As ours was one of very few independently funded social science projects on changes in primary schools following the Education Reform Act, we felt that we had a particular responsibility to stand back from simple evaluation of the innovation and to attempt to discern and articulate more fundamental developments and consequences.

In this we were able to build on some of our previous work. For instance, one of our major theoretical concerns was the influence of external constraints on teacher professionalism and here it was possible to develop work from the ESRC project 'Teachers' Conceptions of Their Professional Responsibilities in England and France' (Broadfoot and Osborn, 1993). Another theoretical issue centred on teacher–pupil interaction and strategies in classrooms, on which we were able to develop the work of Pollard (1985) and others in tracing the changes in classroom practices adopted by teachers and children as they responded to new curricular and assessment arrangements. These concerns emerged, as has been reported in Chapter 3, as a set of 'dimensions', against which, we believe, it is possible to map change in primary school practices and experiences over time.

The findings reported in this book thus also provide a basis for the next phase of the study: PACE 2. This will continue the process of describing and analysing the innovations of the National Curriculum and its assessment procedures as they impact on both schools and the cohort of children in this longitudinal study.

Chapter 5

The Perceptions and Strategies of Headteachers

5.1 INTRODUCTION

We begin our extensive account of empirical findings with this chapter on headteachers' perceptions of school change. This provides an important school-level context to the later chapters and draws on our wider sample of interviews with 48 headteachers.

All 48 headteachers of the schools in the study were interviewed twice: in the summer term of 1990 and again in the summer term of 1992. They were asked a variety of questions about their school and their approach to education, the changes they had made and those they were planning in response to the National Curriculum, their strategies for change and their views on current developments in primary education. In this chapter we shall consider overall perspectives on the nature of change and the pressures on headteachers, and also issues of school strategies for change and the relationship of these to the substance of change.

The broader context of these changes was a series of developments in educational policy, which have already been touched on in Chapters 2 and 3. Of particular relevance to the discussion in this chapter are changes in the governance of schools, and these can be related to the dimensions of power that were considered in Chapter 3.

Before the 1988 Education Reform Act schools had relative autonomy with regard to curriculum and pedagogy but were relatively constrained with regard to resources and management. They had close relationships with their local authorities, and these could be characterized as being most directive in the areas of resources and management, and usually least directive in the area of curriculum and pedagogy. They had much more distant relationships with central government, which did not impact directly on any aspect of the work of the school. While government determination of resources was mediated for schools by local authority processes, central government influence on the curriculum and teaching was mediated by teachers' own professional practice.

Following the 1988 Act we can identify a dual shift in control. First, there was a gradual transfer of power away from local authorities and towards central government; second, there was an extension of the agenda beyond resources and management to include curriculum and, to a lesser extent, teaching methods. Thus, after 1988, primary schools were directed regarding curriculum in a way that had never been the case in the past, but, at least in principle, they had greater freedom to manage their own resources, staffing and other responsibilities. The latter, though something of an illusion given constrained budgets and new accountability requirements to parents and governors, was reflected through the introduction of local management of schools and school development planning (Hargreaves and Hopkins, 1991).

Within primary schools the role of the headteacher is absolutely central, with regard to legal powers and responsibilities and, usually, with regard to informal influence and interpersonal relationships. Handy and Aitken (1986) have detailed this centrality in terms of organizational theory, and Jones and Hayes (1991) in terms of current educational developments. Nias *et al.* (1992), in a study that is mainly concerned with democratic and collaborative approaches to school management, emphasize that, even in schools characterized by high degrees of staff participation in decision-making, the role of the head is crucial.

All the headteachers interviewed in the present study saw themselves as having a central role in responding to educational initiatives such as the National Curriculum. Even those who were least happy about the changes being made, or (apparently) least well-prepared to make them, were clear that the school response was their responsibility. Conversely, all the teachers interviewed took the centrality of the headteacher's role for granted, even when they were emphasizing the collective nature of their school's response.

In this chapter we shall first describe in a factual manner the content of change as it was seen by the headteachers, its relationship to other pressures on them, how they felt about different changes and their experience of changing patterns of constraint and autonomy. We shall then use the interview material to delineate different strategies pursued in schools in order to manage change, and shall look at the relationship between these strategies and the extent of the changes being made. We shall also consider these changes in terms of the dimensions for school change identified in Chapter 3. In particular, in terms of the operation of power in the educational system, we shall consider the extent to which changes were imposed or negotiated and whether school responses can be characterized as forms of compliance, mediation or resistance. Within schools, we will be considering the extent of management by imposition or management by participation. At various points in the chapter, we will note a further dimension with regard to the operation of educational values in relation to the extent of individualism and collegiality in the operation of schools.

5.2 WHAT CHANGES DID HEADTEACHERS PERCEIVE FOLLOWING THE INTRODUCTION OF THE NATIONAL CURRICULUM?

Fundamental to the National Curriculum introduced following the 1988 Act was a common school curriculum consisting of the three core foundation subjects (English, mathematics and science) and six other foundation subjects (technology, history, geography, art, music and physical education). The headteachers were asked in both rounds of interviews about changes in curriculum balance as a result of the National Curriculum. In Table 5.1 their replies are summarized in terms of more or less time being spent on particular curriculum areas. It should be noted that the heads were not asked subject by subject whether more or less time would be spent, but were asked in an open-ended way about curriculum balance. Their replies were then categorized according to subject. In this sense, the figures in Table 5.1 differ from those in Table 7.9, which summarize the teachers' account of curriculum change. Teachers were asked subject by subject whether more or less time would be spent, while the headteachers' answers reflect the changes in curriculum balance they gave in response to an open-ended question.

As Table 5.1 shows, the areas where heads were most likely to see the need for an increase in curriculum time were science and technology. In the first round of interviews (summer term 1990) almost three-quarters of heads mentioned science as an area of increase. In the second round of interviews (summer 1992) this had fallen to under a half of heads saying they needed to increase science. Presumably the fall indicates that many schools achieved the necessary increase in science content in the intervening period, but although the figures are lower in 1992, science is still the area of the curriculum most likely to be mentioned as requiring expansion. In both rounds of interviews just over 40 per cent of the heads said that technology needed to be increased. In the first round

Table 5.1 *Headteachers' perceptions of curriculum change (percentages)*

Curriculum subject	1990		1992	
	More	Less	More	Less
English	12.5	20.8	8.3	27.1
Maths	2.1	16.7	6.3	10.4
Science	72.9	2.1	43.8	0.0
Technology	41.7	0.0	41.7	2.1
History	10.4	6.3	31.3	0.0
Geography	6.3	6.3	31.3	0.0
Art	4.2	20.8	0.0	10.4
Music	4.2	16.7	2.1	0.0
PE	2.1	6.3	0.0	2.1
RE	4.2	2.1	4.2	2.1

Source: PACE 1 headteacher interviews.
Sample: 48 headteachers.
Date: summer 1990 and summer 1992.

of interviews science and technology stand out in the responses as areas for increase, but in the second round, although they are still the most likely to be mentioned, history and geography also appear as subjects where an increase is needed. In 1992 just under a third of heads said that each of these would need to be expanded, indicating that as the core subjects became established heads were beginning to look ahead to foundation subjects that would be the subject of future assessments.

Table 5.1 also shows the curriculum areas where heads thought there had been a reduction in curriculum time. In both years English was identified by a substantial minority as an area of the curriculum that was having less time devoted to it, and the proportion of heads saying this increased over the two interviews. Other areas identified as experiencing a decrease in time were mathematics and art. In 1992 there was less mention of curriculum areas in which time was being reduced than there had been in 1990, possibly indicating that necessary reductions had already taken place. It is also worth noting that the percentages in the 'more' column sum to a much higher value than the percentages in the 'less' column. This reflects the fact that headteachers were more likely to talk about areas for increase than they were about areas for decrease, and this was especially so in the second round of interviews. However, this effect was moderated by the existing imbalance in the time devoted to different curriculum areas and the fact that English and, to a lesser extent, mathematics were particularly likely to be mentioned as decreasing. As the observation data presented in Chapter 7 show, English and mathematics made up a high proportion of the curriculum. Thus a relatively small decrease in the time available for these subjects could provide space for a relatively large increase in the time available for subjects such as history and geography.

Headteachers had given a lot of thought to the curriculum adjustments they had made. They were conscious of the pressure on the time teachers had to cover the curriculum and the importance of trying to find an appropriate balance. A typical comment was: 'I have had to think very carefully about curriculum balance and the best use of time. I try to identify areas where subjects cover a lot of attainment targets.' Although the developments in the science curriculum that most schools found necessary were generally welcome, the pressures on other areas of the curriculum were experienced as a problem by many heads. For example: 'Ironically we are having to spend less time on the basics. A broader curriculum is good in principle but not necessarily for these children – they need a lot of time on basic number and language.'

In terms of the dimensions of change identified in Chapter 3, the understanding of curriculum content, as expressed by headteachers in interviews, had clearly shifted in the direction of a more subject-centred curriculum and subject specialism. The identification of subjects as a way of thinking about curriculum change was a noticeable feature of the interview and was a change in discourse that some headteachers found uncomfortable.

As would be expected, all the headteachers talked about changes in curriculum and in assessment as consequences of the National Curriculum. They were also asked explicitly about other possible changes that were not directly required by the National Curriculum but were possible consequences of it. Their responses to these questions are given in Table 5.2 for both rounds of interviews. Staff development was the area that heads were most likely to identify as this sort of indirect consequence of the National Curriculum. Indeed, over 80 per cent of heads identified staff development as an area of change in the first round of interviews and 90 per cent in the second round, with over half identifying it as an area of 'great change' in 1992.

Table 5.2   *Headteachers' perceptions of non-curriculum change (percentages)*

Non-curriculum change	1990		1992	
	Great change	Moderate change	Great change	Moderate change
Teaching methods and staff organization	8.3	43.8	25.0	31.3
Staff responsibilities	20.8	39.6	25.0	41.7
Staff development needs	16.7	66.7	54.2	35.4
Changes in relations to parents	8.4	43.8	33.3	27.1

Source: PACE 1 headteacher interviews.
Sample: 48 headteachers.
Date: summer 1990 and summer 1992.

Related to staff development was the degree of perceived change in staff responsibilities. Sixty per cent of heads said these had changed in the first round of interviews and this increased to two-thirds in the second round. Teaching methods and staff organization were also identified as areas of change by about half the heads in the first interview and slightly more in the second. Changes in relation to parents were also identified by about half the heads in the first interview and this had increased to about 60 per cent in the second interview. In both these areas heads were strikingly more likely to describe 'great changes' in the second interviews.

It is evident that the great majority of schools had experienced changes associated with but not directly required by the National Curriculum, and that aspects of staff development, staff responsibilities and teaching approaches had figured prominently in these changes. Changes in relation to parents had also taken place in the majority of schools, and it was interesting to see that heads were more likely to describe such changes as having occurred after a period of experience of the National Curriculum than they were relatively early in the implementation period. Even more striking was the increase in the perceived extent of these changes, with a considerable shift from describing such changes as 'moderate' in the first round of interviews to describing them as 'great' in the second round.

The changes associated with curriculum, assessment, school organization and so on all have potential influence on the nature of relationships in schools. Primary schools have traditionally put considerable emphasis on the quality of relationships: in particular, the relationships between teachers and pupils, but also relationships among the staff and between the school and parents. For example, when asked about their major priorities, heads talked about 'a happy, relaxed atmosphere' and 'close staff relationships'. In the interviews the heads were asked about the influence the National Curriculum was having on various sorts of relationships: on the relationships between teachers and children, the relationships between teachers and parents and the relationships between the head and the staff.

As the figures in Table 5.3 show, the perceptions of headteachers of changes in relationships varied considerably. In the case of all three patterns of relationship a majority of heads felt either that there had been no influence from the National Curriculum or that the influence had been mixed, having both positive and negative aspects. However, in both rounds of interviews over a third of heads felt that the influence of the National Curriculum on teacher–pupil relationships had been negative. These heads stressed the emphasis on assessing the pupils and the tension that had introduced into the

Table 5.3   *Headteachers' perceptions of changes in relationships (percentages)*

Changes in relationships	1990		1992	
	Better	Worse	Better	Worse
Teacher–pupil	12.5	35.4	22.9	35.4
Teacher–parent	20.8	18.8	16.6	27.1
Headteacher–staff	22.9	12.5	12.5	20.9

Source: PACE 1 headteacher interviews.
Sample: 48 headteachers.
Date: summer 1990 and summer 1992.

relationship, and they also drew attention to the way that the constraints of the National Curriculum prevented teachers from responding to children's needs. Further, they suggested that teachers would have less time for children as individuals. In contrast, a minority of heads thought that the National Curriculum had improved the quality of teacher–pupil relationships. In the first round of interviews one head in eight suggested that this was so and in the second round the proportion had risen to nearly a quarter. These heads tended to stress the way that teacher assessments of individual children had given teachers the opportunity to get to know children's academic needs in more detail than before and had improved the range of curriculum coverage.

Perceptions of the influence on teacher–parent relationships were more balanced. In the first round just over one in five heads thought these had improved and just under one in five thought they had got worse. In the second round there was something of a shift to perceiving a worsening of relationships. Heads who thought that relations had improved generally spoke about increased levels of parental interest coming about as a result of meetings to explain changes and the reporting of children's SAT results. Heads who thought relations had deteriorated saw the increased parental involvement more negatively, as driven by pressure for results rather than by a more rounded concern for the child's development.

Finally, Table 5.3 shows the heads' perception of the impact of the National Curriculum on their own relationships with their staff. Most thought that this had not changed or that any changes had been mixed. However, a minority of heads thought that relationships had improved. They tended to point to the process of working together, of responding as a whole school and turning the staff into more of a team. Other heads felt that the relationship had been adversely affected. Their experience was of having to push staff in unwelcome directions and having to implement unpopular changes. Although the number of heads involved is relatively small, it is worth noting that heads were more likely to say that the influence on their relations with staff was positive in the first round of interviews and more likely to say that the influence was negative in the second round. Parallel data from teachers will be considered in Chapter 6.

5.3 WHAT CAUSED MOST PRESSURE ON HEADTEACHERS?

The substantive focus of the research was on the National Curriculum, and the interviews inevitably concentrated on National Curriculum issues. However, in order to get a slightly different perspective on contemporary change in the primary school, in the

Table 5.4 *Problems causing the headteachers concern, 1992 (percentages)*

Problems causing concern	
LMS-related	75.0
National Curriculum content	22.9
National Curriculum assessment	20.8
School organization	31.3
Staff development	29.2
Parental pressure	10.4
Personal/social problem (child-related)	2.8
Personal/social problem (staff-related)	6.9
Relations with LEA	2.8

Source: PACE 1 headteacher interviews.
Sample: 48 headteachers.
Date: summer 1992.

second round of interviews heads were asked an entirely open question about the problems that had caused them most concern in the previous year. As the results in Table 5.4 show, although the National Curriculum was an important cause of concern, it was not the one that had caused the most immediate problems for headteachers. The issues that had most dominated the heads' work of the previous year were related to the introduction of local management of schools, and it was concerns over financial management, levels of resources, dealing with contractors and so on that the majority of heads mentioned as creating problems for them. Three-quarters of the headteachers described LMS as a major source of concern, while about 40 per cent described National Curriculum issues as a major problem. About a third of the heads described aspects of school organization as a major problem and much smaller proportions identified issues with staff, parents or pupils.

LMS was typically the factor that had had most impact on the headteachers' working day, as well as having a major impact on the problems that concerned them: 'It's not the curriculum changes. It is because of LMS that I have less time in the classroom.' 'The working day hasn't really been changed by the National Curriculum – LMS has made much more difference.' As well as noting the predominance of LMS, it is also worth noting the predominance of 'new' problems in the heads' concerns. It was the recently introduced changes of LMS and the National Curriculum that heads said had caused them most difficulty and which appeared to have overtaken 'traditional' concerns about pupils and staff as issues for the heads. Perhaps it is inevitable that it is the new which dominates, but the responses in Table 5.4 give a striking indication of the extent of primary school change in recent years and the impact it has had on the work of the headteacher.

5.4 HOW DID HEADTEACHERS FEEL ABOUT THE CHANGES THAT HAD OCCURRED?

In order to look at heads' feelings about these changes, after asking respondents to describe them and towards the end of the second round interview, we asked the heads which of the changes they had been describing were most welcome to them and which

Table 5.5   *Headteachers' response to change (1992) (percentages)*

Issues faced	Most welcome	Least welcome
Local management of schools	25.0	29.2
Curriculum	72.9	47.9
Assessment	25.0	52.1
Teaching methods	8.3	6.3
Relations with parents	4.2	8.3
Relations with children	0.0	4.2
Relations with LEA	2.1	2.1
School organization/planning/consultation	13.2	10.4

Source: PACE 1 headteacher interviews.
Sample: 48 headteachers.
Date: summer 1992.

were least welcome. This was an open-ended question and the replies are categorized in Table 5.5.

As Table 5.5 shows, the aspects of change that predominated in headteachers' replies were LMS, curriculum changes and assessment. These three areas figure in the lists of changes described as 'most welcome' and as 'least welcome'. They were overwhelmingly the features of the previous year that figured in headteachers' minds and this was so regardless of whether the changes they had brought were welcome or unwelcome.

Most headteachers welcomed some aspects of recent changes and most also considered some aspects unwelcome. Feelings were most evenly balanced with regard to LMS, where only slightly more headteachers found aspects of these changes 'least welcome' than found them 'most welcome'. The balance of response was most positive in the area of curriculum change, with considerably more 'most welcome' than 'least welcome' changes. It was least positive in the area of assessment, where heads were more than twice as likely to describe changes as 'least welcome' than as 'most welcome'.

Most headteachers welcomed at least some aspects of the curriculum content associated with the National Curriculum. Nearly three-quarters mentioned this as being among the most welcome changes. In particular, the increased emphasis on science and technology and the increase in curriculum planning were welcomed. However, about half the heads also identified aspects of curriculum content as being among the least welcome changes. Here heads were concerned about the threat to the depth of curriculum activities brought about by the increased range of curriculum coverage, the loss of flexibility and the opportunity for creativity by teachers: 'The best teachers are responsive to children's needs and can see the possibilities that situations in the classroom create. This is much harder now.'

The balance of feeling about the changes in assessment was the reverse of the responses to curriculum content. Over half the heads described the changes in assessment as among the least welcome, while a quarter identified them as being among the most welcome. The inappropriateness of SATs and, especially, the time-consuming and disruptive aspects of standardized assessment were particularly problematic for heads. A few welcomed standardized assessment, but headteachers who described aspects of assessment as welcome changes were more commonly referring to the teacher assessments.

The third major area addressed in these responses is LMS. A quarter of heads described the LMS-related changes as being among the most welcome while slightly more regarded them as among the least welcome. This is the area where responses from the headteachers were most polarized. Heads who welcomed LMS generally did so enthusiastically and commented on the greater freedom and autonomy it had given them, and the capacity they now had to maximize the use of resources. One head said: 'I welcome LMS. There is satisfaction in being able to make things happen. It is good for my motivation and job satisfaction.' This head was one of those for whom the freedom from LEA management of resources had been experienced as liberating.

On the other hand, many headteachers felt that they had been restricted in the time they had available for the educational aspects of their role: 'It is LMS that has changed my job. A complete reversal, from in the classroom to in the office.' 'I am really a classroom person. This is not what I came into teaching for.' In some cases the changes in curriculum practice and the perceived loss of teacher creativity linked to the changes in management practice and the heads' role to give an overall feeling that working in schools was less fulfilling than in the past: 'We have lost the excitement – the feeling that there is exciting work and that teachers are excited. Now I am more worried about whether the caretaker has cleaned the floor.'

5.5 HOW AUTONOMOUS DID HEADTEACHERS FEEL FOLLOWING THE INTRODUCTION OF THE NATIONAL CURRICULUM?

One of the themes of discussions over recent educational changes was constraint and autonomy within the education system. The implementation of the National Curriculum has increased one aspect of central control because schools were very much more constrained with regard to the content of the curriculum than they had been previously. Similarly, centrally imposed assessment arrangements introduced government control into an area where primary schools had enjoyed autonomy, at least since the end of 11 plus selection.

However, other aspects of the changes introduced by the Education Reform Act were supposed to give schools greater autonomy, and much of the rhetoric of education policy of the late 1980s and early 1990s had been concerned with releasing schools from bureaucratic control. The headteacher quoted above on the liberating effect of LMS is an example of this latter aspect of the impact of recent change.

In both rounds of interviews headteachers were asked how free they felt to act as they thought best in their schools, and also whether this had changed recently. The results showed a marked shift in heads' perceptions between the two rounds of interviews. In the first round (of 1990), over a half of headteachers (54.2 per cent) said that they felt free to act as they thought best, while in the second round (of 1992) this figure had gone down to only a third of headteachers (33.4 per cent). Some heads were unambiguous about the constraints they were working under: 'I am very much less free than I used to be. Central initiatives mean that schools have little autonomy.' Other headteachers felt that although they were working under constraints they had still been able to protect substantial areas of autonomy: 'Less [freedom] than before but we still have a lot of autonomy in how we do things.'

A similar pattern emerged when the heads were asked if their freedom to act as they thought best had changed recently. In the 1990 interviews exactly two-thirds thought that they had less freedom to act for the best, with the majority of these saying that they had 'rather less' rather than 'much less' freedom. In the second round of interviews three-quarters (76 per cent) said they had less freedom and the great majority of these, half of all headteachers, said that they had 'much less' freedom. In both rounds of interviews most of those who did not say they had less freedom said that it had not changed or they were unsure. Only two headteachers in the first set of interviews and one in the second set said that their freedom had increased.

It is clear that, from the perspectives of headteachers, the constraining and directive aspects of the National Curriculum and associated changes had a strong impact. On the other hand, aspects of the educational reforms that were intended to free headteachers had, at the point of our data-gathering in 1992, had little effect on schools. With regard to external pressures the autonomy experienced by headteachers had clearly decreased and in important and educationally central areas we can identify a shift towards imposed rather than negotiated or school-based change. On the other hand, those headteachers who welcomed and used LMS experienced an increase in their autonomy within their schools and the possibility of school-based developments in this aspect of their work.

5.6 HOW DID SCHOOLS MANAGE NATIONAL CURRICULUM CHANGES?

In this section we will address a series of questions about how primary schools have attempted to manage the various changes that have come about following the Education Reform Act. These questions relate to the kinds of management strategies employed by schools and to the relationship between different management strategies and the substantive content of change. We will also be concerned with broader issues about the nature of primary schools as organizations and with the relationship between organizational development and teachers' individual professional activities and identities.

A traditional model of the primary school as an organization emphasizes, on the one hand, the individual autonomy of the teacher in the classroom, and, on the other, the individual autonomy of the headteacher with regard to the management of the school. Teachers worked on their own in their own classes on a rather isolated basis and had relative autonomy with regard to the learning of their pupils. A number of studies of primary education have drawn attention to this rather solitary nature of teaching as an activity and to the way in which many teachers rarely saw colleagues teach or worked collaboratively with them (e.g. Galton *et al.*, 1980). Paralleling this individualistic model of the teacher in the classroom is the individualistic model of the headteacher as responsible for the school. In their study *Understanding Schools as Organisations*, Handy and Aitken (1986) describe a typical model of primary school organization as one that revolves around a single authority figure using a very personal approach to management and a notion of 'his' or 'her' school. An example of this individual and personal approach to school management can be found in an NFER study of streaming and de-streaming in primary schools conducted in the late 1960s (Barker-Lunn, 1970). Three case studies of schools making the decision to stream or de-stream are described. In one the head saw each teacher individually to explain the decision. In another the head announced the decision by a notice pinned up in the staffroom. In the third the staff 'had to find out for themselves'! Staff apparently accepted these arrangements as natural. A teacher is quoted as saying: 'When streaming was introduced it was without consultation, which the head, of course, had a perfect right to do' (Barker-Lunn, 1970, p. 255).

The fact that such arrangements now sound an extraordinary way to manage a major change in school practice reflects two developments in the organization and management of primary schools. The first can be broadly described as managerialism and the second as collegiality. These developments have different emphases, but also points of overlap, and both turn our attention away from the very individualistic model of the school as an organization.

In terms of the broad analytic themes of this book, managerialism relates to the operation of power as something imposed on teachers, while collegiality relates to the operation of power in a way that can be collectively empowering. However, these are not simple dichotomies. Collegial solutions may come about as part of a management strategy by headteachers and others and certainly do not imply an absence of management. Thus, 'managerialism' must be understood as only one of the ways in which management may operate.

We see managerialism as a bureaucratic solution to the problem of bringing coherence and direction into organizational activities. It emphasizes formal structures, the explicit and public delineation of organization structures and purposes, and of roles and responsibilities within the organization. In primary schools, management-centred approaches have led to greater differentiation of staffing; for example, through the use of posts with particular designated responsibilities for areas of the curriculum and attempts to direct in-service work to reflect identified school needs rather than the individual interests of teachers. Such developments are not incompatible with participative and collective approaches to school development, but they can imply a directive and controlled model of primary schools that impinges on some of class teachers' professional autonomy.

Collegiality is a difficult and somewhat contentious concept that we have used to describe approaches to managing primary schools that emphasize the common and cooperative aspects of teachers' work. It is a response to the relative isolation of much of what teachers do, which looks to develop schools by encouraging school staff to work together in a collective approach to school development, rather than by treating staff as 'human resources' to be managed more and more 'effectively'. Studies such as those of Nias and her colleagues (Nias *et al.*, 1989, 1992) have described a 'culture of collaboration' as the prevailing organizational style in a number of primary schools. This culture does not dispense with leadership from the headteacher and often derives from the head's approach, but it places emphasis on whole-school staff approaches to developing schools collectively. In such approaches, in moving away from purely individualistic notions of teachers' work, a degree of autonomy is surrendered collaboratively rather than managerially.

These distinctions between managerial and collegial approaches to management emerged clearly in the interviews with headteachers, although it must be emphasized that the discussion below is based on the accounts we were given rather than on direct observation in schools.

As is apparent from the discussion above, issues of managerialism, collegiality and so on are not easy to operationalize in a straightforward manner, and the analysis of approaches to managing change draws upon answers to several questions. Heads were asked about their personal approach to their leadership role in the school and also about their schools' strategies for managing change in response to the National Curriculum.

Their answers to these questions were recorded in an open-ended fashion and then coded. For our analysis, heads were located on the basis of these coded responses on a continuum defined in terms of a 'more managerially directed' or 'more collegial' approach to managing change.

At the directed end of the continuum are headteachers who identified the school's strategy for change as essentially top-down. It should be noted that these heads did not typically see this top-down approach in simple terms. Most of them also emphasized that they involved staff fully in consultation and often that they also relied on a senior management team. However, all these heads firmly emphasized their personal role and the importance of centrally directed change to the way the school had responded to the National Curriculum. Comments were made such as:

> These are changes for which I am legally responsible, I want to carry the staff with me but in the end it has to happen and I have to make it happen.

> The time scale really does not allow for much discussion. My approach has always been that I carry the can and so I decide.

> Much change was needed and I had to impose it. I probably went too fast but I did try to communicate.

Such statements indicated an approach that relied on the head, or the head and a few senior colleagues, to carry changes through.

Heads were sometimes conscious of having moved into a more directive and authoritarian mode:

> When I came here I was very autocratic in the 'charismatic head' tradition. I have mellowed but have needed to go back to that to some extent.

> Decisions are now made by me to a much greater extent than in the past. I have to meet legal obligations and have had to impose decisions in order to do it.

Another element of some of the responses of heads who identified their approach as a top-down one was a concern to protect staff from the stress and pressure of making difficult and sometimes unwelcome decisions. There was a concern among some heads to insulate staff and protect them from the responsibility of decisions that might conflict with educational values. For instance, 'I'd rather they grumbled at me than [have them] feeling they have let the children down.' 'It's my responsibility to run the school and make decisions. I think the staff are pleased that I have taken responsibility.'

A middle point on the continuum was identified in terms of heads who emphasized the collective and consultative aspects of the way the school went about responding to the National Curriculum, but also emphasized that, because the final responsibility was theirs, the final say had to be theirs. These headteachers were similar to those identified as 'top-down' in terms of the stress they placed on the role of the head in making sure that changes happened in an appropriate fashion. However, they differed from them in terms of emphasizing that the head's role was to guarantee effective change, rather than necessarily to direct it. We have described this approach to management as 'managed participation'. The following comments illustrate managed participation:

> Our natural priorities are child-centred and I support the staff in this. But in the end I have to make sure that we conform with the legislation.

> It is not an autocratic approach. I take the lead but we work as a staff. I try to lead by example.

I have to be a leader but it is important to take the staff with me. I am influenced by staff views.

A third group of heads came closest to the collegial model of school management. These heads were clear that they were leaders in the school, but wanted to be leaders of a group of colleagues working together. They emphasized the collective and participative approach within the school and the way in which all colleagues were involved in decision-making. An aspect of the way these heads saw their role was in facilitating the changes the staff saw as necessary and as helping the teachers to work together. A number of heads referred to 'democratic' leadership styles and others were aware of the limitations on what they could achieve if they were not working collaboratively with the staff.

It is a consultative one [management approach]. We are very much a democracy. I do not want to make decisions without consultation. It is important to be able to say to staff, 'We decided this'.

Basic approach is collegiate. It is not quite democratic but with a strong emphasis on consultation and decision-making by staff. The staff need to have ownership of change if it is to work.

We work as a team. Democracy is time-consuming but is worth it.

In Table 5.6 headteachers have been categorized along this continuum from 'top-down management' through 'managed participation' to 'managed collegiality'. A small number of heads could not be classified in this way, either because of very limited responses to these questions or because of idiosyncratic responses that did not relate to the dimension. Heads were categorized independently in terms of their response in the first interview and in the second interview. The column entries in Table 5.6 are based on the 1990 interviews and the row entries are based on the 1992 interviews. This makes it possible to look at the distribution of management approaches in the two years and also at the shifts between them.

The overall figures for 1990 are the column totals at the foot of Table 5.6, and it can

Table 5.6 *Management strategies for change*

Management strategies for change		1990				
		Top-down management	Manage participation	Collegial management	Mixed/ unclear	Totals for 1992
1992	Top-down management	2	2	1	1	6 (12.5%)
	Managed participation	0	7	5	1	13 (27.1%)
	Collegial management	0	1	21	0	22 (45.8%)
	Mixed/unclear	0	2	2	3	7 (14.6%)
	Total for 1990	2 (4.2%)	12 (25.0%)	29 (60.4%)	5 (10.4%)	

Source: PACE 1 headteacher interviews.
Sample: 48 headteachers.
Date: summer 1990 and summer 1992.

be seen that, in 1990, by far the largest group of heads were categorized as 'collegial' in their management style. Twenty-nine heads, 60.4 per cent of the total, were categorized in this way. A further twelve, 25.0 per cent of all heads, were categorized as responding to change through 'managed participation' and only two had a 'top-down' approach to managing change. A further five headteachers did not describe their practice in ways that allowed them to be placed in one of these categories.

A comparison of the figures derived from the 1992 interviews with the figures from 1990 shows something of a shift away from collegial and participative approaches and towards more directed approaches, although participation and collegiality still predominated. The 1992 figures are the row totals on the extreme right of Table 5.6. While 60.4 per cent of heads (29) were collegial in 1990, this had reduced in 1992 to 45.8 per cent (22). In contrast, the number of heads describing their approach as top-down had trebled to six, although this was still only 12.5 per cent of the total.

The cell entries in Table 5.6 show the individual changes which contributed to this aggregate shift in approach. Entries on the diagonal of the table (from top left to bottom right) represent headteachers whose strategies had remained constant over the two years. Other entries represent movements from the category identified by the column in which they are located, into the category identified by the row. Analysis shows that, while there had not been a wholesale shift in management strategies by heads, a minority had moved towards a rather more directed managerial strategy. Three heads had moved from collegial management or managed participation approaches to a top-down approach, and five had moved from a collegial to a managed participation approach. Only one head had moved in the other direction, from managed participation to a collegial approach.

The relative consistency of the categorization of management strategies over the two years gives confidence that what is being described is a reflection of real differences in school approaches that can be captured in interviews. The approaches are fairly stable over time and they have shifted in a fashion that suggests similar pressures on schools and heads. In both rounds of interviews a substantial majority of heads were placing emphasis on staff involvement and consultation as their strategy for managing change, although in some cases they emphasized that this was a 'managed' involvement. However, the experience of implementing the National Curriculum has tended to push at least some heads in the direction of a more managed and more top-down approach to change.

The limitations of our data cause us to be cautious about interpreting these findings too much but two underlying factors can be identified. First, there is what we shall call a 'work experience' factor. On this, we have in mind the gradual divergence in role expertise and experience of class teachers and headteachers. While these were, in a sense, fairly close in the past, the Education Reform Act caused significant differentiation. Headteacher concerns with management, finance and accountability are a long way from the classroom concerns of their staff. At the same time, the latter became expert, in a way that most headteachers were not, in the details of attainment targets, programmes of study, assessment procedures and other technical necessities of the National Curriculum. A more distanced form of management reflected the realities of these changed forms of work experience. The second interpretive factor we offer we shall call 'headteacher survival'. It is almost impossible to overestimate the quantity of paperwork, regulation and administration that was passed to headteachers over the period of study and the escalation in their responsibilities as LEA powers and support structures were weakened. In this context, becoming more 'top-down' is a form of coping strategy rather than an indicator of a fundamental change in values.

In summary, the within-school approaches analysed here indicate a movement on the dimension discussed in section 3.3, of managerial imposition–participative negotiation, in the direction of a greater imposition, although more schools were still located towards the participative end of this dimension. There was also a movement away from individualist, and towards more collective, ways of achieving change.

5.7 WAS THERE A RELATIONSHIP BETWEEN STRATEGIES FOR CHANGE AND THE SUBSTANCE OF CHANGE?

School strategies for change reflect management and organizational strategies but also reflect (and may in turn influence) the substance of the changes being made. As we saw earlier in this chapter, schools varied in terms of the degree and nature of the changes they felt would be required of them. Such changes also involved a complex set of responses in terms of their impact on working practices and the relationship of change to the values and identity of the school. In Chapter 3, one of the dimensions relating to power in the educational system was given as compliance–mediation–resistance, denoting a range of school responses to externally imposed change. We have considered aspects of the impact of change on schools using these concepts to classify the types of response to emerge from interviews with the headteachers. However, none of the heads interviewed could be classified as resisting or contesting change. The responses emphasized the extent to which changes were being incorporated into previous practice (a form of mediation) or were superseding previous practice (compliance).

As we saw earlier, a fairly typical initial response of headteachers (and teachers) to the National Curriculum was that much of it was an extension of existing good practice. Breadth of curriculum coverage, careful curriculum planning and recording, assessment of pupils' progress and so on strongly related to the ways in which they saw their work and the work of their staff.

> We have tried to be true to our own philosophy. We do not want to change the basic system and have not had to change radically. It has been possible to keep our basic approach.

> There is a sense of achievement that we have influenced how the National Curriculum works here. The sense of something out of our control has gone.

> We were all well aware of what was coming and were also confident of our own practice. We can take it in our stride. I think we were well placed to cope with change.

These are the sort of approaches we have characterized as 'mediation'. This does not necessarily mean that little change was planned or that the heads were happy about the way in which the National Curriculum was imposed. However, they emphasized the continuity between their existing practice and what was required of them.

The National Curriculum impacted more radically on those schools whose strategies we have characterized as 'compliance'. Headteachers of such schools emphasized the scale of the changes that would be necessary and also emphasized the disjunction and discontinuity between their response to the National Curriculum and their previous practice. These heads saw the impact of the National Curriculum in terms of relatively

Table 5.7   *Strategies for management and the accommodation of change, 1990*

Strategies for change	Management strategies			
	Top-down management	Managed participation	Collegial management	Totals for 1990
Mediation	0	12 (100%)	23 (79.3%)	35 (81.4%)
Compliance	2 (100%)	0	3 (10.3%)	5 (11.6%)
Mixed/unclear	0	0	3 (10.3%)	3 (7.0%)

Source: PACE 1 headteacher interviews.
Sample: 43 headteachers.
Date: summer 1990

Table 5.8   *Strategies for management and the accommodation of change, 1992*

Strategies for change	Management strategies			
	Top-down management	Managed participation	Collegial management	Totals for 1992
Mediation	1 (16.7%)	6 (46.2%)	14 (63.6%)	21 (51.2%)
Compliance	4 (66.7%)	5 (38.5%)	7 (31.8%)	16 (39.0%)
Mixed/unclear	1 (16.7%)	2 (15.4%)	1 (4.5%)	4 (9.8%)

Source: PACE 1 headteacher interviews.
Sample: 41 headteachers.
Date: summer 1992

fundamental changes and saw implementation very much as a response to external requirements rather than as a development of internal practice. Comments included: 'It has had to be completely different. We are now subject dominated, which is the reverse of previous practice.' 'Much change was needed and I had to impose it.'

It should be noted that this was not always a hostile reaction from headteachers, although it certainly was in some cases. Some heads saw the National Curriculum as a lever they could use to make changes that they judged to be needed and where they had encountered resistance in the past. One recently appointed headteacher expressed this: 'There are a lot of changes happening, almost a reversal of some practices, but most of it is for the better. To some extent I have used [the National Curriculum] to get the school moving.' However, others saw the changes in much more negative terms: 'It has been like going over Niagara Falls – going over and coming up again – battered against the rocks.'

In Tables 5.7 and 5.8, the types of management style described above are cross-tabulated against the extent to which schools' responses to change were categorized as 'mediation' or 'compliance'. A comparison of the marginal entries (on the extreme right of the tables) for 1990 with those for 1992 shows the extent of the shift over the period in school perspectives. In the initial round of interviews more than four-fifths of the heads interviewed described their responses to the National Curriculum in terms that were best characterized as 'mediation'. They stressed the aspects of continuity and the way that many of the requirements were developments of existing good practice. Only just over one in ten heads described a response that involved abandoning existing practice and making radical changes in order to comply with the National Curriculum.

However, in the second round of interviews, although mediation and incorporation into current practice was the most common response, it did not predominate to anything like the extent it had earlier. Half the heads gave responses in the second round that could be described as mediation, while two-fifths of heads now responded in terms that were best described as compliance. (Only those headteachers whose management approaches could be categorized are included in this analysis.)

It is clear that in the period between the two sets of interviews, the experience of implementing the National Curriculum had dented some headteachers' optimism that it could be regarded as an extension of good practice, and had pushed a number of schools in the direction of greater changes and a greater discontinuity with previous practice than initially anticipated. One factor in this might be the substantial impact the operation of standardized assessment had on the organization of classrooms and the work of staff, and this will be discussed in Chapter 12.

Tables 5.7 and 5.8 also make it possible to look at the interrelationships of mediation–compliance as strategies and the overall school approach to change. In 1990 very few schools had identified a basically top-down approach to the management of change, and the great majority had identified an incorporative, mediation approach to its substance. However, the two schools with top-down approaches had also identified a relatively major and discontinuous impact on their practice and had been categorized as having an approach based on compliance. In contrast, all the schools with a change strategy based on 'managed participation' and four-fifths of those with 'collegial' strategies had a mediative response to the substance of change based on the development of practice.

The figures for schools using 'top-down' approaches are based on very small numbers, but the same overall pattern emerges in the figures for 1992. In the data from 1992 there is an overall shift towards top-down management strategies and towards a process of compliance rather than mediation of the National Curriculum changes. There were then six heads whose approach was categorized as top-down and four of them described a process of compliance in response to the National Curriculum. Only one of these heads described the changes as mediation through current practice. In contrast, nearly two-thirds of the heads using collegial strategies for change described their approach as incorporation and about a third described their approach as compliance. The heads whose strategy for managing change was characterized as managed participation also fell between the other groups in terms of their relative emphasis on mediation and compliance.

In summary, in the period covered by the two rounds of data collection, schools shifted from an approach to managing change that placed strong emphasis on collegial and participatory approaches towards placing more emphasis on managerial and directed approaches. In the same period they also shifted from stressing the way that the National Curriculum could be mediated and incorporated by building on existing practice to placing more emphasis on discontinuities with substantial change, while schools that had collegial and participative strategies were most likely to emphasize the process of developing and building on their existing practice.

These two shifts occurred at the same period of time, and in each round of interviews the management style and extent of change were strongly related. It is therefore tempting to look for a relationship between the two parallel shifts over time. The most obvious causal explanation is that the experience of finding that more radical change was required pushed headteachers into more directive and managerial strategies. Alternatively, it is possible that schools that had more directive approaches to change found that these moved them in a more radical direction.

The data from the present study do not provide an unambiguous answer to the question of causality and its direction, although there is more support for the first explanation than for the second. In the first round of data collection very few schools were identified as having a top-down approach to managing change, so there is relatively little scope for such an approach to create a shift from mediation to compliance. On the other hand, there are collegial strategies that are associated with compliance in the first round of interviews and that could be associated with a move to a more top-down approach. However, examination of the data from the individual schools involved does not reveal a clear-cut relationship. It is certainly not the case that all the schools identified as undertaking major change in 1990 had found it necessary to move to a more directed approach by 1992, and shifts to more directed approaches were made by schools which were incorporating change in both rounds of data collection. Thus, although we can conclude that, at each of the points in time studied, more radical breaks with previous practice were associated with more directive approaches, we cannot conclude that the shift to more directive approaches was caused by the extent of change.

5.8 CONCLUSION

In this chapter we have seen a school-level view of change from the perspective of headteachers and have looked at some aspects of the impact of change on their role. We have also looked at schools' strategies in response to the introduction of the National Curriculum and related these to the extent of changes being made.

As a result of the introduction of the National Curriculum, headteachers clearly predicted changes in curriculum coverage and assessment practice. At the time our first data were gathered, the major curriculum impact was in the area of increased time devoted to science and, to a lesser extent, technology. However, by the second round of data collection a concern with increased time for history and geography was also apparent. As well as these changes, which were a very direct consequence of the National Curriculum, headteachers had also made changes in the organization of staff and teaching and in staff responsibilities and staff development. It was noticeable that these indirect changes occurred most frequently in the second rather than the first round of interviews. Although the National Curriculum had made a major impact on all of the schools in the study, it was not necessarily these changes that had caused heads themselves the most difficulties. The challenges faced in relation to local management of schools seemed to have caused headteachers the most problems over the period.

Headteachers had mixed feelings about the changes they had had to make. The great majority welcomed at least some aspects of the curriculum changes although many were unhappy about some parts of these. Developments in assessment, particularly forms of teacher assessment, were also welcomed by some headteachers, but over half the heads saw some part of the new assessment requirements as unwelcome. Over the period covered by the two interviews headteachers perceived a loss of autonomy. This emerged both from a comparison of their responses in the two interviews and from their own accounts of the impact of developments over the period.

School strategies for change were located on a continuum ranging from very top-down and directed approaches, through participative approaches with a strongly managed element, to more collaborative and collegial approaches. Most schools were located towards the collegial management end of this spectrum but there was a clear tendency for schools to become more managerially directive over the timescale of the study.

School approaches to the National Curriculum reforms were also identified in terms of whether they essentially built on previous practice to incorporate or mediate new requirements or whether more discontinuous and radical changes from previous practice had been necessary to achieve compliance. An approach based on building on and developing previous practice was the predominant one but, as with management strategies, a shift away from mediation and towards greater divergence from previous practice was apparent over the two rounds of interviews. It was also very clear in both rounds of data collection that there is an association between management strategies and the relationship of change to previous practice. The more the school had moved from previous ways of working, the more directive were the management strategies.

In terms of the operation of power in the educational system and the dimensions of power we have used, we can identify changes in both power over schools and power within them. The great majority of headteachers had experienced a reduction in their autonomy and felt more external constraints and controls. This sense of loss of autonomy grew during the time of the research. Although there was scope for school-based and negotiated developments, the sense of external imposition predominated. Within schools there was a shift from more participatory and collaborative to more directive modes of accomplishing changes. However, despite this shift, there was still an emphasis on participation – although often with a strong managerial emphasis. While some headteachers were conscious of having developed more directive ways of working, others had experienced the achievement of considerable collaborative change with staff. In virtually all schools there was a move away from teacher individualism.

Finally, we should again note that there was evidence of a considerable degree of intensification of many aspects of the pressures that new requirements have put on schools. The more 'obvious' of the National Curriculum changes in the areas of curriculum content and assessment were recognized early on by the headteachers. However, other, less direct changes in the areas of staffing, perceptions of reduced autonomy, shifts in management styles and divergence with previous practice were much more evident in the second round than in the first round of interviews.

Chapter 6

Teachers' Professional Perspectives: Autonomy and Accountability

6.1 INTRODUCTION

In this chapter we discuss the impact of the 1988 Education Reform Act on teachers' views of their role, of their autonomy and of their accountability to others. One of the assumptions underlying centrally directed change is that teachers, where necessary, will be both willing and able to adapt their practices in appropriate directions. Yet there is considerable evidence to suggest that this is not so. Indeed, far from their being mere puppets pulled by the strings of policy-makers, it can be argued that teachers mediate the external pressures upon them through the filter of their own professionalism and practice. The result is a blend of both personal ideologies and external constraints (Fullan, 1982; Grant, 1989; Acker, 1990). Thus, as teachers attempt to reconcile external demands with their belief in professional autonomy and with the practicalities of the working situation, they must make choices about the way in which they carry out their work. In responding to an indefinitely expanding set of tasks and role prescriptions, they have to ration their time and prioritize their tasks. In so doing, they effectively become makers of policy as well as implementers of policy and might be seen as 'practitioner policy-makers' in their own classrooms. It follows that if government policy-making is to be implemented, that implementation will reflect both the general beliefs that inform teachers' practice and the perspectives likely to be held by any particular group of teachers at any given time and place.

The 1988 Education Reform Act provides an ideal focus for exploring the relative significance of teacher professionalism as a mediating influence in the impact of educational policy initiatives. Not only does it mirror an international trend within educational systems towards centrally determined goals and local responsibility for achieving them (Broadfoot, 1990), it also represents a virtually unprecedented attempt to challenge one of the most strongly entrenched elements of English teachers' ideology – that of professional autonomy. Since the 1988 Act, English teachers' freedom of individual judgement regarding curriculum has been substantially reduced and pressure has been exerted in classroom pedagogy (Alexander *et al.*, 1992; OFSTED, 1993). In this chapter, we will be concerned with examining how primary teachers' perspectives of their work have changed in response.

In terms of the dimensions introduced in Chapter 3, we will consider possible changes in the power context of teachers' work, from being relatively autonomous to being relatively constrained. We also discuss teachers' feelings about the nature of their personal commitment to work. This is considered in terms of a value dimension that ranges from expressive commitment to instrumentalism to alienation. A third dimension we discuss relates to teachers' understanding of their professional role in terms of a focus on immediate responsibilities and classroom concerns (restricted professionalism) or an engagement with issues, structures and practices beyond their own classroom (extended professionalism). Later chapters on teachers (Chapters 7 and 9) will consider how these perspectives have influenced, and in turn been influenced by, changes in curriculum and in professional practice.

6.2 FROM PROFESSIONAL TO TECHNICIAN?

This section draws upon previous comparative research (Broadfoot and Osborn, 1993) to provide a baseline on teachers' professional perspectives prior to the 1988 Education Reform Act. This research studied teachers' conceptions of professional responsibility through the comparative focus of the two very different education systems of England and France, before both these systems started to undergo major changes. From this earlier work it emerged that the most significant influence on teachers' practice in both systems was not the formal apparatus of external obligation and control but the personal sense of professional obligation held by the teachers themselves. Thus French teachers were found to be deeply committed to the need for a national curriculum as the basis for equality of opportunity, and in order to relieve them of the burden of both producing and justifying more locally influenced provision. Conversely, English teachers were strongly committed to a notion of teacher autonomy and local responsiveness to children's needs.

Teachers' conceptions of their responsibility in the two countries were characterized by two very different models of professionalism (Broadfoot *et al.*, 1987; Broadfoot and Osborn, 1988). To summarize briefly, French teachers had a narrower, more restricted and more classroom-focused conception of their role, which centred mainly on what they saw as their responsibility for children's academic progress. This restricted network of obligation was firmly rooted in the hierarchy of the system itself. English teachers, in contrast, saw themselves as having a more wide-ranging and diffuse set of responsibilities, which encompassed widely dispersed goals relating to responsibilities outside as well as inside the classroom, including extra-curricular and sometimes even community activities, all aspects of school relationships, accountability to parents, colleagues and the head. They also had a strong consciousness of the need to justify their actions to others.

At their most extreme, a French teacher's perceptions of her role centred on 'meeting one's contractual responsibility', while a typical English teacher characterized her role as 'striving after perfection'. For some English teachers this meant a certain amount of conflict and confusion about their role and a sense that they were setting themselves, and being set, goals they could not hope to fulfil.

We can relate this discussion to the dimension of professionalism raised in Chapter 3: 'extended' and 'restricted' (Hoyle, 1974). In Hoyle's concepts, restricted professionality indicates thought and practice that are largely classroom-based and focused on immediate concerns, while extended professionality takes account of a broader educational context and a wider range of professional activities. Thus, in terms of these dimensions, we can see that teachers in England before the introduction of a National Curriculum had a wide-ranging conception of role, an 'extended' professionality. More recently, Jennifer Nias has used the term 'bounded professionalism' to refer to English primary teachers, who, while adhering to whole-school perspectives and an interest in collaboration and collegiality, may still be largely atheoretical and classroom-focused in their approach to other issues (Nias, 1989).

The research suggests, then, that before the 1988 Education Reform Act, although English teachers were becoming increasingly constrained on all sides, they nevertheless believed strongly in their autonomy, and saw it as central to their 'extended' role that they be able to define and decide for themselves both what they would teach and how they would teach it. However, in the light of the sweeping and comprehensive change introduced by the Education Reform Act, change that brings English education much closer to the French model, some educationists have queried whether 'professionalism' and 'professionality' are still valid concepts in relation to teachers and their work. It has been argued that teachers' work is becoming deskilled, intensified and proletarianized, that teachers' work should be seen in terms of accountability rather than professionalism, and that there has been a move from 'professionalism' to 'managerialism' in English education (Lawn and Ozga, 1981; Apple, 1986; Densmore, 1987). In particular, the intensification thesis put forward by Michael Apple and others suggests that teachers' work is increasingly becoming dependent on an externally imposed apparatus of behavioural objectives, and of instruments for assessment and accountability. This, it is argued, has led to a proliferation of paperwork and administrative tasks, chronic work overload, and the loss of opportunities for more creative work and for developing caring relationships with pupils.

Stephen Ball has suggested that teachers are becoming subject to new relations of production (Ball, 1990). The introduction of management techniques into education, the establishment of a formal contract for teachers with fixed working hours and the reduction in scope for teacher decision-making brought about by the introduction of the National Curriculum and associated assessments have, he argues, severely constrained and delimited the professional role of the teacher. Further, they have emphasized an 'employee' as distinct from a 'professional' perspective for teachers' work. Local management of schools, he argues, has even led to a view of teachers as 'commodities, interchangeable with books, paint, and new desks' (Ball, 1990, p. 21). Thus, for Ball, the Education Reform Act is about

> control over teachers and teachers' work. It rests upon a profound distrust of teachers and seeks to close down many of the areas of discretion previously available to them. In doing this it brings into being a massively over-determined system of education. The National Curriculum and National Testing provide the belt and braces of central control, and the market offers a further carrot-and-stick mode of constraint. Embedded in all this are confused and contradictory views of the 'new teacher', ranging from the innovative and competitive 'petit-professional' to the harassed, reactive teaching technician.
>
> (Ball, 1990, p. 214)

These are powerful and compelling arguments. However, as Ball himself recognizes, they focus only upon what appear to be the 'intended' consequences of the Education Reform Act, and ignore the possibilities of 'unintended' consequences, in particular the gap between central policy and the way it is interpreted and implemented in schools and by individual teachers. Above all, they underplay the role played by teachers' ideologies in interpreting, accommodating or resisting state policy (cf. Chapters 1, 2 and 3).

Other recent work has suggested that while there is real evidence, in both Britain and North America, to support the intensification thesis, intensification may not impact on all teachers in the same ways. Nor can all instances of broadened commitment and heightened 'professionalism' be explained in terms of the intensification of teachers' work or as 'misinterpretation' of the labour process by teachers (Acker, 1990; Hargreaves, 1992). In this chapter, however, we go beyond the study of policy change to examine teachers' own conceptions of how their role and professional responsibilities have changed.

We begin by considering whether there bas been a shift in teachers' feelings of accountability, autonomy and perceptions of role. We also consider the extent to which there has been a move from a personal and expressive commitment to work towards greater instrumentalism or even alienation, and the extent to which teachers have adopted a restricted or extended conception of role. We go on to examine teachers' professional relationships with other adults and how these might be changing from values of individualism towards those of greater collegiality. Finally, we discuss how teachers felt that the changes might affect their work in future and how teachers' perspectives varied.

The findings we present here are based on the two rounds of interviews plus a short questionnaire carried out in summer 1990 and summer 1992. We also draw upon interviews carried out with teachers during the classroom studies in autumn 1990 and autumn 1991. Chapter 4 describes the research design in more detail.

6.3 TO WHOM DID TEACHERS FEEL ACCOUNTABLE?

If teachers were internalizing the policy changes implied in the Education Reform Act, one might expect to observe a shift in teachers' sense of obligation to various groups in the educational process. A change might be anticipated from a personal or moral focus to an external focus in response to increasing demands for external accountability. In the short questionnaire used in 1990 and 1992 with 88 teachers and 48 headteachers, we were able to assess the extent of teachers' feelings of accountability to various groups by means of a question asking: 'As a teacher, to whom do you feel accountable and to what extent?' Replies were measured using a five-point scale ranging from 'not at all accountable' to 'very accountable'. Results are summarized in Table 6.1.

It was clear from the responses in 1990 that most teachers had a strong sense of personal and moral accountability and an internal sense of obligation to, above all, themselves and their own conscience (95 per cent 'very accountable'), followed closely by an obligation to their pupils (86 per cent). Less important, but still significant, was a feeling of accountability to other partners in the educational process: parents (65 per cent), the headteacher (56 per cent) and colleagues (48 per cent). External obligations to employers, i.e. the LEA, to governors and to the government figured to a lesser extent. As one teacher put it, 'I am responsible for the progress, in all areas, of the children in my class, and for their happiness and well-being at school. Also, I am responsible to parents, colleagues, the the head and governors for the same.' When the questionnaire was administered to teachers again in 1992, the findings were remarkably consistent with those of 1990.

No significant differences emerged between older and younger teachers or between those with more or fewer years of teaching experience – except in relation to headteachers or governors, where older teachers with more than 20 years' teaching experience felt more accountable. Many in this latter category may have been deputy heads or even heads, who might be expected to feel this accountability more strongly. There were no significant differences in feelings of accountability in teachers working in different socio-economic catchment areas.

Table 6.2 compares the PACE findings with those from English teachers in the earlier

Table 6.1 *Extent of accountability perceived by teachers (percentages)*

Perceived accountability	Not accountable		Accountable to some extent		Very accountable	
	1990	1992	1990	1992	1990	1992
Yourself/own conscience	0.0	0.0	4.9	4.3	95.1	95.0
To pupils	0.0	0.0	13.8	21.5	86.3	78.5
To parents	1.2	0.0	33.3	3.7	65.4	6.3
To headteachers	0.0	0.0	43.5	43.7	56.4	56.3
To colleagues	0.0	0.0	52.6	57.2	47.5	42.8
To governors	1.3	0.0	77.5	77.7	21.3	22.3
To employers	12.7	14.9	77.2	79.1	10.1	6.0
To society	8.8	1.1	85.0	85.4	6.3	13.5
To the Government	28.8	27.0	67.5	64.0	3.8	9.0

Source: PACE 1 teacher questionnaire.
Sample: 84 Key Stage 1 teachers.
Date: summer 1990 and summer 1992.

'Bristaix' study, which focused on teachers of children aged seven to eleven in 1985. It is clear from these data that, although external obligations still appeared to be less significant for primary teachers in England than internal ones, there had been a shift in accountability since the advent of the 1988 ERA. This represents a noticeable move in English teachers' sense of responsibility, which does not seem explicable in terms of the different ages of the children being taught. The really marked differences were in relation to the feelings of accountability towards the headteacher, colleagues and parents. After the Education Reform Act, teachers felt far more strongly accountable towards these three groups.

A different measure of comparison can be obtained by considering teachers' replies to an 'open-ended' question about the meaning of professional responsibility: 'What does professional responsibility mean to you?' This question was posed to the English teachers in the Bristaix sample in 1985 and to the full sample of PACE teachers in 1990 and 1992. Only spontaneous statements about responsibility to different agencies in the educational process were recorded under this method. In order to be able to compare our findings back to those of this earlier study, we adopted an almost identical coding procedure in which categories were identified within the data rather than imposing a theoretically based coding frame (Table 6.3).

Table 6.2   *Changes in teachers feeling 'very accountable' (percentages)*

Source of accountability	1985 Bristaix	1990 PACE	1992 PACE
Yourself	89.4	95.1	95.0
Pupils	81.8	86.3	78.5
Headteacher	32.9	56.4	56.3
Colleagues	24.3	47.5	42.8
Parents	43.1	65.4	63.0
Society	31.7	6.3	13.5

Source: PACE 1 teacher questionnaires and Bristaix questionnaires.
Sample: 94 Key Stage 1 teachers, 360 English Bristaix teachers.
Date: summer 1985, summer 1990, summer 1992.

Table 6.3   *Accountability to whom: categories mentioned by teachers (percentages)*

Responsibility felt towards	1985 Bristaix	1990 PACE	1992 PACE
Children	91.0	93.5	87.2
Colleagues	29.3	47.2	37.2
Parents	25.4	35.8	34.0
Employers	12.7	2.4	17.0
Headteacher	11.5	11.4	9.6
The school	9.4	12.2	10.6
Myself	7.6	6.5	6.4
Society	6.8	1.6	5.3
Governors	1.9	19.5	14.9
Other professionals	1.7	0.8	0.0
Senior staff	1.3	0.0	4.3
Other	0.0	4.1	1.1

Source: PACE 1 teacher questionnaires and Bristaix questionnaires.
Sample: 94 Key Stage 1 teachers, 360 English Bristaix teachers.
Date: summer 1985, summer 1990, summer 1992.
Note: Totals do not equal 100 per cent since questions were open-ended and multiple coding was used.

It is clear from Table 6.3 that teachers' sense of personal and moral responsibility remained high in terms of an emphasis on responsibility to children, although spontaneous identification of 'myself, my own conscience' did not figure highly in 1985, 1990 or 1992. However, there was a significant increase in feelings of external, contractual accountability. This was most notable with regard to the governors, but it was also clear with regard to parents, who, arguably, may now be considered part of the external, contractual dimension.

Feelings of responsibility to colleagues had also considerably increased, suggesting, as Lawn argued, that cooperativeness between teachers is no longer 'a possible quality a teacher may embody, but a necessary technical requirement in the teaching and management of the curriculum proposed for schoolwork' (Lawn, 1988, p. 162). This finding confirmed other data collected from the interviews, where teachers argued that they now spent much more time working collaboratively with colleagues in planning, assessing and, sometimes, in teaching itself (see section 6.6). For instance, a teacher talked of

> an increase in joint planning and whole-school planning where you know that the children aren't going to be repeating the work which you've done the previous year and you know exactly where the children's education is progressing. I think that has been very useful . . . and that sort of collaboration work between us in getting things together. Well, it's helped to counterbalance the extra demands that the National Curriculum has put upon us.

To summarize, while the strong sense of obligation to children and to partners in the educational process had in no way decreased since our earlier study in 1985, there was a significant increase in the 'external' sense of obligation that teachers felt. Rather than a shift, there was an increase in overall feelings of accountability to others. Teachers are now having to take into account a wider range of what might sometimes be perceived as conflicting obligations. In terms of our dimensions, there has been a noticeable shift in power from independence to greater accountability of teachers. This is reflected in what one teacher said about her obligations to others: 'There is a continual feeling of harassment caused by contradictory signals from the "powers that be". It predates the National Curriculum but it's got worse since . . . At the same time, we have got parents' expectations to think about – they may be different again – and, most important of all, there are the needs of the children.'

Section 6.6 of this chapter considers relationships with others in more detail. First, however, we will examine in the next section the extent to which teachers perceived changes in their work and role.

6.4 HOW DID TEACHERS PERCEIVE THEIR ROLE CHANGE?

In the two rounds of interviews with 88 classroom teachers, we asked teachers to talk in an open-ended way about their role and how it might have changed as a result of the introduction of the National Curriculum and assessment. Nearly two-thirds of the teachers (65 per cent) felt that their role as a teacher had changed to some extent, and for some these changes were fairly profound.

Although many teachers felt positive about the overall structure provided by the National Curriculum, for the majority of teachers in 1990 the impact of the changes was perceived to be largely negative. As Table 6.4 shows, they mentioned more

Table 6.4 *Impact of change on teachers' role (percentages)*

Changes in teacher role	1990	1992
More administration	46.8	64.8**
Increased time on planning	39.0	46.2
Increased stress and anxiety	24.7	35.2*
Loss of spontaneity and child-responsiveness	23.4	22.0
Imposition of priorities on teacher from outside	19.5	42.9***
More mechanistic and less opportunity to be creative	13.0	9.5*
Close cooperation with colleagues	39.0	45.1
Has focused and confirmed role	18.2	20.9
Accountability increased	16.9	22.0

Source: PACE 1 teacher interviews.
Sample: 88 Key Stage 1 teachers.
Date: summer 1990 and summer 1992.
Note: Totals do not equal 100 per cent since questions were open-ended and multiple coding was used.

administration (47 per cent), increased planning (39 per cent), a loss of spontaneity and child-responsiveness in their teaching (23 per cent), increased stress and anxiety (25 per cent), a strong sense of the imposition of external priorities (20 per cent) and a feeling of loss of autonomy and of creativity (13 per cent). As one teacher put it,

> I'm just more stressed now. I feel pulled in different directions and I feel the need to fulfil attainment targets and to cover the core subjects as a constant unspoken pressure. The relaxed atmosphere I used to have in my class is gone. I can't spend so much time with individual children and I don't feel able to respond in a spontaneous way to some initiative introduced by the children. I no longer have the luxury of being responsive and creative.

These strongly negative feelings were counterbalanced to a limited extent by the positive feelings of those who saw the changes as having the effect of focusing and confirming their instructional role or of leading them towards closer cooperation with colleagues.

By 1992, a number of these changes were perceived by teachers to have intensified, in particular the time spent on paperwork and administration, the level of stress and anxiety experienced and the sense of externally imposed priorities on the teacher. As one explained,

> It's just a different pace. There's a pressure and a feeling that you're never doing enough . . . You look at the documents and you think, 'How can I possibly fulfil all these demands? How can I fit all this in?' It's just overwhelming sometimes. You feel you're just going through a wheel. You're desperately covering stuff because you must give an assessment for it, and you think, 'This is just not what it's about. Learning is not about this and this is not what it should be like.'

On the other hand, between 1990 and 1992 a slightly increased proportion of teachers felt that the changes had helped to focus and confirm their role and that close cooperation with colleagues had been maintained or even increased. For many teachers these were perceived as positive developments.

In both 1990 and 1992, it was teachers who perceived themselves as strongly child-centred, creative and spontaneous in their approach who often felt that they had the most to lose under the National Curriculum. For example, where a high value had been placed on the quality of children's learning experiences, this was now felt to be eroded by time pressures. A number of these teachers expressed a feeling that the things that were of central importance to them in teaching were under attack, but they also asserted that they would defend them no matter what. As one teacher argued in 1990, 'I am not prepared to become somebody walking round with a checksheet, and I will fight it . . . I think my place is with the children, making a relationship with them. It's not fiddling around with bits of paper or spending all my time talking with their parents.'

It was striking that, when asked about their own strengths as a teacher, 75 per cent in 1990 emphasized skills such as being good at developing relationships with children, colleagues and parents, which we coded as 'affective skills', compared with only 34 per cent who mentioned classroom management skills. Yet, at the same time, 48 per cent of teachers perceived management skills to be of increasing importance under the National Curriculum (Table 6.5). It is not surprising, therefore, that 22 per cent felt that their strengths and skills were being eroded by the National Curriculum. Thus one teacher argued that, to be a good teacher,

> It's got to be first of all an ability to have a good relationship with children, to be able to encourage, cajole them into working hard, to be lively, full of fun, to provide a stimulating environment where they want to come to school and they want to learn. Some of one's spontaneity gets dampened by the rigorous demands of the National Curriculum. Some of the very special times in a primary classroom are when you just respond spontaneously to children's ideas. There is not much time or scope for that now.

By 1992, far more teachers emphasized cognitively related teaching skills (58 per cent compared with 24 per cent) as a strength, although in other ways their perceptions of their own strengths were little changed. What is more, an increasing proportion of teachers (50 per cent compared with 22 per cent) felt that their strengths and skills were being eroded by the National Curriculum (Table 6.6).

While many teachers were clearly not happy with the early impact of the changes on their work, it seems that fewer than a quarter felt strongly enough in 1990 to see this in terms of 'deskilling'. However, by 1992 virtually half the teachers had some perception of being 'deskilled'. Into this description of professional concern, we should note that, in both 1990 and 1992, there remained a proportion of teachers (around one-fifth) who saw the National Curriculum as complementing and enhancing their skills and strengths or providing the opportunity to develop them further. As one teacher put it, 'The National Curriculum has been useful in giving us targets and a framework to work within. In a way, it's a bit reassuring. It gives me a focus and another reason for doing

Table 6.5 *Teachers' perceptions of their teaching strengths (percentages)*

Teaching strengths mentioned	1990	1992
Classroom management skills	34.1	36.6
Cognitively related skills	23.9	58.1***
Affectively related skills	75.0	68.9
Curriculum-related skills	46.8	41.9
Assessment-related skills	1.1	2.2
Life experience	3.4	5.4
Hard work and enthusiasm	12.5	18.3
Enjoyment of teaching children	36.3	28.0

Source: PACE 1 teacher interviews.
Sample: 88 Key Stage 1 teachers.
Date: summer 1990 and summer 1992.
Note: Totals do not equal 100 per cent since questions were open-ended and multiple coding was used.

Table 6.6   *Teachers' perceptions of the influence of the National Curriculum on their strengths (percentages)*

Perceived influence on strengths	1990	1992
Complemented by NC	21.6	18.3
Eroded by NC	21.6	49.5***
No influence from NC	42.0	25.8
Possibly an influence in future – positive	5.7	3.2
Possibly an influence in future – negative	5.7	2.2
Other	3.4	1.0

Source: PACE 1 teacher interviews.
Sample: 88 Key Stage 1 teachers.
Date: summer 1990 and summer 1992.

things. It helps me feel as though I'm on the right track and releases me to work out new ways of teaching.'

We believe that there were two sub-groups here. Some teachers drew on the 'emergent professionalism' that we described in section 2.4, and felt positively about processes of reviewing and reflecting on their practice that they believed the National Curriculum had made necessary. They also believed that it had raised awareness among teachers of the importance of providing progression and continuity for children. Similarly, a need to read more widely was suggested and the need to collaborate more closely with other teachers was perceived as an enhancement of professionalism. It is significant that this proportion of teachers persisted from 1990 to 1992 in seeing positive outcomes for their professionalism, indicating that there was some enduring optimism regarding professionalism being enhanced by the consequences of the Education Reform Act. However, another sub-group of teachers were simply compliant because they saw the Act as endorsing traditionalism – particularly with the debates on subject specialization and whole-class teaching that were current at the time of our second interview.

To summarize, although some teachers may have felt empowered or affirmed by the changes, on the whole there was a noticeable shift towards perceptions of deskilling among teachers. Most teachers felt that their professionalism was under attack. The loss of responsiveness teachers perceived in their work with children was associated, regretfully, with a shift from an expressive towards a more instrumental role commitment.

6.5   DID TEACHERS FEEL THAT THEIR PROFESSIONAL AUTONOMY AND PERSONAL FULFILMENT WERE THREATENED BY THE CHANGES?

Although at the onset of the implementation of the Education Reform Act it was apparent that the imposition of a National Curriculum would reduce individual teachers' freedom to choose the 'content' of the curriculum, it was not so clear to what extent it might affect their freedom over how they taught. For example, it was argued by Hargreaves (1988) that having less responsibility for deciding curriculum content would release teachers' energies to engage in developing new pedagogic approaches. Others, however, have argued that external pressures would compel teachers to change their teaching methods (Osborn and Broadfoot, 1990). In 1990, 45 per cent of the teachers we interviewed perceived some loss of autonomy over teaching methods, although only 14 per cent said that their autonomy had been *considerably* reduced and nearly half felt no change in their freedom to select teaching methods. However, while many in 1990 still retained a considerable degree of autonomy over their teaching methods as individuals, there was more whole-school planning of topic work than previously and more collective curriculum decision-making by the school as a whole rather than by individual teachers. Most schools had appointed 'curriculum coordinators' for each National Curriculum subject area, whose role it was to advise and work with colleagues on the implementation of that subject area. However, this was seldom mentioned by teachers as a constraint on their freedom and was generally seen in a positive, constructive light.

By 1992, with the publication of the 'Three Wise Men' report (Alexander *et al.*, 1992), the debate over subject specialism and teaching methods in the primary school had moved on to centre stage and may have begun to affect how teachers saw their classroom autonomy in this area. Forty-seven per cent of teachers (compared with 31 per cent two years earlier) then spoke of having rather less freedom in choice of teaching methods than previously. Thus, nearly half the teachers felt a loss of autonomy in their pedagogic decision-making following the advent of the National Curriculum, and saw it as to some extent eroding professional judgement. A large number of teachers talked of a loss of freedom and creativity in their teaching, of feeling increasingly like 'a machine for delivering a prescribed curriculum', as well as the loss of a career structure and of the feeling of doing a valued and worthwhile job. One teacher said:

> I knew that teaching was going to be about long hours and a lot of preparation. That was always my inclination and I knew the demands of working with young children, but I never for one moment thought that there wouldn't be a feeling of doing an important job. I don't think that feeling is there any more and I think that has come through more and more since the National Curriculum.

However, we must again note that in both 1990 and 1992 a significant minority continued to speak of the positive effect of having a structure and guidelines to work within. This, they felt, released them to be creative in the way they worked with individual children rather than worrying about whether they had covered what should be covered. As one teacher put it,

> I feel that at least now there is some guideline as to what you should have achieved in the amounts of time that you have had with children . . . Up till now I have always felt that in teaching I'm not doing enough. I could always be doing more, which I think every teacher feels. Things were so open that you could never feel you had done a good job.

Such feelings of uncertainty and anxiety among primary teachers prior to the implementation of the National Curriculum were not uncommon. Indeed, several previous researchers have pointed to the insecurity experienced by individual teachers about whether they were covering the right things or whether they ought to have been doing more (Broadfoot and Osborn, 1988; Nias, 1989). Another teacher in the PACE study talked of the 'vulnerability' of teachers before the National Curriculum, when 'You had very little framework, you were very much left to yourself to decide what's to do and I think that is quite hairy really when you look back.' As a result of this previous uncertainty, the majority of teachers (68 per cent) welcomed the structure and guidelines introduced by the National Curriculum, although not its over-prescriptive nature, the rapid pace at which the changes were introduced or the sheer volume of work and pressure that resulted (see Chapter 7).

The degree of freedom teachers have and the sense of enjoyment and fulfilment gained from work are likely to be closely related. On the one hand, too little freedom may leave a teacher feeling like 'a machine for carrying out a prescribed curriculum', as one teacher put it, while too much can for some lead to feelings of being overstretched and of conflict and confusion about their role (Broadfoot and Osborn, 1988; Nias, 1989).

When we talked in more depth to our nine classroom study teachers in 1990 and 1991, it seemed that, as with the larger sample, the majority of these teachers perceived a loss of freedom in their teaching. Accompanying this was a loss of enjoyment, a lessening of the sense of fulfilment in their work that most had previously felt. Most expressed at least some negative feelings about the effect of the changes on job satisfaction. For several, the loss of freedom and increasing sense of constraint took the form of a feeling of being forced into 'an unnatural way of teaching', of having to be increasingly didactic in their teaching, rather than what they believed they should be, 'a facilitator of learning'. As one teacher put it,

> It's definitely not me, because that is not my way. I have never been a fountain of knowledge. I've usually tried to go side by side with the children because it's exciting. For them it's the first time they've experienced that. I might have done it a hundred times, but I must make them believe that they're the person that's invented it or thought it up.

Closely related to this was a sense of constraint experienced as a constant pressure to move on in order to cover everything, rather than being able to explore one idea to the full, as they once might have done. The Year 1 teacher at Orchard Primary School argued: 'I feel a little bit that I'm just trying to do too much, I'm much more structured in my work now. Previously, I might have deviated from my plan in order to make full use of an idea. Now I feel more pressure to move on to the next thing, to cover everything that's on my plan.' Sometimes, this even meant not being able to give the time they would like to the 'core subjects'. As the Year 1 teacher from Greenmantle Primary argued,

> There seems to be so much more to fit in. And I also feel that the three core subjects, you don't seem to be able to do those in as much detail as I would like to, because all the time you are worried about 'they should be using the computer, they should be using the cassette recorder and taping and that sort of thing'. It just seems an awful lot to try and keep going all at one time.

For some of the other teachers there had overwhelmingly been a sense of loss of enjoyment. The demands of change and the initial bombardment of teachers by the media were experienced as 'endless' and as eating into teachers' personal resources and personal life. As the Year 2 teacher at Lawnside Primary School put it, 'I still enjoy teaching very, very much. I do get a great deal of satisfaction from it but I do wonder how much more I can ignore . . . I just feel that sometimes I can't really give any more than I'm giving at the moment.'

The Year 1 teacher at Valley Primary, Sally Jones, whom we met in Chapter 3, felt that she was no longer able to carry out her 'personal philosophy on what I believe is right for children'; and she experienced this as very destructive of enjoyment and job satisfaction. In addition, teaching, she felt, was 'eating into my own life' and into the creative things she used to do at home. 'I've not made any wine at all . . . I don't read at all now, except educational documents . . . I never pick up a novel from one fortnight's summer holiday to the next.' Thus, not only had she experienced severe loss in her teaching, she also felt a sense of loss in her personal life, to the extent that she compared it with religious commitment: 'I do think you need to switch your mind off. I've become a teaching machine. I mean I can fulfil the National Curriculum by pure dedication only. I mean a nun hasn't . . . I don't believe a nun has any more dedication to her duties than I do.'

The Year 2 teacher at St Anne's also felt very strongly:

> I can see no bright areas of the job whatsoever. Even the simple pleasures of seeing children achieve things. It's more a case of, 'Oh well, I can cross that off my list, mark that box', and it's not a personal development shared between two people. It's just another task out of the way. It's becoming easier in a sense because you start the day, you know exactly what you're going to do, but then one of the joys as well as one of the nightmares of infant teaching was you didn't know how the day was going to develop.

This teacher would not now choose teaching as a job,

> which is a shame because at times I've enjoyed it. I've realized that I'm good at it, and I've sort of found out what I was meant to be, and it's very disheartening that I'm not allowed to enjoy what I'm doing any more. But, having said that, you know, when I wake up in the morning and think, 'Would I rather go to work in a library, would I rather go to work in an office, would I rather go to work in a school?' School comes down last on the list.

For some of these teachers, then, the satisfactions derived from teaching were ebbing away, while the frustrations were increasing. In terms of the values regarding commitment to role discussed in Chapter 3, teachers were being propelled towards alienation or instrumentalism rather than their previously expressive and moral commitment to their roles. If the heavy investment of these teachers' selves in teaching (Nias, 1989) does not continue to pay off in terms of rewards from their work, then we must ask ourselves whether committed teachers will continue to stay in teaching, and, if they do, whether their effort and motivation will decline. Certainly there is some evidence that such classroom teachers are no longer seeking to move up the career structure to become deputies and headteachers (Campbell *et al.*, 1991).

On the other hand, as the National Curriculum became more accepted, two of the nine classroom teachers interviewed in 1992 found that the sense of constraint they had experienced had begun to lessen as they became more familiar with the National Curriculum and had the confidence to deviate from it where they felt it appropriate. For example, the Lawnside Year 2 teacher argued:

> Now, I don't necessarily think, 'Oh, I shouldn't do that.' I don't feel the restraint in that sense now. I don't feel that it's wrong to go off on to something which maybe has been inspired by the children, whereas before [i.e. in the first few months of the National Curriculum] I used to think, 'I don't have time to do that.' I'm not so frightened at going off on a tangent now. I feel as long as it's worthwhile . . . that the children can get as much from going off the topic for a while . . . So much is covered over and over again. Practically everything is repetition in different ways.

For this teacher, rather than a lessening of enjoyment and fulfilment in work, there had merely been a change in the gains she felt. She now derived satisfaction from working out new creative ideas for meeting the National Curriculum requirements. 'Personally,

I find it very stimulating because I look at documents and I look at the things that are required and I try to think of ideas and ways of doing things that meet the requirement . . . I find it very challenging to work within a frame but at the same time I want to be free to go outside it to some degree if I think it's worthwhile.'

A second teacher, working in the inner-city context of Meadway Infant School, argued that:

> Before, I felt our goals were becoming woolly and that we had run out of steam with the child-centred approach . . . As long as I can continue my way of working and implement the National Curriculum as I see fit . . . Sometimes it's [the National Curriculum] easy to assimilate and sometimes difficult. [The National Curriculum] as a whole is welcome but it's hard work.

These teachers' responses suggest again that some teachers were gaining the confidence to interpret and actively to mediate the National Curriculum in ways that suited their own professional ends.

As a whole, however, teachers felt that their professionalism and classroom autonomy had been eroded and their sense of fulfilment in work reduced. In terms of the key dimension of power discussed in Chapter 3, teachers experienced a shift from having relative autonomy to experiencing greater constraint and control.

6.6 HOW DID TEACHERS THINK THE CHANGES INFLUENCED THEIR PROFESSIONAL RELATIONSHIPS WITH OTHER ADULTS?

One possible outcome of the recent policy changes, in particular the emphasis on teachers' responsibility for implementing a prescribed, predetermined curriculum, was that teachers might narrow and restrict their professional goals in the way we found French teachers had done, focusing down on their responsibility as a classroom teacher, responsible mainly for the subject teaching of their pupils within the classroom and placing less emphasis on the other related aspects of professional life (Broadfoot and Osborn, 1993). However, our data suggest that this was far from the case. As section 6.3 suggested, compared with 1985, English teachers in the 1990s felt responsible to a far wider range of people, but feelings of responsibility to children had in no way decreased. The elements of responsibility that might be termed 'external' or 'contractual' had increased, while the informal 'moral' dimension had also remained of high importance.

These findings were confirmed in teachers' responses to an open-ended question about the meaning of professional responsibility, which was posed to the Bristaix teachers in 1985 and to the PACE teachers in 1990 and 1992 (see section 6.3). Only issues spontaneously mentioned by teachers were recorded under this method. Professional relationships with other adults, which might form part of a wider or 'extended' professional responsibility, had increased in importance for teachers since the implementation of the Education Reform Act (Table 6.7).

Table 6.7   *Teacher relationships with others (percentages)*

	1985	1990	1992
Relationships with colleagues	23.1	47.3	43.0
Relationships with parents	19.0	29.1	29.3
Relationships with pupils	15.0	30.0	28.7

Source: PACE 1 teacher questionnaires and Bristaix questionnaires.
Sample: 94 Key Stage 1 teachers, 360 English Bristaix teachers.
Date: summer 1985, summer 1990, summer 1992.

Teacher relationships with colleagues

Responsibility for maintaining good relationships with colleagues had more than doubled in the proportion of times it was mentioned, while responsibility for relationships with parents had also significantly increased. At the same time, relationships with pupils were seen as more important, indicating again that they had not been displaced by pressure from other areas.

When we asked our nine classroom study teachers how the reforms were influencing their relationships with colleagues, most confirmed that there had been considerable changes in the way they worked with colleagues and with the headteacher, but that there had been less effect on their relationships with parents. Three key themes in teachers' conversation about colleagues were those of 'cooperation', 'support' and 'awareness'. All 18 teachers felt that, as a result of the National Curriculum, they were cooperating and working more closely with colleagues, and this was often seen to be a positive outcome, to give 'a feeling of ownership and sharing'.

As the Year 1 teacher at Kenwood put it, 'Now we have a lot more staff meetings when curriculum leaders talk about curriculum areas. We all go on the latest courses . . . We have in-service days regularly. There is an increase in working together. Last year we visited each other in classrooms and we ask each other for help a lot more often now.' The Year 2 teacher at Orchard Primary School said:

> We always have worked closely together but we are doing so even more now. We're discussing our own topics together far more and making sure too that we're not all covering the same thing, and we're very much more aware that we're planning to cover the whole of the curriculum . . . Initially, when the science curriculum came out, all the teachers made all their projects science-based . . . Just recently we've dealt with humanities; suddenly science is being pushed to one side and humanities is coming to the fore.

However, some of the increased cooperation was a response to the stress and overload that colleagues were feeling and an attempt to alleviate this. Maintaining an increased level of support was tiring and an extra strain. Teachers talked of 'forever throwing lifelines to your colleagues' and of exhaustion at the end of a day spent sharing colleagues' worries as well as one's own. The Year 1 teacher at Valley expressed herself as follows: 'We have to be really aware to help each other out when we're feeling low about it, and really put the effort in to talk to your colleagues and console them and say, "Look, I feel the same way", and "Yes, it's not just you". "If you can't do it, well, hard luck, don't do it".'

At the same time, most teachers felt that they were far more aware of what their colleagues were doing and more concerned to keep up with any new ideas or methods a colleague might be introducing. 'There's that underlying worry, "Am I doing the right things, should I be doing things that way as well?" I think there is always this underlying current, this nagging doubt.' The Year 1 teacher at Greenmantle said: 'I feel everybody's a lot more tense and a lot more stressed than they ever used to be. Everybody's very aware of what they feel they should be doing and what they're achieving.' Closely related to this was the knowledge that the children would be moving on to a colleague next year and must have covered the right preparatory ground: 'In the past everyone just got on with whatever topic they wanted. Now we have to be aware of what children will do next year and must try not to repeat ourselves from year to year.'

In one of the schools, collaboration between teachers had often taken the form of supporting one another to resist aspects of the National Curriculum that were felt to be inappropriate for inner-city children. These teachers, with the tacit support of the head, saw themselves as 'conspirators' working together to implement the National Curriculum selectively in a way they felt would protect the children and avoid overload. For example, a decision had been made in 1992 to ignore the history and geography programmes of study, except where they 'fitted naturally' into topics planned for the core subjects.

There was certainly evidence from the classroom studies and from the larger round of teacher interviews that teachers were moving towards more collaboration in their professional work, but few signs that this was beginning to take the form of shared teaching or more subject specialism. This is clearly a complex issue. For instance, a number of researchers have commented on the limitations of viewing whole-school planning as a move towards real collegiality (Warren-Little, 1987; Wallace, 1991; Hargreaves, 1989). One recent ethnographic study has suggested that teachers, trying in their own classrooms to implement topic work planned on a whole-school basis, found difficulty in presenting such curriculum ideas in a creative and interesting way (Stone, 1993). It seems that enforced collegiality can sometimes lead to a lack of ownership in the planned work and hence a loss of interest and spontaneity. On the whole, however, most of the teachers welcomed the increase in collaboration and partnership with colleagues, and felt that it added a new dimension to their professionalism.

Teacher relationships with headteachers and deputy headteachers

When we asked teachers in the 1992 rounds of interviews whether the relationship between the head and the staff had changed, slightly over half felt that there had been no change, but roughly one-fifth felt that relationships had worsened. Only 2 per cent felt that relations with the head had improved, while another fifth remained 'neutral', or unable to express an opinion.

Headteachers were perceived by their staff to be under more strain and, reciprocally, some had adopted an increasingly protective role towards their staff, attempting to organize things so as to put the least possible strain on class teachers. One of the Valley Primary School teachers described her head as putting 'an extra burden on herself'. In her own office time she did extra teaching in the classroom. 'When she should be doing work with administration she leaves it and does it at home in her own time, so that she can give the teachers time to do planning. She knows it's not enough, but she feels that it's necessary just to keep us all on an even keel, or else we'd be inundated with the whole task at weekends.' Teachers who were deputy heads were often taking extra responsibilities, as well as some of the head's overload, which devolved upon them.

At St Anne's another teacher argued:

> Yes, things have changed considerably. I mean the head seems more like a manager now. Quite against his will he's had to devolve responsibility into subject meetings and management teams and department groups, and there are times when one just longs for the old days when the boss would come in and say, 'Look, we're going to do this, we're going to do that' . . . because that's what he's getting paid for. He's had the role of accountant, and manager, and chairman of the board, as it were, thrust upon him and he's not trained for it . . . It is becoming a business, which is, I suppose, what the Government wanted.

Teacher relationships with parents

Teachers' relationships with parents were not seen to have changed in any fundamental way as a result of the reforms. Roughly 20 per cent of teachers in both 1990 and 1992 felt that their relationship with parents had improved because of the National Curriculum. Some of these teachers argued that parents saw teachers as more professional now that they reported back on individual children and used written records and schemes of work. Although in 1992 parents' level of awareness and anxiety was perceived to have increased as a result of the publication of SAT results (29 per cent in 1992 saw parents as anxious compared with 20 per cent in 1990), in both years nearly 20 per cent of teachers felt that parents were more supportive now that the sheer volume of teachers' work was more visible to them. At St Anne's, an inner-city school in a disadvantaged area, a teacher said:

> A number of parents are becoming more aware of what they should be getting from school and from the teachers, and they're not, sort of, coming up demanding their rights, but they're coming up showing an understanding of what's happening, and fortunately, they're showing a sort of appreciation of what we're doing and saying, 'Gosh, we didn't realize you had so much to do. Is there any way we can help?' We only had one example, last year, of 'Why is he on Level 1 when he should be on Level 2 and I'd love him to be on Level 3!'

Some inner-city teachers feared that continued publication of SAT results, plus the effects of local management of schools, the publicity over teaching methods and the financial gap that was likely to develop between inner-city schools and those in more privileged areas, could lead to the development of 'sink' schools through the exercise of parental choice and the operation of educational markets. A contrasting set of concerns was expressed by teachers and headteachers in schools in the most affluent areas, those in leafy suburbs and attractive commuter villages. Teachers feared increased parental pressure, both on the children and on themselves, as well as a 'flight to private education if the published results did not come up to scratch'.

To summarize, teachers had increasingly developed and valued collaborative relationships with other colleagues. Relationships with parents were little changed, although there was concern about the publication of assessment data. In terms of the dimensions discussed in Chapter 3, there was a shift in values from individualism towards greater collegiality.

6.7 HOW DID TEACHERS FEEL THAT THE CHANGES WERE LIKELY TO INFLUENCE THEIR WORK IN FUTURE?

In 1990, we were aware that we were asking teachers about the effects of the changes in education at a very early stage of implementation, when their impact might not be fully felt. Indeed, many teachers who felt reasonably comfortable with what had happened so far nevertheless expressed fears about the future. When asked how they thought primary education would develop in the next five to ten years, most were pessimistic (47 per cent) or had mixed feelings (34 per cent). Over 67 per cent predicted that the degree of teacher stress would be such that there would be heavy drop-out from the profession, and nearly a quarter predicted further constraints, loss of autonomy and a narrowing of the teachers' role (see Table 6.8).

On a more optimistic note, 33 per cent felt that the changes would soon lessen in intensity, things would sort themselves out, and the worst aspects of the National Curriculum and assessment would disappear. A small minority once again saw things in a more positive light and predicted more collaboration between teachers and more review and reflection by teachers on their practice.

In spite of largely pessimistic predictions about the future, 46 per cent said that if they had to choose again they would still choose to be a teacher, while 25 per cent were undecided. However, a number of the former group said that they would not encourage a son or daughter to enter teaching and some had already actively discouraged a child with plans for teaching. Perhaps their feelings were well expressed by one inner-city teacher from our larger sample, who said:

> I've got a tremendous amount out of teaching, a tremendous amount, and I think that's partly the reason why I feel so strongly about this, and why I've got so depressed about it all is because I can see what's being destroyed. I've thought seriously several times this year about throwing it in because I can't stand it any longer. On the other hand, that seems defeatist . . . if it becomes more and more inflexible and we get less and less control over the way we teach, and the children become less and less important then I shall leave, because there'll be no pleasure in it any more and I shan't feel that I'm doing a worthwhile job. It's not what I consider to be education.

In 1992, more teachers had become pessimistic about the future. Fewer teachers predicted stress and drop-out, although well over half still saw this as a real possibility. Possibly the slight drop is a reflection of the high unemployment figures in 1992, making it less likely that disaffected teachers would be able to find a job elsewhere. Strikingly,

Table 6.8 *Changes predicted by teachers in the nature of their work (percentages)*

Type of change	1990	1992
More teacher stress/drop-out	66.7	55.8
More constraints/loss of autonomy	25.9	79.2***
Less personal fulfilment	17.3	35.1***
More collaboration among teachers	11.1	7.8**
More reflection, review of practice	6.2	7.8

Source: PACE 1 teacher interviews.
Sample: 88 Key Stage 1 teachers.
Date: summer 1990 and summer 1992.
Note: Totals do not equal 100 per cent since teachers could predict more than one change.

however, in 1992 almost 80 per cent of teachers predicted more constraints and greater loss of autonomy for teachers in the future, compared with only 26 per cent in 1990. Similarly, the proportion of teachers expecting to find less personal fulfilment in their work was doubled in the 1992 sample. Both the increases noted above are statistically significant.

This increasing pessimism about the future may have been fuelled by the publication of the report of the so-called 'Three Wise Men' (Alexander *et al.*, 1992) and the debate in the media over teaching methods in the primary school, which immediately preceded our 1992 interviews. A teacher argued:

> With the publication of results, with the minimizing of local authority support, with the removal of professional expertise being equally available to schools, and with requirements of new legislation and the induction of all sorts of different schemes, I think one thing I foresee is that schools will become progressively more different from each other in terms of resources, staffing, advantages and disadvantages. I think there will be more schools that are disadvantaged than advantaged. I think there will be less equality of opportunity for children and I think children will become more competitive – it will become more competitive throughout primary education, it will be rather divisive. I see schools being divided from each other and there being less cohesiveness among professionals.

Nevertheless, a proportion of teachers still saw some positive outcomes emerging in future, in particular in terms of the emphasis placed by the National Curriculum on collaboration between teachers and on the need for teachers to reflect upon and review their practice. One such teacher argued that the National Curriculum would release teachers from anxiety and vulnerability,

> because you've got a framework and you've got a reference, and provided it's used as a tool, which I think perhaps we do here, it can actually release you . . . you can relax more because you know that you've got things keyed in at the planning stage . . . You can focus much more in depth on areas . . . provided that you use it as a tool, and you don't change what you believe is the best way children learn.

Another argued that standards would be pushed up in primary schools, leaving secondary education with less to do: 'Like the science we've been doing over the last couple of years, we've been doing some of the work that would have been done in the first two years of secondary schools, so there ought to be things rebounding off it. Standards should be going up. I think the children are going to be better prepared.'

To summarize, as a whole, there was an increase in teachers' sense of pessimism about the future of primary education and a sense that constraint would increase still further and autonomy be reduced. Many expected fulfilment in work to continue to decline.

6.8 HOW DID TEACHER PERSPECTIVES VARY?

There are many variables at both institutional and individual level that might influence a teacher's stance towards change. Among these are the school ethos and strategy for change, the socio-economic catchment area of the school, the teacher's ideology and previous beliefs about teaching, as well as the teacher's age and years of teaching experience. For example, Bowe and Ball (1992) argued that schools which are already well adapted to making changes, and where a collaborative culture has been fostered, are in a better position to make a 'creative' response to change that will involve and support the staff. There was some evidence from our interviews with classroom teachers that teachers who had perceived themselves as strongly child-centred, creative and spontaneous in their approach were those who often felt they had the most to lose under the National Curriculum, and were, as a consequence, less positive about it.

Conscientiousness, or even over-conscientiousness, may be an issue too. Campbell *et al.* (1991) cite such internalized commitment to high personal standards as a factor in teacher stress and consequent demoralization, because it made it difficult for teachers to limit their workloads. In contrast, some teachers had developed coping strategies that enabled them to constrain impulses to over-conscientiousness in order to protect their personal time, social life and 'sanity'. In terms of our dimensions, such teachers had begun to accept a shift in values from an expressive to an instrumental commitment. For some of the teachers in our study, the ability to adopt such a stance enabled them to make a more positive, creative response to the National Curriculum by exercising choice and rationing and prioritizing the workload. Some of these teachers, like those identified by Fullan (1991) as 'interactors' or by MacCallum *et al.* (1993) as 'systematic planners', were able to make a conscious decision about how to proceed rather than allowing themselves to be 'swamped by change'. We return to this point in the concluding section of this chapter.

Our data showed no difference between teachers of different ages and experience in terms of the accountability they felt to children, headteacher, parents, colleagues, governors, etc. (see section 6.3). However, there is some evidence that younger teachers and new entrants to teaching felt more positively towards the changes being introduced and more ready to internalize them and develop their practice from them.

Schools in different types of socio-economic catchment area experienced very different pressures as a result of the changes, and consequently their teachers often expressed a different set of concerns and anxieties. Thus, in many schools in disadvantaged inner-city areas, anxiety centred on the difficulty of adapting teaching to the perceived needs of the individual children. The National Curriculum was not seen as relating well to the children's needs. It was felt that there was a need for time in order to allow infant-school children to adapt to classroom life and to become ready to learn, and that this time was no longer available under the pressures of the National Curriculum. As one inner-city teacher put it,

> There are social and economic difficulties here. You can't start where you would hope to. You have to start building up closeness to the child first. If you don't do that you might as well not bother. I'd hate to get to the point where I think, 'I must do that today and I'm sorry if Emma comes in crying, but she's just got to sit and do it, because the law says I must be doing it.'

In 1992, 62 per cent of teachers in inner-city schools expressed the view that the demands of the National Curriculum took no account of the real classroom situation, compared with 43 per cent of teachers in affluent, middle-class areas and 21 per cent of rural teachers (Table 6.9). More inner-city teachers also felt that the National Curriculum was unsuited to special needs children, and more teachers from the inner city (94 per cent) and from settled working-class areas (82 per cent) thought that, in the future, primary education would be less able to adapt to children's needs, compared with 73 per cent of teachers in middle-class areas and 60 per cent of rural teachers. Because of their situation, and the very real constraints under which they operated, these teachers often adopted coping strategies similar to those of the 'autonomous' teachers identified by Fullan (1992), who 'cannot be forced to be involved and may very well be doing a good job'. They were often likely to articulate their position in terms of responding to the needs of the children and protecting children's interests.

Teachers in affluent middle-class catchment areas were the most likely to see the changes as enhancing their teaching qualities and skills, in terms of enabling them to reflect on their practice (33 per cent of teachers in middle-class areas compared with 11 per cent of inner-city teachers) and collaborate with other teachers (47 and 4 per cent respectively). Those teaching in rural and in middle-class areas were also more likely to perceive the National Curriculum as enabling them to provide greater continuity and progression for children (see Table 6.10).

Teachers in the inner city had very justifiable concerns about the financial effects of LMS, the publication of league tables of standardized assessment results and the effect of such comparisons with schools in more advantaged areas. These, they felt, could in no way take into account the progress individual children had made or the enormous efforts made by teachers. Comparisons in the media, which began to emerge over the period of data-gathering, were perceived by many teachers as demoralizing and insulting to both staff and children. Such findings suggest that as the effects of the educational market continue to operate, and teaching in the inner city becomes a harder and less

Table 6.9 *Teachers' opinions of the relevance of the National Curriculum: by school location and socio-economic circumstances (percentages)*

Teacher view of relevance of the National Curriculum	Rural area	Settled blue-collar/ white-collar area	Inner-city area	Middle-class/ professional area
NC takes no account of real class situation	21.4	33.3	61.5	42.9
NC overcrowded/difficult to cover	64.3	72.2	46.2	57.1
NC not suitable special needs	21.4	16.7	26.9	14.3
NC consolidates present practice	0.0	5.6	7.7	21.4

Source: PACE 1 teacher interviews.
Sample: 88 Key Stage 1 teachers.
Date: summer 1992.
Note: Totals do not equal 100 per cent since questions were open-ended and multiple coding was used.

Table 6.10 *Teachers' perceptions of the influence of change on their qualities and skills: by school location and socio-economic circumstances (percentages)*

Influence of change on teachers	Rural area	Settled blue-collar/ white-collar area	Inner-city area	Middle-class/ professional area
More reflection on own practice	13.3	10.5	11.1	33.3
More collaboration	6.7	21.1	3.7	46.7
More continuity for children	21.4	5.9	4.5	16.7

Source: PACE 1 teacher interviews.
Sample: 88 Key Stage 1 teachers.
Date: summer 1992.
Note: Totals do not equal 100 per cent since questions were open-ended and multiple coding was used.

rewarding job, the eventual outcome might be a flight of teachers from the inner-city schools to 'easier', more affluent areas, as often occurs in France as a primary teacher's career develops. This could mean a considerable loss to inner-city children of committed, confident and experienced teachers.

All these factors apart, the teachers who felt able to make a creative response to the National Curriculum were those who felt confident and sure enough about their own practice to enable them to make choices and to be selective in how they implemented the programmes of study. They were often supported by a strong, collaborative school culture. Their responses were characterized by a confidence that they could benefit from the structure and guidelines of the National Curriculum without letting it drive them or destroy what they knew to be good about their practice. Examples of such teachers' beliefs and classroom practice are given in Chapter 9 and in the case study of Sally Jones in Chapter 3.

In summary, there were differences in perspectives between older and younger teachers and between teachers in different socio-economic catchment areas. Teachers in inner-city schools felt the National Curriculum to be particularly inappropriate for their pupils' needs, and were no longer able to provide a differentiated pedagogy in the way they felt appropriate.

6.9 CONCLUSIONS

The evidence presented here suggests that even at an early stage in the implementation of the reforms most teachers felt that they had to change their teaching approach, their classroom practice and their perception of their professional role in ways they would not have chosen for themselves. This resulted in pressures from lack of time, an intensification of workload and a loss of job satisfaction. By 1992 there were increasing perceptions of a loss of autonomy and fulfilment in teaching. In terms of the dimensions introduced in Chapter 3, teachers were feeling more controlled and less autonomous. There was some evidence of a move from an expressive commitment to work to more instrumentalism, and even alienation. Thus, on the face of it, the data appear to support the intensification thesis. However, this impression does not fully take into account teachers' capacity to take charge of events, and to mediate change rather than simply to respond to it. A significant minority of teachers felt that a new professionalism, involving creative ways of working with individual children and of assessing them, was possible provided they had the confidence to shape the imposed changes to more professionally acceptable ends. As Hargreaves (1992) demonstrates, this emergent perception of a 'new professionalism' cannot simply be dismissed as 'false consciousness' on the part of teachers.

There was little evidence that teachers in England were moving towards a 'restricted' model of professionalism, akin to that prevalent in France, centred only on classroom teaching and 'fulfilling one's contractual responsibility'. Rather, the indications were that teachers were taking on an increasing range of responsibilities, both 'internal' and 'external' and that there was a strong move towards increased collaboration and interchange with colleagues. Often this was evident only at the planning stage of work, and there were limits to its effectiveness, but it nevertheless represents an important development of collaborative professionalism.

In his 1991 study of educational change, Fullan identifies various responses to change often made by teachers. Particularly relevant to our data are his dimensions of 'receivers' who are 'ready to implement received material', 'participators' who are willing to take part but 'have yet to learn to work with change in a balanced way', 'interactors' who are 'keen to be involved in change and to interact with the change process in a balanced way', and 'autonomous' teachers who 'cannot be forced to participate and may well be doing a good job'.

The responses to change of the PACE teachers can be categorized into five similar categories and in this we also build on our discussion of dimensions of school change in section 3.3 and the empirical consideration of school strategies of section 5.6. Our five strategies are 'compliance', 'incorporation', 'mediation', 'resistance' and a fifth dimension, not identified by Fullan, which we have identified as 'retreatism'. These responses are explained as follows:

- *Compliance*: acceptance of the imposed changes and adjustment of teachers' professional ideology accordingly, so that greater central control is perceived as acceptable, or even desirable.
- *Incorporation*: appearing to accept the imposed changes but incorporating them into existing modes of working, so that existing methods are adapted rather than changed and the effect of change is considerably different from that intended.
- *Mediation*: taking active control of the changes and responding to them in a creative, but possibly selective, way.
- *Retreatism*: submission to the imposed changes without any change in professional ideology, leading to deep-seated feelings of resentment, demoralization and alienation.
- *Resistance*: resistance to the imposed changes in the hope that the sanctions available to enforce them will not be sufficiently powerful to make this impossible.

Compliance was most noticeable among young teachers who had newly entered the profession, most of whom had never experienced teaching before the Education Reform Act. It was also evident among older returners to teaching who had been out of the profession for a number of years.

The response of the majority of teachers in our study appeared to be one of incorporation. For instance, there was a common feeling that 'I'll accept the changes, but I won't allow anything I consider to be really important to be lost.' As one headteacher explained,

> I think I feel less uncomfortable than I did. Just about this time last year I wrote a letter to my senior adviser telling him that I was very seriously thinking of resigning because I was not prepared to have a dictated curriculum and I was not prepared for somebody to change the job I loved into one I didn't even recognize. He was very good about that and we had a long talk about acting subversively – it sounds awful – but if you were really convinced that what you were saying was right, then you looked at the National Curriculum and you used it as a tool really, rather than letting it drive you . . . I feel happier about it than I did a year ago.

Several other teachers talked of using the National Curriculum as a tool, 'taking what is best from it, and leaving the rest' and 'not letting it govern everything I do'. As one teacher put it, 'I'll never sacrifice the children. I'll go on doing what I think best for them regardless.'

For a small proportion of teachers (about one-fifth) the response was stronger than simply incorporation. These teachers could be seen as active mediators, taking ownership and control of the innovations and working to develop new forms of practice in pedagogy and assessment while building on what they felt to be good about their existing practice. One example of such a teacher was a deputy head who argued that the National Curriculum facilitated his role as a manager as well as a classroom teacher: 'It's a powerful lever for me in getting things done in school. It would be a harder struggle without the National Curriculum in getting any change. I use it as an enhancer for what I want to do anyway. It's an enhancing process because it forces us to be clearer about what we want to do. It gives a clearer focus to work.' Further examples of active mediators can be found in the chapters on pedagogy and assessment.

There was considerable evidence of retreatism among teachers, particularly among some older teachers who, at the time of the interviews, were about to take early retirement or were strongly considering it. One such teacher, with 34 years of experience, expressed her feelings in this way: 'It has changed my job to a job I detest from a job I loved and I've been a teacher since 1957. It's taken me away from the people I was trained to help . . . It is my whole job satisfaction, my whole outlook, everything's gone. My joy has gone.'

Resistance, in the form of total refusal to implement the National Curriculum or assessment, was almost non-existent, but decisions to resist where it was felt children's interests would be particularly ill-served were not uncommon. For instance, there was the group of 'conspirators' who identified themselves in one inner-city school (p. 93). This form of response was particularly noticeable among teachers who were strongly child-centred in their approach, and it was justified by them in terms of the children's needs. MacCallum *et al.* (1993) have called such teachers 'children's needs ideologists'. However, the spring 1993 decision by the teaching unions to boycott national assessment procedures (which occurred outside the time period on which this book reports) could be seen as the beginning of a significant collective movement towards resistance. However, the unions were clear that such action would in no way affect the *teaching* of the National Curriculum. It was perhaps significant that this move to resistance only occurred as national assessment reached the secondary school, when cross-phase support was harnessed.

While only a small proportion of teachers could be directly categorized as mediators, there were many more, in fact a majority, who welcomed the guidelines and structure provided by the National Curriculum (cf. sections 7.2 and 7.6). Indeed, it is likely that if such teachers had not been swamped by the sheer pace of change, and if they had been given an opportunity to take ownership of the innovations, mediation might have been the predominant response. Most teacher disillusion related to the pace of change, the nature of recording and assessments, and, at later stages, to the overcrowded nature of the curriculum.

If a future review of the curriculum and assessment requirements results in a reduction of workload, many more teachers may feel able to make a positive and creative response to educational reform. Thus, in spite of the pressures and the generally inept central management of the introduction of the Education Reform Act, our 1992 findings suggest that there was a continuing potential for constructive professionalism. Some teachers still saw a way through the changes to some growth and development in their practice. They envisaged the possibility of a movement forward, after previous uncertainty, to a new clarity about their role.

To summarize overall, teachers' work had intensified considerably, but most teachers remained unwilling to give up their moral commitments to pupils and to their extended professional role. In terms of our dimensions, there was no noticeable shift from an extended to a restricted conception of role, although, as section 6.7 suggested, some teachers feared that this might happen in the future. There was, however, evidence of a shift towards a more collaborative professionalism.

In Chapter 7 we go on to examine teachers' initial and later views of the National Curriculum, their goals and priorities for the children, and the impact of the changes on their classroom planning and curriculum provision.

Chapter 7

Teachers and the Curriculum

7.1 INTRODUCTION

The introduction of the National Curriculum clearly emphasized the primacy of separate subjects and had associated with it a distinct subject-based structure within NCC, SEAC and LEAs. One of the aims of the PACE research was to monitor how this impacted on the forms of knowledge that had previously been adopted by primary schools. These, in general terms, could be characterized as endorsing a considerable degree of subject integration through the use of 'topics' and projects for non-core subjects. We were interested in how far teachers were changing their priorities and their practice in line with these new curricular structures. In this chapter, in terms of the dimensions that were introduced in section 3.5, we consider the extent to which there was a shift from integrated curricular provision, or low classification of subject knowledge, to more subject-based provision with high classification of curricular knowledge.

In addition, again focusing on a dimension that is highlighted in Chapter 3, we consider here the issue of curriculum balance and the ways in which teachers attempted to resolve the tension between the requirement to cover nine subjects, and thus provide a broad curriculum content, and the need to give priority to the basics, even where this means emphasizing a narrower curriculum content.

Associated with the above two issues is the question of the extent to which there was a shift in schools towards perceptions of knowledge as 'established' in the National Curriculum and as representing bodies of thought into which pupils should be inducted, perhaps through didactic or 'whole-class' teaching methods. The contrasting element of this dimension, of course, is a view of knowledge as socially or individually constructed, probably through more fluid teaching–learning processes and with more teaching of individuals or groups.

This chapter is presented in two main parts. Sections 7.2 to 7.6 consider teacher perceptions of the introduction of the National Curriculum and of the ways in which it has impacted on their priorities for the children and on their classroom provision. This account draws mainly on data collected in two rounds of interviews with 88 teachers from our main national sample, conducted in 1990 and 1992. The second part of the chapter, sections 7.7 to 7.11, reports what the PACE team recorded happening in classrooms. It draws mainly on systematic observation data derived from classroom studies of nine Year 1 classrooms observed in autumn 1990 and nine Year 2 classrooms, from the same schools, observed in autumn 1991. Chapter 4 gives more details of the sample and methods used.

As we saw in Chapter 6, teacher values, ideologies and views of professionalism vary considerably. This variation is echoed in the many views that were taken of the National Curriculum. However, even where it is possible through the PACE research to identify broad patterns in perspectives, it is necessary to be very specific about the time of data collection. Teacher views, concerns and priorities have, in other words, changed rapidly over the past few years. This is hardly surprising given the progressive nature of the implementation of the National Curriculum, spread over many years, revised several times, and subject to heated debate at almost every point.

Our account of PACE findings concerning teacher perspectives thus reflects successive phases of National Curriculum implementation. We have also tried to deal specifically with teacher views of the National Curriculum *in principle* and to make these data distinct from teacher views of National Curriculum *implementation*.

7.2 WHAT WERE TEACHERS' INITIAL VIEWS OF THE NATIONAL CURRICULUM?

The most striking feature revealed by our interview data on Key Stage 1 teachers' initial responses to the National Curriculum was their general acceptance of it. Teacher views of the work of the National Curriculum Subject Working Parties, which met during 1989 and 1990 to construct the National Curriculum, were certainly often forthright, but the overall feeling, subject by subject, was remarkably positive. 'It's what we are doing already' or 'It's just good practice' were common responses. Primary teachers, in the initial phase of implementation, thus tended to treat the challenges of the National Curriculum as 'private troubles' (Mills, 1959). They accepted its legitimacy, the principle of entitlement that it enacted and the 'reasonableness' of its expectations. Most teachers took on the personal challenges that the National Curriculum brought.

Many teachers particularly welcomed the curricular clarification that the National Curriculum offered, despite the time pressure and hard work that was evidently going to be involved in implementation. Indeed, by the time of our first round of interviews in 1990, the need for curricular breadth and progression seemed to have been largely accepted in principle. Two national surveys, however, confirmed that, even at this early phase, primary school teachers were becoming aware of weaknesses in their subject knowledge, particularly in science and technology (Wragg *et al.*, 1989; Moses and Croll, 1990).

The initial analysis of interview data thus reflected a generally constructive reception for the changes. In the case of the overwhelming majority of teachers interviewed, the introduction of the National Curriculum was supported in principle and it was evident that a very great deal of thought and work was going into its implementation. This was clearly indicated in teachers' responses to our enquiry of the relevance of the National Curriculum to the needs of the children in each teacher's class. In 1990, 16 per cent of teachers thought that the National Curriculum was 'very well matched to the needs of all children' and another 39 per cent saw it as 'well matched to the needs of many children'. A further 28 per cent felt that the National Curriculum related 'well to some needs but not others'. Only 14 per cent declared that it was 'not well matched' and just 3 per cent that it was 'irrelevant'. In only a small number of cases was active opposition to the National Curriculum apparent.

The issue that aroused massive opposition even in 1990 was assessment, with 83 per cent of teachers mentioning the requirements as being unrealistic and many others objecting in principle to formal assessment of seven-year-olds. There was also concern about the applicability and effect of the National Curriculum for children with special educational needs. Nevertheless, the overall picture in 1990 was of teachers in primary schools accepting the broad terms and principles of the National Curriculum and seeking to implement it.

Within this general support for the curriculum there was also dismay at the ways in which it was being implemented. First there was irritation and anger at some statements by Government ministers and officials, which seemed to be unnecessarily disparaging of teachers and their work – feelings that were often aggravated by media treatment of such remarks. Furthermore, whatever the responses to the National Curriculum of different groups and individuals, there was universal awareness that it was being introduced with great speed. Schools reported receiving 'huge' quantities of documentation from national and LEA sources. It was felt that instructions were issued and often countermanded a few days later, and that teachers had to come to terms with a whole new vocabulary of programmes of study, attainment targets, levels and assessment tasks. 'Too much has been happening too quickly' was the way many teachers put it. They reported feeling 'swamped by change' and 'simply overwhelmed' by the amount of documentation that accompanied it.

Nor was there much appreciation of the quality of what was on offer. In our 1990 interviews 61 per cent teachers said that national documentation was 'not very helpful' in planning their work and no less than 78 per cent said that there was simply 'too much' to assimilate. Perceptions of the support offered by LEAs varied considerably, with over half of those questioned finding it unhelpful or being unaware of what was on offer. Feelings about school-based training, though still very variable, were slightly more positive. Nevertheless, the overall impression of this initial phase of National Curriculum implementation is that most teachers simply felt bewildered by a combination of external criticism, unreasonable demands and confused guidance.

Many teachers, heads and LEA advisers thus found the situation difficult and stressful. The time needed to solve the problems was simply not available, as was reported by HMI from a survey of 1000 classes of five- to seven-year-olds: 'A pressing problem for almost all of the schools was the lack of time for teachers to plan and prepare work, and in the case of subject coordinators to assist their colleagues at the end of the day' (DES, 1989, para. 10). There was considerable evidence of an intensification of teacher workload. In a study of teacher workload at Key Stage 1 carried out by Campbell *et al.*, over half the teachers in 1990 reported working more than 50 hours per week (Campbell *et al.*, 1991). In 1991, Year 2 teachers were working an average of 58.1 hours per week, with those in the highest 20 per cent working nearly 72 hours per week (Campbell and Neill, 1992).

In a situation such as this, it would be surprising if teachers were not being compelled to reprioritize their educational aims, and in the next section we go on to consider this.

7.3 WHAT CHANGES OCCURRED IN TEACHERS' EDUCATIONAL AIMS AND PRIORITIES?

Through the Education Reform Act a statutory obligation was imposed on teachers to meet academic objectives as prescribed in the attainment targets specified in the National Curriculum. For the first time, teachers in England had clear-cut, prescribed attainment targets in nine subject areas to cover for each child in each academic year, and a direct form of accountability through the SATs, by which the attainments of all children were to be measured at ages seven and eleven. One possible result of these changes was that teachers in England might adopt a view of their work that was more closely related to that of teachers in other countries, such as France, where there have long been clearly defined objectives and attainment targets to be met for children. This would mean a more restricted conception of teachers' role in terms of the adoption of a narrower set of objectives for the children, centred more on academic goals rather than goals of personal and social development, i.e. a shift from expressive to instrumental concerns.

In order to examine the extent to which a shift in teaching objectives and priorities might have taken place, we have drawn upon three sets of related data. Two questions on teaching objectives and on the meaning of professional responsibility are drawn from a short questionnaire administered to 88 teachers and 48 headteachers in 1990 and 1992, and we have also analysed a question about teachers' priorities for the children in their class, drawn from the two rounds of interviews with 88 teachers in 1990 and 1992. Further, we have made comparisons with data gathered prior to the introduction of the Education Reform Act on teachers of five- to eleven-year-olds by Ashton *et al.* (1975) and by Broadfoot *et al.* (1987).

It is notable that 42 per cent of our sample in 1990 and 51 per cent in 1992 felt that their objectives for the children had had to change to some extent. Table 7.1 shows the teachers' spontaneous responses to an open-ended question about their priorities for the

Table 7.1 *Teachers' academic and non-academic priorities (percentages)*

	1990	1992
Academic priorities		
Emphasizing basic skills	47.5	46.7
Developing individual potential	42.5	45.6
Matching work to children	32.5	22.2*
Listening and communication skills	20.0	5.6**
Broad, balanced curriculum	16.3	44.4***
Affective, creative curriculum	6.3	8.9
Achieving NC attainment targets	2.5	13.3***
Other	12.5	0.0
Not mentioned	9.1	3.2
Non-academic priorities		
Happiness, enjoyment in learning	65.3	53.8
Social skills, cooperative attitudes	41.7	32.3
Independence, autonomy	40.3	49.2
Moral, religious education	6.9	3.1
Other	5.6	4.6
Not mentioned	18.2	30.1

Source: PACE 1 teacher interviews.
Sample: 88 Key Stage 1 teachers in 8 LEAs.
Date: summer 1990 and summer 1992.
Note: Figures do not equal 100 per cent because of multiple coding of open-ended responses.

children. Both academic and non-academic priorities are listed in the order of importance in which they occurred in 1990.

It is particularly striking that, by 1992, almost one-third of teachers mentioned no non-academic priorities (30 per cent in 1992 compared with 18 per cent in 1990). The importance of providing a broad, balanced curriculum, however, had increased as a priority from 16 to 44 per cent ($p < 0.005$) and achieving National Curriculum attainment targets had increased from 3 to 13 per cent ($p < 0.005$). At the same time, the development of children's listening and communication skills had declined as a priority mentioned by teachers, from 20 to 6 per cent ($p < 0.01$). Certainly there is some evidence here of a redefinition of teachers' aims in accordance with the pressures of the National Curriculum and assessment. Some teachers were concerned to point out, however, that these were the areas to which they felt compelled to give priority, rather than goals they would ideally have prioritized.

In a separate short questionnaire, the PACE teachers were presented with 20 possible aims for primary education, taken mainly from Ashton *et al.*'s 1975 study, but also incorporating a few aims from the Bristaix study and an update of aims that might be seen as relating to the National Curriculum. Table 7.2 shows the mean score given to each aim by the sample of 94 teachers. The PACE teachers' mean scores, which are ranked in descending order of priority, are compared with those of the teachers in Ashton *et al.*'s 1975 sample and in a few cases with Broadfoot and Osborn's 1985 sample (Broadfoot and Osborn, 1988).

These findings articulated with other sources of data. For example, in response to an open-ended question about their professional responsibility, 69 per cent of teachers in 1990 and 58 per cent in 1992 mentioned the importance of providing an 'all-round' education (i.e. a broad, balanced curriculum), compared with only 41 per cent in 1985 before the introduction of the National Curriculum.

Table 7.2 *Teachers' educational objectives (mean scores)*

Teachers' educational objectives	Ashton *et al.* (1975) or Bristaix	PACE 1990	PACE 1992
Essential/major importance			
Develop full potential	–	4.86	4.83
Basic skills	4.46(B)	4.82	4.68
Happy, well-balanced	4.47	4.79	4.63
Arouse interest in learning	4.71(B)	4.73	4.58
Develop capacity to think	–	4.65	4.52
Develop self-confidence	3.85	4.60	4.54
Foster moral, social development	4.36	4.59	4.44
Child organize work	4.01(B)	4.55	3.98
Enjoy school	4.32	4.54	4.50
Kind and considerate	3.91	4.52	4.29
Equip with skills/attitudes for society	4.09	4.48	4.53
Develop as individual in own way	4.09	4.40	4.32
Cooperative work	–	4.35	4.17
Respect for property	4.09	4.28	4.23
Less important			
Speak clearly and fluently	3.18	4.15	3.85
Capable of hard work/effort	4.61(B)	4.01	3.93
Obedient (parents/teachers/authority)	3.87	3.86	3.89
ATs achieved	–	3.57	3.37
Neat and presentable work	–	3.56	3.39
Minor importance			
Fit for occupational role in society	–	2.48	2.66

Source: PACE 1 teacher questionnaires and pre-ERA Ashton *et al.* and Bristaix questionnaires.
Sample: 94 Key Stage 1 teachers in 8 LEAs.
Date: summer 1990 and summer 1992.
B = Bristaix (Broadfoot and Osborn, 1993); others are Ashton *et al.*
Change in importance, objectives PACE 92: no change = 69.1; some change = 22.3; considerable change = 2.1.

The short questionnaire given to the PACE sample in 1990 and 1992 also asked teachers about their objectives for the children. Considering Table 7.2, it is striking that the highest-ranking goals of the PACE teachers in 1990 and 1992 (those which scored higher than 4.0 in both years) are concerned either with academic goals, such as achieving basic skills, capacity to think and arousing an interest in learning, or with individual personal development, such as being happy, well balanced and self-confident, and developing children's full potential (which is also an academic goal).

Of substantially less importance were aims that were related to an emphasis on the product of education and the National Curriculum, such as achieving neat and presentable work and achieving as many attainment targets as possible. Least important of all was what might be termed the 'societal' aim of fitting children for an occupational role in society.

The incidence of complete rejection of aims follows the above rank order closely. The aims shown in Table 7.3 were rejected by an appreciable portion of the sample. On the whole, teachers who rejected aims were not so much at variance with the rest of the sample as holding the same kinds of opinions more strongly. It should be borne in mind that teachers who rejected aims may have done so because they felt them to be unrealistic rather than because they disagreed with them. This may be particularly true where only one or two of the sample rejected an aim.

Table 7.3 *Educational aims rejected by teachers (percentage)*

Educational aims rejected	1990	1992
Obedience to parents, teachers, and all reasonable authority	4.0	2.1
Achieve attainment targets for as many children as possible	5.6	2.1
Fit children for an occupational role in society	20.0	19.1

Source: PACE 1 teacher interviews.
Sample: 88 teachers in 8 LEAs.
Date: summer 1990 and summer 1992.

Five aims were accepted by all teachers in the 1990 and 1992 sample, and these were all related either to social and personal development or to attitudes to learning. These were that all children should:

* develop their full potential;
* be happy and well balanced;
* have their interest in learning aroused;
* develop self-confidence;
* be kind and considerate.

It is clear that in 1990, in spite of external pressures, teachers as a whole did not prioritize goals relating to the National Curriculum or some notable societal or instrumental goals. In 1992, there appeared to be a slight movement towards raising the priority of National Curriculum goals. Nevertheless, the evidence suggests that many teachers were resistant to pressures moving the infant school closer to an 'instrumental' rather than an 'expressive' order (Bernstein, 1975).

Comparing our findings with those of Ashton *et al.* and Broadfoot and Osborn (Table 7.2), it is clear that teachers' main priorities were very similar in 1990 and 1992 to those in 1975 and 1985. Ashton *et al.*'s highest priority aims were those relating to personal development and enjoyment of school, academic goals related to reading and basic skills and aims relating to social and moral development. However, a very significant difference is the higher number of aims in PACE that achieved a mean score of at least 4.00. Sixteen objectives in 1990 and thirteen in 1992, compared with eight in Ashton *et al.*'s study, came into this category. This suggests that, since the Education Reform Act, teachers see themselves as having to take on a larger range of objectives that are very important or essential.

7.4 HOW DID TEACHERS' GOALS AND PRIORITIES VARY?

The most significant difference in goals and objectives in Ashton *et al.*'s study occurred between older, more established and more experienced teachers and younger, less experienced, less established ones. Broadly speaking,

The older, more experienced, more established teachers strongly preferred a socially oriented concept of education concerned with equipping the child, both personally and practically, to fit into society. They emphasised aims related to the personal/moral and spiritual/religious areas. The younger, less experienced, less established teachers . . . were inclined to give more room to the individually oriented purpose than their older colleagues. They stressed emotional/personal development as an important aspect. The longer established teachers strongly favoured the basic skills group of aims, while the less established and less experienced favoured the intellectual autonomy aims.

(Ashton *et al.*, 1975, p. 87)

When a factor analysis of the PACE data was carried out we found a strong tendency for teachers' responses to be grouped together on a number of objectives that could loosely be described as goals directed towards society rather than towards the individual. Table 7.4 shows those objectives which were associated in a dimension that might be termed 'societal'. As in Ashton *et al.*'s study, there were significant differences between PACE teachers along the dimensions societal–individual between older, more experienced and younger, less experienced teachers.

When we examined the extent to which teachers' age and years of teaching experience influenced their objectives, we found some specific variations, as Tables 7.5 and 7.6 show. In particular, older and more experienced teachers were more likely to adhere to the 'societal' goal of 'encouraging children to be obedient to parents, teachers and all reasonable authority'. In the case of 'fitting the child for an occupational role in society', in 1990 it was the youngest and newest teachers and the oldest and most experienced who were likely to see this 'societal' goal as fairly important or of major importance; other teachers were less likely to emphasize it.

These findings resonate with those of Ashton *et al.*, who found older and more experienced teachers to be 'societal' in their ideology, while younger teachers were more

Table 7.4   *Teachers' societal objectives (varimax rotated factor matrix)*

	Societal dimension
0.71619	Obedient to parents, teachers and all reasonable authority
0.61470	Moral and social development
0.57932	Acquire respect for own and others' property
0.44113	Fitted for an occupational role in society
0.43816	That children should be kind and considerate to others

Source: PACE 1 teacher questionnaires.
Sample: 94 Key Stage 1 teachers in 8 LEAs.
Date: summer 1991.

Table 7.5   *Teacher responses to the objective 'to fit the child for an occupational role in society', by age of teachers (percentages)*

	Age of teachers (years)					
	30 or under		31–45		Over 45	
Importance attributed	1990	1992	1990	1992	1990	1992
Should not be an aim of primary education	20.0	0.0	24.2	24.0	13.0	15.0
Not important	16.7	0.0	3.2	18.0	6.5	20.0
Fairly important	40.0	75.0	53.3	30.0	45.6	23.0
Major importance	33.3	25.0	19.3	28.0	34.7	42.0

Source: PACE 1 teacher questionnaires.
Sample: 94 Key Stage 1 teachers in 8 LEAs.
Date: summer 1990 and summer 1992.

Table 7.6 *Teacher responses to the objective 'to fit the child for an occupational role in society', by years of teaching experience (percentage)*

| | Years of experience | | | | | | | |
| | 0–4 | | 5–10 | | 11–20 | | Over 20 | |
Importance attributed	1990	1992	1990	1992	1990	1992	1990	1992
Should not be an aim of primary school	0.0	0.0	35.0	26.6	18.4	30.3	20.5	9.3
Not important	20.0	33.3	5.0	13.3	0.0	15.2	6.8	20.9
Fairly important	40.0	33.3	35.0	40.0	67.3	21.2	31.9	30.2
Major importance	40.0	33.3	25.0	20.0	14.2	33.3	40.9	39.5

Source: PACE 1 teacher questionnaires.
Sample: 94 Key Stage 1 teachers in 8 LEAs.
Date: summer 1990 and summer 1992.

'individualistic'. Ashton *et al.*'s young teachers would now be in the middle of their careers. However, it seems that a new generation of entrants to the same profession are not following the same pattern.

By 1992, however, the differences between older and younger PACE teachers were less clear-cut. It is possible that by this stage there had been a slight cross-over effect attributable to the retirement or early retirement of older teachers and the movement into older groups of younger, less experienced teachers.

An even more striking finding is the variation in perceived importance of 'achieving as many attainment targets as possible for each child', as shown in Tables 7.7 and 7.8. In 1990, under 25 per cent of teachers as a whole perceived this as essential, while this had increased to 39 per cent in 1992. However, younger teachers and teachers with less than five years of teaching experience saw this as being of far greater importance than did their older or more experienced colleagues. Eighty per cent of those under 30 stressed the importance of achieving attainment targets, compared with only 50 per cent of those aged 31 to 45 and 54 per cent of those over 45. Similarly, 80 per cent of those with less than five years of teaching experience emphasized this goal compared with 55 per cent or less of more experienced groups of teachers. By 1992, these differences had once again become blurred, with older and more experienced teachers, if anything, more likely than others to emphasize this National Curriculum-related goal.

These findings suggest that in the initial phase of the reforms younger and newer teachers were more likely to have been socialized into instrumental concerns and to have internalized goals closely related to the National Curriculum. Perhaps those whose initial training or early socialization into the profession included specific preparation for the National Curriculum were closer to accepting a shift from expressive to instrumental concerns. However, the shift between 1990 and 1992 suggests that, with the movement out of the profession of some of the older and more experienced teachers, these differences largely disappear. This may indicate that over time, and with the departure of those who are perhaps most disenchanted, there will be greater acceptance by teachers as a whole of instrumental goals related to the National Curriculum (see also Packwood, 1992).

To summarize, while there was no evidence that teachers as a whole had begun to perceive individualistic and expressive goals as in any way less important after the

Table 7.7   *Teacher responses to the objectives 'attainment targets should be achieved for as many children as possible', by age of teachers (percentages)*

	Age of teachers					
	30 or under		31–45		Over 45	
Importance attributed	1990	1992	1990	1992	1990	1992
Should not be an aim	0.0	0.0	0.0	4.0	0.0	0.0
Unimportant	6.7	0.0	6.4	14.0	10.9	2.5
Fairly important	13.3	100.0	43.5	50.0	34.8	45.0
Very important	80.0	0.0	50.0	32.0	54.3	52.5

Source: PACE 1 teacher questionnaires.
Sample: 94 Key Stage 1 teachers in 8 LEAs.
Date: summer 1990 and summer 1992.

Table 7.8   *Teacher responses to the objective 'attainment targets should be achieved for as many children as possible', by years of teaching experience (percentages)*

	Years of experience of teacher							
	0–4		5–10		11–20		Over 20	
Importance attributed	1990	1992	1990	1992	1990	1992	1990	1992
Unimportant	0.0	0.0	10.0	0.0	6.1	3.0	13.7	2.3
Fairly important	20.0	66.4	35.0	86.0	44.9	51.5	31.8	53.5
Very important	80.0	33.4	55.0	14.0	49.0	45.4	54.5	44.2

Source: PACE 1 teacher questionnaires.
Sample: 94 Key Stage 1 teachers in 8 LEAs.
Date: summer 1990 and summer 1992.

introduction of the National Curriculum, the findings presented here suggest that teachers have taken on an increasing range of goals they see as important or essential. Further, an increasing number of these are societal or instrumental. This pressure to attempt to meet a wider range of goals, both externally imposed and self-imposed, may be a major cause of stress and anxiety for teachers, as Chapter 6 suggests, contributing significantly to intensification of workload.

Our findings also suggest that at an early stage of the reforms younger and newer teachers accepted societal or instrumental goals and goals related to the National Curriculum more readily than older or more established teachers. However, these differences tended to disappear over time, with older teachers also becoming more concerned with societal or instrumental goals. It is likely that, as more new teachers enter the profession and older teachers leave it, a shift in emphasis from expressive to instrumental values may become more apparent with regard to the infant teacher's role commitments.

7.5   WHAT CHANGES IN CURRICULUM CONTENT DID TEACHERS PERCEIVE?

One of the first questions addressed by the PACE project was how far teachers shared fears, expressed when the National Curriculum was being initiated (Haviland, 1988), that the balance of the infant school curriculum was likely to shift towards the 'core'

Table 7.9 *Curriculum changes perceived by classroom teachers by subject (row percentages)*

	More		Same		Less	
	1990	1991	1990	1991	1990	1991
Maths	9.1	20.4	79.5	65.6	11.4	12.9
English	20.5	14.0	69.3	63.4	10.2	21.5
Science	84.1	73.1	14.8	21.5	1.1	4.3
Technology	60.2	67.7	29.5	23.7	1.1	5.4
History	34.1	50.5	54.5	37.6	4.5	7.5
Geography	36.4	54.8	51.1	36.6	5.7	5.4
Music	3.4	1.1	67.0	54.8	29.5	43.0
Art	2.3	1.1	68.2	44.1	29.5	53.8
PE	3.4	2.2	85.2	78.5	11.4	18.3
RE	6.8	4.3	8.3	72.0	8.0	22.6
Other	3.4	1.1	11.4	4.3	1.1	1.1

Source: PACE 1 teacher questionnaires.
Sample: 94 Key Stage 1 teachers in 8 LEAs.
Date: summer 1990 and summer 1992.

subjects laid down by the Act and away from some of the potentially expressive and creative areas, like art and music.

Dramatic indications of changes perceived by teachers were revealed by questions we put to our sample of 88 classroom teachers. In both 1990 and 1992 they were asked whether each subject was being taught 'more', 'the same' or 'less'. The results are given in Table 7.9. The continuation of previous priorities regarding 'the basics' is clear for English and mathematics, with little perceived change from 1990 to 1992.

In contrast, perceived increases were particularly notable for science, which shows a massive increase recorded by 84 per cent of teachers in 1990, with only a slight falling off in 1992. Technology, history and geography were all seen as having increased a good deal in 1990, but they were felt to have increased still more in 1992. In fact, many teachers explained that these areas had always been covered in topic work without being *called* technology, history and geography. A more conscious labelling of the subject areas of topic work may have been taking place, rather than a real increase. As we shall see, these perceptions of the extent of history, geography and technology work are hardly borne out by findings from PACE systematic observation, during which they were recorded very rarely. However, this could be a sampling problem. Certainly many curriculum plans showed that these subjects were expected to provide a focus at other points in the term.

Four subjects were perceived as having less time spent on them. In the case of English, a fifth of our 1992 teachers perceived less teaching. This trend was also noted by NCC (1991) and offered as a partial explanation of the concern about standards of reading of seven-year-olds, which followed the standard assessments of summer 1991. The 'basics', it was asserted, were being squeezed out by the other demands of the broad National Curriculum.

Two other salient subjects that teachers felt were receiving less attention were, as early critics of the Education Reform Act had suspected, music and art. Initially they were thought to be suffering in the move to embrace science, but the continued squeeze on these subjects suggests that by 1992 they were also losing out to the growth of technology, history and geography.

Our interviews revealed the feelings of many teachers that there were other, more subtle ways in which the 'creative' side of the curriculum was affected. For instance, although the time spent on English had not changed, for most teachers the type of activity upon which children were engaged as part of English work *had* altered. Many teachers repeated that they were doing far less creative writing with their children. Similarly, art may well have been eroded even more than is apparent from the dramatic 1992 response, when 54 per cent of teachers said they were doing less. A large number of teachers said they were doing less 'art for art's sake' with their children. Many said that writing, painting and drawing were now related to subject and topic areas that formed part of their National Curriculum work rather than being open to children's free choice, inspiration or imagination. As one teacher put it, 'It's less fun now. Everything has to be specifically related to the topic.'

The other two subject areas where teachers perceived a decrease in coverage were physical and religious education, particularly by 1992. This is a little curious, since our 1990 and 1991 classroom observations do not show the same trend. However, our sample of data on these subjects is small and for this reason we tend to think that the teachers' perception is more reliable on this particular issue. Certainly concern about religious education emerged strongly in 1993, so much so that it was noted by the Secretary of State and resulted in advice to schools from the National Curriculum Council (NCC, 1993).

Overall, it seems that the perceptions of Key Stage 1 teachers regarding changes in curriculum content showed clear signs of content overload. This may partially account for the overall cooling in teacher support for the National Curriculum that we recorded in 1992.

7.6 WHAT WERE TEACHERS' LATER VIEWS OF THE NATIONAL CURRICULUM?

Data from our 1992 interviews show that a good many teachers remained positive about the principle of the National Curriculum. Indeed, our evidence suggests that, in its broadest terms, it continued to be accepted as an important and worthwhile educational development. The key strengths identified by teachers continue to lie in the clarification of specific aims and in the provision of an overall structure that could facilitate progression. One teacher expressed herself as follows:

> Since I came back to teaching in 1981, I've had to be adaptable, but I've been glad to have the National Curriculum to give me a target to work to and now I'm in that mode. I have the Attainment Targets in the back of my mind for all my planning, then I just get on with it and enjoy it and I know it's covered overall.

However, for many teachers serious misgivings had developed. For instance, by 1992 teachers' opinion of the relevance of the National Curriculum to the needs of their pupils had fallen significantly. The percentage of teachers thinking it 'very well' or 'well' matched had dropped from the 1990 figure of 55 to just 24 per cent. The percentage thinking it 'not well matched' had risen from 14 to 29 per cent. Three per cent continued to think it 'irrelevant', while those believing the National Curriculum to be of 'mixed relevance' had increased from 29 to 41 per cent.

As the curriculum requirements for history, geography and other subjects outside the 'core' were published during 1991 and 1992, the issues of curriculum overload, over-prescription and inflexibility began to surface as important concerns. The scale, complexity and apparent impracticality of the National Curriculum were debated, marking increasing awareness of the changes as 'public issues' rather than as 'private troubles' for which individual teachers should accept responsibility (Mills, 1959). As challenges to the structure and content of the National Curriculum were made and debated in public (e.g. Campbell *et al.*, 1991; Campbell and Neill, 1992), teachers were no longer willing simply to regard themselves as being personally deficient in, for instance, subject expertise.

Such concerns were reflected by the 51 per cent of teachers who, in 1992, felt that the National Curriculum restricted their capacity to adapt their teaching to the children's needs. Only 17 per cent had felt this in 1990. As we saw in Chapter 5, many more teachers also began to feel that their own roles were more constrained: a rise from 24 to 66 per cent between 1990 and 1992.

One teacher, whose careful planning is illustrated later in this chapter, was asked about these issues and recounted her frustration at being forced, as she felt it, to 'cover too much content'. She said:

I find I have to stick to my timetable much more rigidly than I ever did in the past; it's the only way I can fit everything in.

Are you changing activities more often, then?

Very much so, and I don't think it's good for the children. There are often times when an activity is going really well and I know they're enjoying it and I'd like to go on and develop it, but I have to urge them to finish off because there's something else I need them to start. I feel they're getting lots of short bites and that isn't the way I normally like to teach.

You sound as though you're worried about achieving breadth at the expense of depth.

Yes, I am. I feel we're being asked to pack so much into each week that I do think we're in danger of being shallow.

Other teachers made similar statements:

I feel far more constrained. We must follow the syllabus and the artistic, creative side is being squeezed out. It's less experimental and creative than it was once.

The curriculum is so full. Having to teach the whole curriculum I feel there is no choice of topic – we must just fit in with the whole school scheme. I had to teach the Stuart period and we had no resources available, so many schools were teaching the same topic. I find this sort of history very difficult, so abstract. Science is easier because we can create our own resources.

Considerable doubts and concerns thus remained among teachers in the later stages of the implementation of the National Curriculum. Of course, by 1993 both NCC (1993) and OFSTED (1993) had recognized the same points and were articulating a fear that curriculum coverage might be compromising the quality of children's learning. Most of the teachers from whom we gathered data had known this much earlier and were sad and frustrated that their professional judgements had been ignored for so long.

There were many other issues about which Key Stage 1 teachers were concerned in 1992. Was the primary school curriculum becoming more subject-centred? Would the topic-centred approach survive? Were more didactic teaching methods being introduced as result of time pressure? Would the perceived warmth and closeness of teacher–pupil relationships, on which primary school teachers prided themselves, survive the changes?

Evidence on such questions is offered in the chapters that follow, beginning with the results of our observations of classroom curriculum practice.

7.7 WHAT WAS THE OBSERVED CONTENT OF THE CLASSROOM CURRICULUM?

We now move on to consider the findings of curriculum-based systematic classroom observation, rather than teacher interviews. In one sense, this is likely to be a more objective source of data in that it explores the extent to which teachers' beliefs about the effects of change are reflected in actual classroom practice. On the other hand, it is dependent on the strengths and weaknesses of our sample, observation schedule and observers, as described in Chapter 4. In fact, there were very few significant discrepancies between teacher perspectives and classroom observations, though we will highlight those that did occur. Overall, we feel that the data sources complement each other in providing a description of curriculum practice.

There are considerable problems in classifying school knowledge and activity so that the balance of the curriculum can be described, and we faced this issue very directly in collecting data on the curriculum content of teaching and learning activities. In our observations we used the subject classifications of the National Curriculum to code each ten-minute period of pupil and teacher observation by 'curriculum context'. We could show when single or several subjects were being drawn on by coding 'main' or 'part' contexts for the activities that had been observed. However, this was by no means easy and considerable researcher judgement was involved. Where there was uncertainty, the classroom teachers were consulted before coding was confirmed. We should note that the data are derived from observation of the time children were actually working in their classrooms. Thus, in terms of the school day as a whole, they exclude administration, dinner time, breaks, lining up and other non-work activities.

The content of the curriculum is a crucially important question, given the explicit aim of the Education Reform Act 1988 that a broad and balanced curriculum should be provided for all pupils. This created a tension for teachers, as Chapter 3 argues, between meeting the requirement to extend the range of subjects offered to all pupils and the perceived need to give a high priority to the basics. As we have seen, while teachers supported the principle of a broad, balanced curriculum, they felt that the ways in which they were being required to implement it were, in practice, leading to an over-specified and inflexible curriculum.

Table 7.10 shows the results of our 1990 and 1991 observations in the 18 study classrooms. The most noticeable findings here are the dominance of work in English and the preponderance of work in the core National Curriculum subjects, in particular, English and maths. It is interesting that the systematic observation did appear to confirm a slight decrease in time spent on English in 1991. This was the time when other foundation subjects of the National Curriculum were being introduced. It should be noted that these aggregated figures conceal considerable variations between the classrooms studied in different schools during each period of data-gathering. For instance, in 1990 maths as a main curriculum context occupied just 9 per cent of the observation periods in one school but over 20 per cent in another. English occupied a range between 23 and almost 66 per cent.

Table 7.10 *Curriculum subject content (percentage of observed time for main and part curriculum subjects: column percentages)*

	1990		1991	
	Main curriculum	Part curriculum	Main curriculum	Part curriculum
English	38.3	20.0	34.2	14.1
Maths	14.1	10.0	15.9	7.4
Science	8.1	9.0	9.3	6.5
History	2.8	3.0	0.6	3.1
Geography	0.5	1.4	0.4	2.5
Technology	4.6	10.0	5.1	3.9
Art	6.2	17.2	2.7	8.8
Music	2.8	1.8	3.2	4.7
PE	3.0	0.0	3.0	0.6
RE	1.8	1.6	4.4	5.3
PSE	0.9	8.0	1.5	1.2
Non-curricular	5.3	5.0	6.3	6.0
No main curriculum	11.6	NA	13.4	NA

Source: PACE 1 systematic observation data.
Sample: 9 year 1 and 9 year 2 classrooms.
Date: autumn 1990 and autumn 1991.
Note: Part curriculum observations do not equal 100 per cent as it was possible for several part curriculum contexts to be coded at the same time.

In interview, many teachers had said that they were teaching more science. However, science was observed as the main curriculum content for less than 10 per cent of the time, while historical and geographical content was rarely visible. In several schools, however, wall displays provided evidence of historical and geographical content in recent work and teachers' curriculum plans almost universally made appropriate provisions. Such work may have been undertaken in blocks of time that our research design did not enable us to sample.

How justified were apprehensions that the National Curriculum would threaten children's experience of art and music? In 1990, art and music formed the main curriculum content for 6 and 3 per cent of the time respectively, certainly not large proportions, though art was very often combined with other subject work. However, our 1991 data show a halving for art, both as a main curriculum context and as a part curriculum context. This perhaps reflects a particular vulnerability of this subject within a curriculum that was becoming progressively more packed with the subject-content requirements of more highly prioritized subjects. Music seems to have borne up, perhaps through the protection afforded it by timetabled hall and resource allocations.

The very small proportion of time spent in religious education, particularly in 1990, is deceptive, since observations were not recorded during school assemblies. Those assemblies that were attended by members of the research team were often used as opportunities for general reflections on behaviour, kindness and cooperation, for promoting social values and for emphasizing the academic standards of the school community. The 'good work' of pupils was often highlighted. Sometimes there was more explicit religious education. Most assemblies were regularly complemented by singing of appropriate hymns and songs and by prayers. This was so in monocultural schools, as well as in those with mixed ethnic populations. The exceptions, not unexpectedly, were the two Roman Catholic aided schools in our sample. In these schools religious instruction was very explicit and provided the focus of curriculum work for significant proportions of time. In 1991 the recorded time spent on religious education doubled, and this could reflect ministerial statements prior to data collection.

The variations between subjects that were found from 1990 to 1991 were probably only to be expected at a time of progressive implementation of the new National Curriculum structure and it would be unwise to make too much of them without further evidence. However, they do illustrate the compromises that have been made to 'fit in' the National Curriculum. In particular, they document the very small proportions of curriculum time that teachers felt able to allocate to some subjects. Indeed, curricular breadth and balance were proving hard to provide given the extent of specification of subject content. Having said that, we should note that there is nothing unusual in such patterns. Indeed, a recent international comparison of primary curricula in 70 countries (Meyer *et al.*, 1992) shows that the officially planned distribution of time in many countries is similar to these observed findings for infant schools in England, perhaps, if anything, with a little more physical education and aesthetic education (art and music) and a little less language work.

The PACE results show considerable continuities with previous research and HMI findings in the UK (e.g. DES, 1978; Bennett *et al.*, 1980; Galton *et al.*, 1980; Tizard *et al.*, 1988; Alexander *et al.*, 1989; OFSTED, 1993). For instance, Tizard *et al.* (1988) observed top infant classrooms in 1985 and found a comparable emphasis on 'three R' activities. These accounted for 64 per cent of classroom working time, 17 per cent of which was spent in maths, 20 per cent in writing, 27 per cent in reading, discussion, stories and other language activities. Children were engaged in art and craft or construction activities of various kinds for 21 per cent of their classroom time and in free play for only 3 per cent.

Taken overall, there is no evidence that basic subjects were being neglected in the sample schools. The three Rs were dominant, and perhaps it should also be explicitly stated that this empirical research, as opposed to rhetoric, provides no justification for the view that children in English infant schools spend large proportions of their time in unfocused, undirected play.

7.8 WAS THE CURRICULUM TAUGHT AS SINGLE SUBJECTS OR THROUGH COMBINATIONS OF SUBJECTS?

This issue has provided a focus for considerable public debate in recent years and seems to have been taken as a key indicator within the crude rhetoric of 'progressivism' and 'traditionalism'. In a sociological sense, as we saw in section 3.5, the question concerns the degree of 'classification' of the curriculum: the degree to which knowledge is highly classified and is thus bounded by subjects, or is treated in integrated ways, with low levels of classification. The nature of subject classification is something that Bernstein (1971) saw as relating to different views of knowledge and thence to educational codes and social values. It is for this reason that we identified it, in Chapter 3, as a key dimension with regard to which change can be described and mapped.

Educationalists have more commonly linked the issue to different ways of learning and, while accepting the strengths and weaknesses of single subject and more integrated approaches, have argued for a particular balance of advantage at some ages.

One classic example of this is provided by the Plowden Report, in which it was argued that

> Children's learning does not fit into subject categories. The younger the children, the more undifferentiated their curriculum will be. As children come towards the top of the junior school . . . conventional subjects become more relevant. Even so, subjects merge and overlap. Schools and individual teachers group subjects in various ways, as well as allowing for work which cuts right across them.

(CACE, 1967, para. 555)

Here we see the common professional judgement that integration provides a more meaningful curriculum for younger children.

In fact, almost all the research evidence of the 1970s and 1980s shows that the basic subjects of English and mathematics have been taught to young children as single subjects, while it is the 'other' subjects of history, geography and the arts that tend to have been integrated (Alexander, 1984). Examples of innovative integrated work are certainly available (Armstrong, 1981; Rowland, 1984) but topic work has also been consistently criticized. For instance, HMI's 1982 survey of first schools suggested that 'Too much of the work on topics selected by individual teachers or suggested by television programmes was not part of a co-ordinated school plan and tended to be fragmented and superficial' (DES, 1982, para. 2.111).

After sustained criticism of 'topic work' from ministers and many in the media, the report of Alexander *et al.* (1992) presented the most direct challenge to teachers by asserting that 'A National Curriculum conceived in terms of distinct subjects makes it impossible to defend a non-differentiated curriculum' (p. 17). They also suggested that 'Too many topics amount to little more than aimless and superficial copying from books and offer negligible opportunities for progression from one year to the next' (p. 18).

So, what were infant school teachers actually doing in 1990 and 1991? Table 7.11 provides some strong indications. This table displays the percentages of subjects observed as 'part curriculum' in Year 1 classes in 1990, with equivalent data for Year 2 classes in 1991. The first thing to be said is that the data are not strictly comparable because of the different age of the pupils studied. For this reason one might expect curriculum

Table 7.11 *Curriculum subject classification (percentage of part curriculum context, by subject)*

	1990 (% part/total obs.)	1991 (% part/total obs.)	1990 and 1991 (% change)
English	0.35	0.18	−49
Maths	0.42	0.19	−54
Science	0.53	0.31	−41
History	0.52	0.73	+40
Geography	0.75	0.60	−20
Technology	0.70	0.44	−37
Art	0.73	0.67	−9
Music	0.40	0.44	+10
PE	0.00	0.00	0
RE	0.47	0.30	−36
Totals	0.48	0.28	−41

Source: PACE 1 systematic observation data.
Sample: 9 Year 1 and 9 Year 2 classrooms.
Date: autumn 1990 and autumn 1991.
Total no. of observations in year = 432.
Note: These are the percentages of part curriculum to the total number of observations for each subject.

classification to increase a little. We must also recognize again the difficulty in making the necessary judgements that are involved in the collection of these data. However, the actual finding on data gathered before the publication of the report by Alexander *et al.* (1992) is so large that in our view it sweeps away these qualifications.

In 1991 the curriculum experienced by these six- and seven-year-old children was taught *far more* as single subjects than it had been in 1990. In fact, the overall percentage of recorded times in which subjects were taught as a 'part' of some other subject decreased by no less than 41 per cent. If this is the case in infant classes, then it suggests that junior classes are likely to move in a subject-based direction even more rapidly as the National Curriculum impacts on them.

Changes relating to each subject are also interesting. Data on English, mathematics, science, technology and religious education show the major trend towards single-subject learning tasks, with maths leading the way. Raw data for history and geography are hardly copious enough to be considered valid, but art is still shown to be among the subjects most likely to be combined. Interestingly, the combination of music with other subjects actually increased between 1990 and 1991, perhaps reflecting its incorporation into the National Curriculum. Physical education continued to be taught exclusively as a single subject.

So what might this mean? One interpretation is that many teachers are receptive to the call for more single-subject teaching – an interpretation that could highlight the perspective of relatively traditionalist teachers. After all, in one sense the adoption of subjects simply builds on common practice, particularly for the 'basics' of the core subjects. However, there is also a possibility that the subject expertise of what we called 'active mediators' (see section 6.9) has now developed to a point where pupil motivation can be sustained within single-subject work and where other benefits of subject focusing are apparent. Such teachers may no longer feel that subject-based teaching undermines essential characteristics of childhood and children's learning.

The situation regarding history and geography remains a little unclear, particularly in the context of National Curriculum review (NCC, 1993), but the humanities may well remain relatively integrated at Key Stage 1. The position of art remains difficult. Our data support other findings in suggesting that art has been the major integrative subject, organized largely on an individualized basis in infant classes. Teaching art as a single subject is likely to pose serious resourcing and organizational problems and, in future, art may face a considerable decrease in curriculum time.

In terms of the dimension of high–low curriculum classification to which we have drawn attention as a means of mapping change, the pattern is clear. The implementation of the National Curriculum in infant classrooms brought about a decisive move from the low classification of integrated work towards more highly classified single subject work.

7.9 HOW DID THE TEACHERS PLAN THEIR CLASSROOM CURRICULUM?

Curriculum planning has been identified as a crucial factor in providing progression, coherence and differentiation in the learning experiences that are provided for children (DES, 1985a). Over the period of the PACE research, considerable developments in curriculum planning were noted. This was graphically indicated by the massive increase between 1990 and 1992, from 8 to 41 per cent, in the proportion of teachers who identified at interview the pressure of changes in classroom planning. There is no doubt, then, that teachers believed that they have tackled the issue of planning their classroom curriculum with great seriousness.

Evidence from the PACE study of whole-school changes indicates that there was a steady move away from teachers working with their own, individual curriculum planning systems towards more coordinated, whole-school approaches (see Chapter 5). In this, of course, the gradual publication of National Curriculum documents provided a strong framework. That having been said, it is hard to generalize about the strategies adopted by teachers, for, over the period of data-gathering, there was still a considerable amount of experimentation and development going on. This was combined with concern about the 'overload' of some of the National Curriculum and uncertainty about its detailed future.

Many teachers felt constrained by the overall effect of this increased planning in terms of its limiting their capacity to make individual decisions and to respond to immediate pupil interests. As one of them put it,

> it's changed dramatically; there's no longer the great freedom to do what you would like to do with the children. This is controlled by the policy that the school has adopted in whole-school planning and in termly forecasts, where topics are determined two years in advance. I think we have to guard against not picking up on opportunities when they present themselves because you have to get through your topic or your theme for that term. Teachers must be allowed that spontaneity because often those are the moments the children will remember and learn from.

We will return to such concerns, but will meanwhile illustrate some of the curriculum planning methods that were adopted and, in so doing, will highlight some of the challenges and workloads the teachers faced.

In our 1990 round of classroom studies we noted that teachers recorded their plans of work in very varied ways: for a week, a month, a half-term or a whole term, and by means of lists, grids and webs. Nevertheless, some relatively common aims of the plans seemed to be:

- to start with familiar experiences and gradually to extend the curriculum in time, space and abstraction;
- to draw as many curricular areas as possible into a meaningful topic.

Given these concerns, there was also evidence of teachers' efforts to relate National Curriculum subjects to children's interests. Of course, within the nine classrooms in our detailed sample, there were wide variations in the amount written in the plans and in the degree of detail entered.

As an example, we can take one Year 1 teacher in a large suburban primary school who, when forecasting the work for the winter term of 1990, produced a type of topic web amplified by ten pages of detailed notes (see Figure 7.1). This teacher taught at a Roman Catholic aided school and it was not surprising to find considerable emphasis on religious education. Colour and pattern has always been a popular topic for infant classrooms. It occurred in several other schools and clearly lends itself well to activities in science and in art and craft, as is shown in Figure 7.1.

The timetable for this class was firmly demarcated into periods. As can be seen in

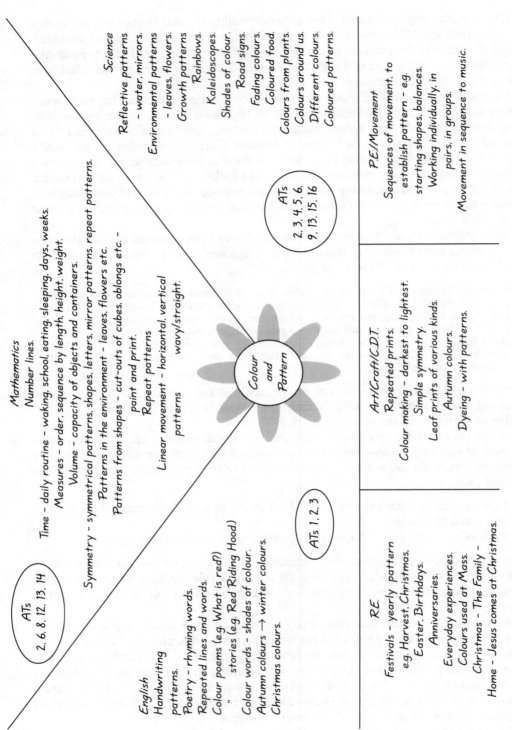

Science
Reflective patterns
- water. mirrors.
Environmental patterns
- leaves. flowers.
Growth patterns
Rainbows.
Kaleidoscopes.
Shades of colour.
Road signs.
Fading colours.
Coloured food.
Colours from plants.
Colours around us.
Different colours.
Coloured patterns.

ATs
2, 3, 4, 5, 6,
9, 13, 15, 16

P.E./Movement
Sequences of movement. to
establish pattern - e.g.
starting shapes. balances.
Working individually. in
pairs, in groups.
Movement in sequence to music.

Mathematics
Number lines.
Time - daily routine - waking. school. eating. sleeping. days. weeks.
Measures - order. sequence by length. height. weight.
Volume - capacity of objects and containers.
Symmetry - symmetrical patterns. shapes. letters. mirror patterns. repeat patterns.
Patterns in the environment - leaves. flowers etc.
Patterns from shapes - cut-outs of cubes. oblongs etc. -
paint and print.
Repeat patterns
Linear movement - horizontal. vertical
patterns   wavy/straight.

ATs
2, 6, 8, 12, 13, 14

English
Handwriting
patterns.
Poetry - rhyming words.
Repeated lines and words.
Colour poems (e.g. What is red?)
"   stories (e.g. Red Riding Hood.)
Colour words - shades of colour.
Autumn colours → winter colours.
Christmas colours.

Colour
and
Pattern

ATs 1, 2, 3

Art/Craft/C.D.T.
Repeated prints.
Colour making - darkest to lightest.
Simple symmetry.
Leaf prints of various kinds.
Autumn colours.
Dyeing - with patterns.

R.E.
Festivals - yearly pattern
e.g. Harvest. Christmas.
Easter. Birthdays.
Anniversaries.
Everyday experiences.
Colours used at Mass.
Christmas - The Family -
Home - Jesus comes at Christmas.

Figure 7.1 *Teacher's curriculum plan, St Bede's School, 1990.*

Figure 7.2, half of every morning, apart from one radio and one television programme, was devoted to 'basic subjects'. Three afternoons began with 'basics and creative work', one with science, followed by PE – its only appearance on this timetable – and one with a radio music and movement programme, followed by 'phonics'. Each day began with 'prayers and RE' and ended with 'story, prayers, etc.'. The timetable gives a clear indication of the dominance of the three Rs in primary school work. Nevertheless, it displays a much greater emphasis on science than would have been expected in an infant school ten years previously, with a science-based television programme, a period of 'follow-up' and two other science periods.

Between 1990 and 1991, as the subject documentation of the National Curriculum was published and awareness of the issues of progression and differentiation increased, classroom curriculum planning became noticeably more complex and sophisticated in most of our classroom study schools. This is well illustrated by the four levels of planning undertaken in 1991 by Sally Jones, the teacher in a rural primary school whose approach to teaching was reviewed in section 3.7. She taught a mixed class of reception, Year 1 and Year 2 children.

This teacher prepared:

- a form of topic web, related to National Curriculum subjects;
- a week-by-week plan of work for each subject for each half term in relation to programmes of study, attainment targets and links with other foundation subjects;
- a standard weekly timetable showing hall periods, broadcasts etc., plus subject-based activities;
- a day-by-day plan for each week, which enabled differentiated planning of each session for each pupil, both as part of a group and in relation to their age and attainment.

The week-by-week plan and the day-by-day plan are reproduced in Figures 7.3 and 7.4.

The week-by-week plan in Figure 7.3 shows the enormous influence of the National Curriculum: subjects are named, programmes of study and attainment targets are listed and related to work plans. However, there is no attempt to force artificial links: the overall theme was 'our senses', and drawing in substantial historical content was thought to be difficult, although there are strong geographical elements. Presumably history would have featured in the previous or subsequent plans, with the aim of keeping a balance over longer periods.

Differentiation and practical implementation was planned at a further level of detail in the day-by-day forecasts. These were specified for small groups of children, of similar age or levels of attainment, as Figure 7.4 shows. The demands on this teacher's time in terms of curriculum planning and provision for groups, individuals and the whole class may be imagined. However, confirming the account in Chapter 3, her timetable additionally shows that on four days each week the period immediately after school ended was occupied by football practice with junior children or with meetings with staff or parents. In addition she routinely marked children's written work at home and prepared for the next day. At weekends she completed evaluations and other records.

Such examples resonate with the work of Campbell and Neill (1992), whose 1991 sample of 105 Key Stage 1 teachers from 61 LEAs worked on average for 52.4 hours per week. Only 18 hours of this time was spent in actual contact with children. Preparation and administration combined to take no less than 28 hours of work each week.

★ - Mrs Lavelle   ✳ - TV   ✴ - Radio

	Monday	Tuesday	Wednesday	Thursday	Friday
9.15	Registration and Prayers R.E. etc. "Storytime" 10 am B.B.C.	Registration and Prayers Hymn Practice Science	Registration and Prayers R.E. and Follow-up Science-T.V. 9.45 am	Registration and Prayers and R.E. "OUR WORLD" ✴	Registration and Prayers and R.E. HALL TIME Assembly
10.35	B ✴	R ✴	E	A	K
	Basic subjects Mrs Austin's Group	Basic subjects	Basic subjects Words & Pictures T.V. 11 am Mrs Austin's Group	Basic subjects Listening & Reading-Radio	Basic subjects Mrs Austin's Group
12.10	L	U	N	C	H
1.00 -2.00	Basics and Creative work	Music and movement Phonics	Basics and Creative work Science T.V. "Follow-up"	Science 2.00 P.E.	Basics and Creative work
2.00 -3.00	✴ B	R	E ✴	A	K
3.30	Follow-up to Words & Pictures Story Prayers. etc.	Story Prayers, etc.	Story Prayers, etc.	Science "Follow-up" Story Prayers, etc.	Story Prayers etc.

Figure 7.2   *Teacher's class timetable, St Bede's School, 1990.*

Classroom curriculum planning and preparation formed a significant part of this workload and, as we have seen, developed in association with more concerted whole-school planning and with a gradually emerging and occasionally revised National Curriculum. Until the later phases of the PACE project, we will not have the evidence to evaluate the overall outcomes of these developments in terms of the coherence, progression and differentiation of pupil learning experiences. However, there is no doubt that enormous amounts of teacher effort were directed at curriculum planning and, of course, this was one reason for the common expression of teacher frustration when changes in the National Curriculum framework were proposed or introduced, meaning that planning time had been wasted. On the other hand, teachers continued to face the frustrations of what they saw as an overloaded and over-specified curriculum that reduced their professional autonomy. The dilemma may have had structural and political origins, but it was experienced acutely by teachers at the classroom level.

7.10 DID TEACHERS USE A REPERTOIRE OF TEACHING APPROACHES FOR DIFFERENT SUBJECTS?

One of the most important recommendations of the 1992 discussion document on classroom organization and management (Alexander *et al.*, 1992), which was supposed to generate a fundamental review of pedagogy in primary schools, was that teachers should develop a wider repertoire of teaching methods. It was suggested that teaching methods could then be matched to aims and this would produce an increase in 'fitness for purpose'.

With this issue in mind, we analysed our data on the teaching of different curriculum subjects in terms of the main teaching contexts that were used to teach them. Our coding of teaching contexts recorded whole-class interaction of all sorts, teaching of individuals and group work. Although such an analysis cannot provide perfect evidence of the use, or otherwise, of a repertoire of teaching approaches for different subjects, it does provide indicative data. The results are shown in Tables 7.12 and 7.13.

The most striking finding is that in both years a much wider range of teaching methods was employed to teach the core subjects of English, mathematics and science than for other subjects. Of course, English and mathematics form the traditional 'basics' of the infant school curriculum and it is possible that our data reflect the existence of a more confident repertoire of teaching methods with regard to these subjects rather than others. There are some signs that there was an increase in the repertoire of methods used in the teaching of science in 1991. Other subjects that were taught in relatively diverse ways include art and technology, with technology being the main focus of cooperative group work. For some subjects, such as history, geography, physical education and religious education, the range of teaching contexts observed was very limited.

These data suggest that teachers already had the basic framework of the wider repertoire of teaching methods that might be developed, though they do not provide evidence on the detail of teaching approaches within each context or on the 'fitness for purpose' in terms of the teaching and learning objectives that were actually realized in each case. It seems, too, that this repertoire is stronger with regard to the more frequently taught

	ENGLISH	MATHS	SCIENCE	TECHNOLOGY I.T.
PROGRAMMES OF STUDY	Develop a variety of listening skills Sequencing Reasoning Read & make own books		Collect & find differences & sims in natural materials, include rocks & soils, observe & record changes in weather & relate these to their everyday life	Database Record bird details Use of W.P. for writing stories
NATIONAL ATTAINMENT TARGETS	1. 1a, b, c, 2a, b, c, d. 2. 1a, b, c, d, 2a, c, d, e. 3. 1a, 2a, b. 4. 1a, b, c, 2a, b, c 5. 1a.	1. 1a, b, c, 2a, b 2. 1a, b, 2a, b. 3. 1a, 2a, b, c. 4. 1a, 2a. 5. 2a. 13. 1a 6. 2a. 8. 1a, b, c.	2. 1a, 2a, b, c, 3a, b, c 6. 1a, 2a, b. 3. 1a. 14. 1a. 15. 1a, b, 2a, b. 9. 1a, b 2a, b. 16. 1a.	All targets level 1-2
LINKS WITH FOUNDATION SUBJECTS	Drama Maths Science History Geography	Science English	Maths English Art & Craft	Science Maths
Book Week **WEEK 1** **Nov 5 - 9**	My favourite story, character Make up a story using a story format	Graph work, favourite story From about 5. numbers in poems and nursery rhymes	Science from a story Squirrel Nutkin Things that float/sink	Making rafts
Our Senses Listening in WEEK 2 Autumn Nov 12-16	What do we hear in various places L.D.D. Tapes	Counting – making sets of animals that hibernate – become dormant. migrate	Pinpointing sound. Big ears for wild animals Make some big ears	Which shape is best for a boat – test and design best. make
Seeing/hearing WEEK 3 Nov 19-23	What do we see in the day/night time? Carnival week	Activities sets o'clock 1/2 past 1/4 past day night both	Non topic; moving around Sets noises in school/out Living – non living	Making rafts continue – test best sail Can we make a lighthouse?
Touch– Research Week WEEK 4 Nov 26-30	Things we like/ dislike to touch – clay, fur, etc. Story pasta pot DON'T TOUCH	Making sets from English rough smooth wet, dry soft, hard	Can you guess what things are by touch? Needs for life (assessment 4 tops) Water/sand	Revise circuits (assessment 4 tops) Complete & test rafts
Taste – Christmas food favourites Jelly Smell WEEKS 5 + 6 Dec 3-14	Favourite food – tradition	Shopping for Xmas cards	Smelly pots – use spices etc +coffee, talc etc.	Can we make a pop-up card?

Figure 7.3   *Teacher's week-by-week curriculum plan, Valley School, 1991.*

ARTS & CRAFTS	HISTORY & GEOGRAPHY	PE/ DANCE/ DRAMA	MUSIC	R.E.	RESOURCES
Develop skills with colour mixing – choosing app. materials		–	–	–	
–	Geography At1, 1b, 1c. At3. 1a. At4. 1a. At5. 1a. At6. 1g	History At1 At2 At3 (level 1) At4	–	–	–	
Science Language	Core subjects + art	Language Maths	English	English	
Design and make book covers	Geography A map of story land	PE / Drama – favourite stories/ characters	3.35 Can you march? Can you tap your finger? Repertoire	Stories from the Bible Old & New Testament	
Begin day/ night items for friezes Drawing squirrrel	Where do the birds go – France. Spain. Africa – look at globe	Drama Rainy weather. jumping in and out of puddles PE	1.30 Hickety tickety Listen. listen Keeping a pulse Tick tock	Story Fred squirrel – not prepared for winter	Globe torch
Clay models of squirrel mice: observation work on machines	Night and day – different parts of globe – link to seasons	Drama – Fred squirrel puppet show PE – forwards. backwards. 1/2 turn. whole turn	Hey, hey, look at me Mice 3 Rabbit in the hollow Summer goodbye See my wellies 1.41	Dramatize story and use for assembly	Hairdrier for rafts
Making stained glass window Use various tactile materials	Can you make a map that can be felt?	Lead a blind person – explain and describe objects PE – holding. 2 points. 4 points. make a sequence	Hands are cold and . . . Blackbird	The heapers – blind deaf Revise Helen Keller, Louise Brailee	Various touching items – feely box
Make pomanders (presents for mum) Calendars cards. Begin Xmas frieze	Where do ingredients for an Xmas pud come from?	Snowman story Xmas play PE – practicse terms work	I I me oh my Repertoire so far + Xmas songs	Xmas story	Oranges. ribbon. cloves. pins ingredients Xmas pud

	9.00 9.30	10.00 10.21 10.40 10.55	11.35 11.40	12.15 1.30	2.05 2.45 3.00
MONDAY	assembly	YR1. YR2 ← Maths ← Phonic skills — Reception — Tape MATHS IS FUN I.T.V. Individual handwriting	YEAR 2 to 5 for games/handwriting — creative writing — YR1. YR2 Reception — Reception practical maths/lang.	PROJECT WORK — YR2 Library skills	Story
TUESDAY	R.E.	YR2 Maths — YR1 Maths — Reception handwriting — Reception Dance/drama — YR1 + Y2 - SWIMMING.	YR 2 phonic skills — YR1 phonic skills — Reception story writing	Mrs Jones — YR2 creative writing + handwriting with K — Science Reception + YR1	Story + library skills except YR2 (hymn practice)
WEDNESDAY	assembly	YR2 to Mrs Joy for science — YR1 + Reception + YR1 phonic skills + maths reading skills — Individual handwriting — *Tape words and Pictures — Words and Pictures	creative writing — Year 2 creative writing	YR2 phonic skills/maths — P.E. YR1 + Reception → Music — Reception	Story
THURSDAY	assembly	YR2 to 5 for Science + PE — Reception LDD (listening skills) music — Reception + YR1 maths — Mrs Munn handwriting — YR1 handwriting Reception handwriting	YR2 Maths — phonic skills — Reception language/maths activities YR1 + YR2 + Reception writing → 12.00	YR2 creative writing — Reception and YR1 Science	Story
FRIDAY	assembly	YR2 Maths — YR1 phonic skills — YR1 spring maths — Reception handwriting + maths/lang activities	"Let's move" whole class — Music Box — Handwr Tracing skills	YR2 Project writing — PROJECT WORK	Story

Figure 7.4   *Teacher's day-by-day teaching plan, Valley School, 1991.*

Table 7.12   *Teaching context by main curriculum area, 1990 (row percentages)*

Main Curriculum	Whole-class interaction	All group work	Individual work
English	39.8	13.8	45.8
Maths	14.8	27.9	55.7
Science	45.7	22.9	31.4
History	100.0	0.0	0.0
Geography	50.0	50.0	0.0
Technology	30.0	45.0	25.0
Art	7.4	29.6	63.0
Music	91.7	8.3	0.0
PE	100.0	0.0	0.0
RE	100.0	0.0	0.0
PSE	100.0	0.0	0.0

Source: PACE 1 systematic observation data.
Sample: 9 Year 1 classrooms.
Date: autumn 1990.

Table 7.13   *Teaching context by main curriculum area, 1991 (row percentages)*

Main curriculum	Whole-class interaction	All group work	Individual work
English	24.1	21.0	52.5
Maths	14.7	24.0	56.0
Science	40.9	29.5	29.5
History	33.3	0.0	66.7
Geography	50.0	0.0	50.0
Technology	12.5	29.2	58.3
Art	15.4	15.4	69.2
Music	80.0	6.7	6.7
PE	92.9	0.0	7.1
RE	76.2	0.0	23.8
PSE	100.0	0.0	0.0

Source: PACE 1 systematic observation data.
Sample: 9 Year 2 classrooms.
Date: autumn 1991.

subjects of the curriculum. Perhaps this is so because for more regular work the preparation of materials and development of more diverse pedagogies is more necessary to maintain pupil motivation.

We suspect that the question of teaching repertoire may be related to that of subject expertise. There have been several studies of this topic in recent years. For instance, Croll and Moses (1990) found that, of 50 primary heads whom they interviewed, 56 per cent identified the lack of subject expertise as an anticipated difficulty in implementing the National Curriculum. Bennett *et al.* (1992), in a 1991 sample of 433 teachers, found that 77 per cent felt confident of their teaching expertise in English and 62 per cent were confident regarding mathematics. The proportion of teachers who claimed to feel competent to teach science had risen to 41 per cent from a figure of 34 per cent two years previously. These were relatively high figures. The same study recorded a fall from 1989 to 1991 in the numbers of teachers who felt confident in teaching history and geography, while there was no change regarding technology.

Such findings seem to suggest that publication of some subject requirements of the

National Curriculum in 1990 and 1991 were a considerable challenge to many teachers, and we believe that a lack of subject confidence and expertise is likely to be reflected in a more limited teaching repertoire. Teaching methods, in other words, may broaden, and fitness for purpose will be achieved, only when the subject knowledge to be taught is well understood. Such issues will be considered further in Chapter 9.

7.11 CONCLUSION

In this chapter we have seen how teachers supported the principle of the National Curriculum but, as it was progressively implemented, felt it to be both overloaded with subject content and over-prescriptive. In these circumstances one major objective of the Education Reform Act 1988, of achieving the implementation of a broad and balanced curriculum, does not seem to have been being achieved. There was an emphasis on the core curriculum of English, mathematics and science – an emphasis that, we would speculate, will be amplified in future by the publication of standardized assessment results in these subjects.

Of course, the core subjects represent 'the basics', which, since the Industrial Revolution, have been regarded as an essential foundation for education and work (Alexander, 1984), with science as a late addition. These priorities have been consistently endorsed by many generations of teachers. For instance, King (1978) reported that

> There can be no doubt about the primacy that all the teachers gave to . . . 'the basics' . . . 'the academic side', or 'the three R's'. Whereas children could sometimes choose to paint, draw . . . or dress up, none could refuse to read, write or do mathematical or number work when asked to do so. Sometimes they could choose when they did these things but never whether they did them . . . Of the traditional three R's, reading was given paramount importance.
>
> (King, 1978, p. 24)

The educational value of breadth was promoted by HMI (e.g. DES, 1978), was endorsed by the Educational Reform Act 1988 and has been reaffirmed by NCC (1993) in the context of a review of the extent and detail of National Curriculum subject requirements for primary schools. Our data on curriculum content confirm the need for this review and suggest that breadth can be developed only if the content demands of National Curriculum subjects are reduced.

We have also reported data that show a significant move towards stronger curriculum classification. We found an increasing proportion of subjects being taught alone, and a decrease in teaching and learning activities drawing on and integrating more than one subject. While the prominence of the basic curriculum represents continuity with the past, this change from weak towards stronger subject classification is a major shift along an important analytic dimension.

Other findings, such as the development of more rigorous curriculum planning, acceptance of the associated workloads and the existence and development of teaching repertoires, reflect the considerable commitment and expertise that existed among the teachers we studied. So did their willingness to take on an even wider range of educational objectives. Given their acceptance of the principles of the National Curriculum, most teachers were willing to work very hard to deliver it. However, in the later phases of our study, our evidence began to show that teachers were increasingly feeling that the National Curriculum was flawed, and that, combined with assessment requirements, it could threaten rather than help them to fulfil their basic commitments to the learning and development of young children.

In the next chapter, we consider the pupils' views and experience of the curriculum and the extent to which teachers' fears were well founded.

Chapter 8

Pupils and the Curriculum

8.1 INTRODUCTION

This chapter sets out to answer the question, 'What did the children think of the curriculum?' We believe that this is an important question in at least two respects.

First, there is the question of pupil learning, the ostensible purpose of the Education Reform Act. While the debates around the National Curriculum largely concerned themselves with structures, content and assessment issues, we retain a conviction that the motivation of children is also important. What, as HMI (DES, 1985a) put it, is the 'relevance' of the curriculum? Of course, it was precisely this issue that led members of the Hadow Committee to publish their 1931 statement that 'the curriculum should be thought of in terms of activity and experience rather than as knowledge to be learned and facts to be stored' (Board of Education 1931, p. 93). Both HMI and Hadow had an essentially practical concern here. They wanted children to learn effectively and they were concerned that the curriculum should connect with the concerns and ways of thinking of young children.

A second reason for the importance of pupil perceptions of curriculum follows if one views the educational experiences of childhood as worthwhile in their own right, rather than simply as means to later goals in life. Primary education, for instance, may be seen as something much more than a preparation phase for secondary education or the 'realities' of work. It is a significant part of each child's life and, as parents have consistently recorded (Hughes *et al.*, 1990), pupils' perceived quality of classroom experiences is therefore important.

Blyth (1984) encompassed many aspects of these issues in his conception of curriculum as 'a planned intervention into the interaction of development and experience' (Blyth, 1984, p. 43). This sentence immediately draws attention to issues such as the physical, social, cognitive and affective development of young children and to the ways in which they learn through interaction with their experienced environment – points that seem to have been discussed very rarely by those constructing the National Curriculum in England. Further, curriculum is seen as contributing continuously to both the development and the experience of young children as they grow up. However, while development and experience will occur naturally in one form or another throughout life, curriculum is seen as the outcome of deliberate decisions by others about appropriate provision for learners. The curriculum, as Blyth (1984, p. 43) put it, 'is designed to make a positive impact on children'. This, of course, is exactly what the National Curriculum was intended to do: to provide a broad, balanced, system-wide education and to raise educational standards of achievement.

The rationale of the National Curriculum, in other words, was that it would, ultimately, be reflected in greater clarity of thinking, more knowledge and gradually developing levels of skill among pupils. It was a 'planned intervention' on a national scale. But what would its impact actually be in the realities of classrooms across the country, far from Whitehall? And, further, how would it appear to the pupils, in whose name it was, ostensibly, created? Would they feel motivated by it so that its introduction could contribute to the quality of their learning and of their learning experiences? Our interviews with children were designed to find out.

8.2 WHAT WERE THE MAJOR FINDINGS OF PREVIOUS RESEARCH?

Research on children's perspectives of the primary school curriculum is relatively scarce, and, where it is available, has usually focused on the process of curriculum delivery rather than on the subject content issues *per se*. There are good reasons for this tendency, because children tend to be concerned far more about the implications of a curriculum subject in terms of 'what we have to do' rather than in terms of the subject matter itself. Meaningful curriculum descriptors for young children are thus likely to describe processes – writing, climbing, sitting, doing sums, reading – or qualities of experience – fun, exciting, interesting, boring. Makins (1969), for instance, suggested that what primary school children learn matters to them less than how they are taught.

Cullingford (1990) vividly conveys many aspects of children's feelings of vulnerability in learning, the involvement of self and the defensive strategies that are often adopted. As he writes,

> All children want to remain invisible, unnoticed. For their experience is always private. They do not want to be cajoled into learning. They have the general human tendency to be suspicious of being taught. And when they are learning they know that it is their own. Their ownership of learning makes it real, and private.
>
> (Cullingford, 1990, p. 117)

These are interesting points, for classroom situations are anything but private. Indeed, pupil experience has been powerfully characterized as being of a crowd (Jackson, 1968).

It follows that the learning experiences associated with particular curricular subjects may well be evaluated by the balance of psychological and social exposure and challenge they bring, when compared with the interest and enjoyment they offer.

Good examples of this are provided in the work of Woods (1987, 1988), where the ways in which primary school teachers create classroom contexts that are conducive to learning are explored. Similarly, Pollard (1990) and Pollard with Filer (forthcoming) provide accounts of pupils' learning strategies and relationships to the social contexts of home, classroom and playground. In this ethnographic case study it was the ratio of risk to enjoyment that seemed to determine how children felt about curriculum activity, rather than the nature of the tasks themselves. Further, the significance of the issue is confirmed by Lewis (1993) in her analysis of the views of schooling held by children with moderate learning difficulties. She argues that, rather than curriculum content *per se* being important, such children need a curriculum that addresses social and emotional development, and issues such as friendship and coping with conflict.

More directly, Tizard *et al.* (1988) interviewed 133 seven-year-olds about, among other areas, their work at school. In this case, questions were confined to children's attitudes to reading alone, reading to a teacher, writing and mathematics. The most popular subjects were maths, liked by 71 per cent overall, and reading to the teacher (65 per cent). Writing was appreciated by 56 per cent, while reading to oneself was positively viewed by only 51 per cent of children. Tizard *et al.* speculated that the relative unease over writing centred mainly on the tedium of routine writing tasks and spelling difficulties, while concern over reading to oneself was associated with the difficulty of achieving success with self-selected books.

Goodnow and Burns (1985) produce a rather different account with their interviews with 2000 Australian children. Junior school pupils were unambiguously keen on sport, games and playing at school, and also liked subjects such as art, craft and music. However, they had very mixed views on the standard core subjects of maths and English. Goodnow and Burns attributed this to a discrepancy between the expectations of children regarding their education and the realities of school life. For instance, children expect 'to learn everything', but they are mainly taught basic skills; they expect 'to learn useful things', but the relevance of the curriculum is only rarely apparent; they expect 'to like the work', but it is sometimes 'too hard' and is often 'boring'; they expect the school day to provide variety, but it tends to be very predictable and repetitive.

Clearly there are also likely to be differences among pupils and at different ages. For instance, the responses of the eleven-year-olds interviewed by Pollard (1985, p. 89) showed that by this age children's evaluation of learning is closely associated with the social identities they have acquired, in this case within peer groups of 'goodies', 'jokers' or 'gangs'. Goodies' conformist strategy overrode their feelings about curriculum subjects as they strove to maintain their image in their teacher's eyes. Jokers were likely to try to direct lessons they considered boring into 'more fertile activities', while gangs would, on occasion, become more directly subversive. Unlike the other two groups, they rarely obtained intrinsic satisfaction from their learning unless they saw direct links with future work – a more instrumental approach.

8.3 WHAT WERE PUPIL PERCEPTIONS OF CURRICULUM CONTENT?

We were interested in the children's perceptions of curriculum-related activities in their classrooms, and in the ways in which this related to the findings of our systematic observation of curriculum subject coverage.

With this in mind, we showed the children a collage of pictures of 12 common infant school activities that had been extracted from a book by Ahlberg and Ahlberg (1988). We then asked, 'Which of these activities do you do in your classroom?' This question was asked first in 1990, when the children were in Year 1, and it was repeated in 1991, when they had become Year 2 pupils. From among the large number of activities that the children nominated on each occasion, we coded the first two. In Table 8.1 these nominations have been aggregated and expressed as a percentage of all activities nominated on both occasions by boys, girls and all pupils. We thus have an indicator of curriculum activities as perceived by infant school pupils.

There are several interesting aspects of Table 8.1 but perhaps the most significant is the way in which it resonates with findings from our systematic observations of curriculum content. The three aspects of English identified by the children as taking place in their classrooms (stories, reading and writing) total 30 per cent of the nominations made, compared with 36 per cent of our total observations in the two years. Maths provided 19 per cent of nominations and 15 per cent of observations, while for science the figures were 2 per cent of nominations but 8 per cent of observations. Such figures seem to show a broad mapping of pupil perception and systematic observation regarding the curriculum of 'the basics' at least, though perhaps a lack of pupil awareness regarding the nature of 'science' as a curricular subject. However, the most striking finding is undoubtedly the fact that no fewer than 24 per cent of pupil nominations concerned physical education, far higher than our combined figure of 3 per cent of observations.

Taken together with findings that are reported later in this chapter, we think it likely

Table 8.1 *Classroom activities nominated by pupils in response to the question 'which of these sorts of things do you do in your classroom?' (percentages)*

Nominated classroom activities	Girls	Boys	Overall
Stories	11	11	11
Reading	13	12	13
Writing	7	4	6
Maths	16	23	19
Science	3	1	2
Construction	1	3	2
Sand	2	6	4
Dressing up	2	1	1
Play	2	1	1
Painting	10	4	6
Drawing	2	0	1
Singing	9	3	6
Physical education	22	25	24
Missing data	2	7	5

Source: PACE 1 child interviews.
Sample: 54 Year 1 and 54 Year 2 children.
Date: autumn 1990 and autumn 1991.

that the pattern of children's perceptions of curriculum activities is influenced by subjective feelings that are associated with the experience of these classroom activities. Physical education was seen by many children as a enjoyable source of activity and release from 'work', as other studies have also found (Mortimore *et al.*, 1988), and, while regularly provided, may have been exaggerated in what the children reported. Maths, on the other hand, may have loomed relatively large as a major source of 'work' itself. Aspects of what might be taken as 'play' (sand, 'home corner' play, construction) were, quite accurately, not perceived to occur very often at all, despite the fact, as we shall see, that they were greatly valued by the children.

8.4 WHAT WERE PUPIL PREFERENCES FOR CURRICULUM ACTIVITIES?

In both the 1990 Year 1 interviews and the 1991 Year 2 interviews the children in our longitudinal sample were asked to identify curriculum activities they 'liked best' and then those they 'liked least'. In both 1990 and 1991 they were asked to make selections from the set of 12 activities we had presented to them. Since those activities were not fully comprehensive regarding all infant school activities we cannot treat the data we collected as being totally representative. Nevertheless, they do provide powerful indications of children's preferences for different sorts of curricular activities. We will present the basic findings in this section, while the reasons offered by the children are analysed in section 8.5.

For the purposes of this analysis we coded the activity that was named by each child as 'most liked' or 'least liked'. Table 8.2 provides data on the curricular activities that were most favoured by the pupils. The most consistently favoured activity was physical education. This was liked by boys and girls in both Year 1 and Year 2 and was a first choice for no less than 28 per cent of children. Also clearly favoured were painting and 'home corner' play, though, as for sand, their favoured status was strongest when the children were younger. As the children moved from Year 1 to Year 2, appreciation of

Table 8.2 *Curricular activities 'liked best' by children Year 1 and Year 2 (percentages)*

	Year 1	Year 2	Girls	Boys	Overall
Stories	7	4	7	4	6
Reading alone	4	7	9	2	6
Reading lessons	0	0	0	0	0
Writing	6	2	2	6	4
Maths	2	17	9	9	9
Science	0	4	0	4	2
Construction	6	6	0	11	6
Sand	13	0	2	11	6
'Home corner' play	17	6	13	9	11
Painting	20	7	19	9	14
Singing	4	13	9	7	8
Physical education	22	33	26	30	28
Nothing liked	0	0	0	0	0
Missing	0	2	0	2	1

Source: PACE 1 child interviews.
Sample: 54 Year 1 and 54 Year 2 children.
Date: autumn 1990 and autumn 1991.

maths and singing developed significantly. Girls tended to favour reading, 'home corner' play and painting, while boys prioritized construction activities and sand. Analysis of preferences by pupil attainment showed few differences, though there was a slight preference for lower-achieving pupils to like 'home corner' play.

Data on the curriculum activities 'least liked' are presented in Table 8.3. Overall, the least liked curricular activity was writing, first named by 15 per cent of pupils, followed by maths, science and listening to stories – a finding that made the PACE team immediately wonder about stress on the core subjects of the National Curriculum. The dislike of hearing stories was almost exclusively mentioned by the children when they were in Year 2 and does not undermine the generally positive views of the children when younger. However, there were strong patterns by gender among the activities disliked. Girls disliked construction, science and stories much more than boys, while boys found writing, reading, maths and 'home corner' play more distasteful than girls. Again, analysis of pupil attainment revealed no significant differences.

In keeping with the spirit of the early 1990s, we have produced a 'league table' of Year 1 and Year 2 pupil preferences. This is based on a rank order of the net score when the percentage 'best liked' is set against the percentage 'least liked' for each subject in each year. Table 8.4 sets out the result of this analysis. There are many interesting features of these league tables of pupil preferences. First, we should note that physical education occupies the top of both tables, while writing and science are at the bottom of each. Other curriculum activities that record a change of only two places or fewer are painting, 'home corner' play and singing in the upper half, and reading alone, construction and reading lessons in the lower half. The big 'success story' is mathematics, which rose from twelfth position when the children were in Year 1 to second in Year 2. Conversely, sand and stories fell down the list of pupil preferences as the children aged a year.

It is, perhaps, just as well that recent government policy has not seen pupils themselves as the prime educational consumers in the new market-based model of education that the Education Acts of 1988 and 1993 have introduced. Had this been the case, the National Curriculum core subjects would have been significantly skewed off balance at

Table 8.3 *Curricular activities 'liked least' by children Year 1 and Year 2 (percentages)*

	Year 1	Year 2	Girls	Boys	Overall
Stories	4	17	15	6	10
Reading alone	9	7	2	15	8
Reading lessons	7	2	6	4	5
Writing	15	15	6	24	15
Maths	15	7	9	13	11
Science	7	15	17	6	11
Construction	11	7	17	2	9
Sand	2	2	4	0	2
'Home corner' play	6	2	0	7	4
Painting	4	6	6	4	5
Singing	6	9	7	7	7
Physical education	0	2	2	0	1
Nothing liked	13	7	6	15	10
Missing	2	2	2	2	2

Source: PACE 1 child interviews.
Sample: 54 Year 1 and 54 Year 2 children.
Date: autumn 1990 and autumn 1991.

Table 8.4 *'League table' of pupils' favoured curricular activities*

Rank	Year 1 net rank	Year 2 net rank
1	Physical education	Physical education
2	Painting	Maths
3	'Home corner' play	'Home corner' play
4	Sand	Painting
5	Stories	Singing
6	Singing	Reading alone
7	Construction	Construction
8	Reading alone	Reading lesson
9	Reading lesson	Sand
10	Science	Science
11	Writing	Stories
12	Maths	Writing

Source: PACE 1 child interviews.
Sample: 54 Year 1 and 54 Year 2 children.
Date: autumn 1990 and autumn 1991.

Key Stage 1, with the possible exception of maths. Children, on this evidence, would have done a lot of physical education, painting and playing.

However, this is too simple, for we have already seen in Chapter 7 that 60 per cent of the observed classroom curriculum was in fact devoted to the core subjects in both years and there was, in fact, *very* little time spent on physical education, painting or play. The children, in other words, seemed to dislike things they were required to do regularly but would have liked to do more of the occasional activities, which in their experience provided respite from the more normal routines and curriculum diet of classroom life. More detailed reasons for children's perspectives are explored below.

8.5 WHY DID PUPILS PREFER PARTICULAR CURRICULAR ACTIVITIES?

Two sources of interview data were collected by the PACE team regarding this issue. First, following the identification of 'most liked' and 'least liked' curricular activities, children were asked, 'Why do you like (the most liked) better than (the least liked)?' This sought pupil reasoning concerning activities chosen freely but relatively abstractly. A more contextually embedded approach was also used at the start of the pupil interviews in Year 1 and Year 2, when the children were referred to an activity in which they had participated and that the researcher had actually observed earlier. The children were asked whether they had 'liked' or 'disliked' doing the activity and to explain the reasons for their answer. The activities around which these latter questions were based were the same as those from which our systematic observation findings were derived, and they may be regarded as providing a representative reflection of the Key Stage 1 curriculum. In combination, we believe that pupil responses to these two questions provide a strong data source.

Answers to the two questions were analysed using an identical set of codes and in quantitative terms the results are shown in Table 8.5. These are provided as percentages of the coded responses for each question. Six major pupil criteria for evaluating curricular activities were identified: success/ease, interest, fun, activity, autonomy and long-term education. A seventh major coding, like, was used when pupils affirmed but

Table 8.5 *Pupil criteria for preferred curricular activities (percentages of codings)*

Criterion	Overall preferences
Success/ease	27
Interest	24
Fun	18
Activity	13
Educational	5
Other	7

Source: PACE 1 child interviews.
Sample: 54 Year 1 and 54 Year 2 children.
Date: autumn 1990 and autumn 1991.

did not adequately explain their preference for a curriculum activity. These data have not been used in the subsequent analysis.

'Interest' was an important criterion, used by 24 per cent of children in describing reasons for their curricular activity preferences. From the pupil comments, it could be associated with 'fun' but certainly had an obverse in 'boring'. As other researchers have found (e.g. Goodnow and Burns, 1985), boredom is a child concept that seems, to children, to need little explanation. The pupil use of the concept tended to be brief:

'Cos science is writing and we have to write a lot.

'Cos writing you've just got to write things and grown-ups, like my mum, write all squiggly (shows).

I just don't like singing, it's boring.

The stories can be boring if we all have to listen to them.

More positively, on the other hand, the majority of pupil comments noted aspects of curricular activities that were clearly valued. Some were associated with particular subjects, such as those of the core curriculum.

Regarding English:

Yes, I like it when you can go and read. I like the good stories. We've got the books at home.

Yes, I liked finding out the ideas and I like poems.

Regarding science:

Easy question! I like doing the things we do like making a light-bulb work with a battery and wire. Writing I don't like because we have to write long stories.

Yes, you can watch and see what happens and learn something.

Yes, because I like playing with magnets and I brought a train to school and the back magnets to the front.

Other subject areas were also mentioned. Regarding technology:

Because it's making models and trying to make a machine.

Yes, 'cos it's nice to try and build things.

Regarding art:

Because it was good when you write down and you draw the pictures. I did the grass by – I did light green first and then dark green so it looks like the real grass.

> Yes – I like drawing but not the quiz sheet. Art is my favourite subject and you don't have to add up or write. I like mixing colours and smudging.

More play-orientated activities were also prominent:

> Because you can play schools and stuff in here. Play with all my friends.

> Because you make things good and you play with the train set.

> Because I like making sand castles when it's wet . . . 'cos I've been down to the seaside before, and last year I done a big sand castle . . . and me mum did a big flag so I could do a big flag sand castle and some people played with me and I had a 'turtle' spade and bucket and we dig right to the bottom and we found treasure and silver.

Egan's (1989) argument, that the understanding of young children should be linked, through curriculum, to their interest and facility in fantasy and imagination, takes on a direct significance with play of this sort. The children whom we interviewed confirmed his priority.

The 5 per cent of occasions when long-term educational reasons were cited by the children is a low figure but perhaps one that would be expected from children so young. Their perceptions were of a relatively generalized sort. Something good was being done to them:

> Yes, 'cos I like learning how to add all these things up and I wouldn't know all these things if I don't go to school.

> Yes. I think they're good for you – you learn.

> I like painting because you can be an artist when you grow up, and PE because you can be a PE teacher. Some stories take too long.

> Because you can work harder and I'm going to go to college. You have to work hard for that. That's why I like maths.

The issues of the sense of fulfilment and degree of success and effort that pupils put into their work were also very major criteria in establishing preferences for curricular activities. 'Success/ease' was the primary coding of 27 per cent of pupil responses and there were four major sub-categories of this code.

First, some children were aware of the problem of understanding the tasks set and teacher expectations of them:

> I don't know what to make and what not to make.

> Yes. When Miss tells me to do it, I like it. I like it when I'm doing those numbers.

> No. Because sometimes you don't know what to write.

> In science it's a bit hard 'cos sometimes you don't know what you are doing it in.

Second, there was the issue of just how hard tasks or activities were to complete. There was a variety of views across curriculum subjects and activities but the calculation appeared to concern maximizing the product for a given effort. There was a hint of the need for children to meet teacher-set work quotes or targets here, but also the theme of intrinsic fulfilment from learning itself:

> Because you don't have to do new work [Maths better than writing]. Because you can learn to count like 10 and 10 and I find writing more difficult and takes longer.

> Maths is easier because if we get our writing really spidery we have to write it again. In maths we don't – we just rub out the answers and write them again. Reading is easy 'cos I could read when I was three. I like singing because of learning Christmas songs.

Because, well, I like doing maths and they're easy. Writing is more difficult because I have to keep on going to get words from Miss.

I like sums because they are hard and I have to think. Other things don't take enough time and I get bored when I've done all my 'jobs' and I have to read and you get bored doing that every day.

Because they're quite easy and good fun. I think everybody else likes them as well.

Because I sometimes get it really quickly done. I got ten sums done in five minutes which are hard ones. Writing takes me a long time because the spellings trouble me and I can't rush it. Miss wants it done quick.

The words in my word-building book are hard – like 'alphabet, photograph and physical'. But I like reading stories 'cos most words are easy – and maths has easy answers.

Maths is more difficult.

Because you can draw lots of pictures. Science is hard.

'Cos you paint pictures, writing is hard.

'Cos writing and reading is my favourite things at school. 'Cos at reading you don't have to do any sums, you just write the letters.

Following pupil concern about the process of learning was their awareness of the importance of success. On this, they were concerned with their personal performance in both absolute and relative terms. For instance, some appreciated their attainment in itself:

Yes. I like adding in my head. Getting the right answer: that's what I like.

I quite liked it. 'Cos I knew all the answers – one of them was so easy – it was two add two.

Yes, I like getting on hard books.

Some appreciated completion of work:

Yes. I like finishing things off.

Others drew attention to their achievements relative to others in their classes, and the status that this gave them:

Miss said mine was excellent. She gave me one of the hardest – Simon had the hardest. Because it looks like a tortoise.

Because I like – it isn't really a contest, but I like feeling if you want to win you can do a lot and if you don't win you can say, 'well, I don't mind'.

Yes, 'cos I'm good at writing.

For some, the problem was completion itself:

I don't like writing. I feel that I'm never going to get it done.

There was also the question of 'having fun':

They're fun things and science is good because you learn a lot of things from it. Singing's a bit fun but it's not fun when you're practising for the Christmas Play like now, because you have to keep singing boring songs.

Yes, because it's funny and I like writing and doing puppets.

Yes, like sticking and cutting-out. It's fun and painting too.

Yes, good fun 'cos you can paint and stick things and put wheels on and Sellotaping.

Yes, because it's fun holding the puppets up.

'Cos it's fun, all sorts of hats and clothes and trousers. It's really fun. I like them a lot. Singing is boring. She has to shout and we are too quiet and we don't know the songs. She thinks we should know them.

Beyond 'having fun', however, was a point where a degree of classroom disorder actually became threatening, or problematic to children. This was rare in our data, but the following are examples:

No, because Amanda was getting on our nerves. She wasn't getting on with her writing.

Some of it. Sally and David were messsing about. They wouldn't . . . We didn't do it all.

Autonomy was coded as the main criteria for 5 per cent of pupil answers, though it featured as a factor in many other responses. Children recorded statements such as:

Because you can play in the sand but you can't in science and writing.

It's fun and you can choose what to do.

Because you can choose what to dress up in and it's fun.

'Cos you don't have to do so much work and that stuff.

Because I can build something I like doing – I built a really good ark.

Regarding the pupil criterion we called 'activity' (13 per cent of cold responses), many pupils drew a contrast, which gets right to the point, between physical education and story time.

'Cos you have to sit down when it's story time and when it's PE you can run around.

'Cos you can have a lot of running about in PE and 'cos you can't in the book corner.

Sitting down for long periods of time, such as we had observed in the whole-class sessions on the carpet, was not favoured:

You have to sit down, I get hot, I like to stand up and get cool.

Because you have to sit on the carpet and listen or you get told off and you think 'Oh dear, this is boring'.

We sit on the floor and I get squashed.

In contrast, physical education seemed to provide variety, excitement and a sense of challenge and fulfilment for almost all children:

Because you can run about, go up ladders and swing on the bar and go up the plank. In singing you have to sit still on the floor.

Because we're allowed a crash mat out and you can do hand-stands and can jump on the box and there's a climbing frame and a rope to swing on. Science – we have to do lots of sitting down and writing and going round the classroom looking for things.

'Cos it's good. You practice and you can run.

'Cos you do all sorts of things.

'Cos you climb on things.

Sometimes in PE we have climbing frames, mats, etc. It's like playing, when you read you make mistakes and you don't like it.

Because you do exercises there [points to PE] but I can't get on much there [points to maths].

Our interpretation of these data relates to the context of power relationships between pupils and teachers in classrooms. As one of us has argued (Pollard, 1985), pupils seek to cope in primary school classrooms by juggling major interests-at-hand. Primary pupil interests can be identified as the maintenance of self-image, enjoyment, control of stress and the retention of dignity, and these are satisfied by the enabling interests of peer group membership and learning. All pupils, in other words, have to satisfy three main parties: themselves, their peers and significant adults. Different pupils adopt particular strategies for doing this, as we shall explore fully in future books from the PACE project.

In aggregated and analytical terms, however, we can relate pupil criteria for evaluating curricular activities to the zone of major influence of pupils and teacher respectively – to the power context. This is represented by Figure 8.1. This model locates fun and activity within the pupils' zone of major influence. The criteria relate to the unique sense of humour, mischief and sociability of young children and to the physical energy and developmental stage that set them apart from adolescents and adults alike. Teachers cannot keep up with children as they climb, skip or run about in physical education or the playground, nor can they appreciate their jokes in the same ways the children do. The activities that relate to these criteria are therefore the children's own. They relate to being a child and to child culture.

The criterion of success/ease, on the other hand, is located squarely within the teachers' zone of major influence. Curriculum activities in classrooms yield success or failure, ease or difficulty, depending on the nature of the tasks the teacher sets and the assessment procedures that are implemented. The teacher has the power of structuring and decision and the pupil is maximally exposed – hence the very high proportion of children mentioning this criterion. After all, as Blyth (1984) put it, 'the curriculum is an *intervention* in a child's development and experience'. Of course, it comes as no surprise to realize that the most popular Key Stage 1 pupil activities – physical education,

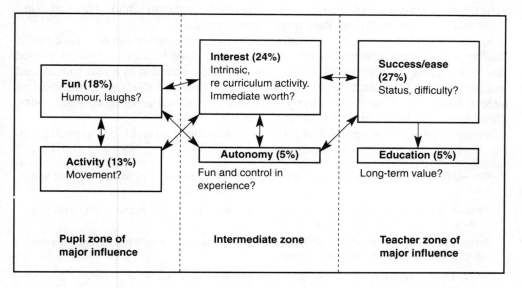

Figure 8.1 *Pupils' major curricular concerns and their articulation with classroom power contexts.*

painting and 'home corner' play – give relatively large scope for fun and activity, while less favoured curricular activities, such as writing, tend to be seen as difficult and as a potential source of failure.

In what we have called the 'intermediate zone' we have located pupil criteria that identify the 'interest' of the curriculum activity and the degree of autonomy provided. Interest is particularly important for, together with its obverse of 'boring', it represents a pupil evaluation of the intrinsic and directly experienced worth of educational activity. As such it is also a pupil concern through which teachers can connect with pupil curiosity and imagination, and can thus support them in moving from the pupil zone of fun and activity towards the more staid goals of the adult curriculum. Nor, it should be said, are pupils unwilling travellers on this developmental and educational track, particularly if it is achieved in ways that leave them appropriate dignity and autonomy. This last criterion, although articulated relatively less often than the others, is important for that processual reason. The fact that it was not cited by more than 5 per cent of pupils could, of course, be taken as another indicator that classroom relationships were seen as good by both teachers and children (see Chapter 10).

Finally we have the criterion that identifies the long-term educational benefits of particular curricular activities. Explicated rarely, it is a good indicator of the extent to which most young pupils do or do not understand the reasons behind the educational experiences to which they are exposed.

8.6 HOW DID PUPILS PERCEIVE TEACHER INTENTIONS?

Research has consistently shown that it is helpful for learning success if pupils understand the specific aims and purposes that teachers have for tasks. However, it has also been shown that such detailed understanding is relatively rare in schools (Bennett *et al.*, 1984) and, unfortunately, our data largely confirm this.

As was described in section 8.3, following systematic observation of a task the 54 children in our classroom studies were asked, 'Why do you think your teacher wanted you to do (the task/activity)?' The question was thus embedded in a real context and was part of the longer interviews that took place in 1990 and 1991, when the children were in Year 1 and Year 2 respectively. The data were coded using seven main codes. These were associated with pupil ideas as follows.

A quarter of pupil answers reflected a belief that teachers set tasks to help pupil learning, in some very general way. For instance:

> 'Cos we're learning to do our letters and write and read. She wants us to learn to read and write.

> Because she wanted us to learn a new story and write it out. *Why?* Because she wants you to learn so when you're older you can write.

> Because she thinks it's good for us. She used to put them on the board but she thinks we've got so good at that, we could do a sheet.

> We're doing it each day. Trying to get better and dead neat and write stories.

> I don't know – get good at writing.

I think it was our maths for today so we can be a bank manager if we like when we grow up. As we get older we get nearer to being very old and ready to work.

So we could learn them.

Many childen thus trusted their teacher's overall judgement in helping them learn. However, for almost a further quarter, tasks were seen more as things that were simply 'required'. Tasks were set because that was what happened in school and reasoning why did not appear to be an educational question. It was more an issue of what the routine or structure of classroom organization was or the moods or preferences the teacher herself came up with.

'Cos everybody in class had to do one.

'Cos we have not done it for a long while.

She just said do it.

(Blank, pause) 'Cos it was on the blackboard.

'Cos I'm on yellow table.

Because she read us . . . Because she read a story and . . . when she reads a story she usually has to let us write it . . . If she thinks it isn't very good then we have to write it out again.

Because we were doing our news and that and then we done our maths. Because she knows what we were doing and that.

Probably she wanted us to do extra work; she couldn't think of any more work because we'd done it all.

She thought it was a good idea to do maths.

Among the numerically significant answers given by children was the simple statement that they 'don't know' why activities were set – proffered on 13 per cent of occasions – or that the task was associated with a class topic of some sort.

Because you've talked about your mums and now you talk about your dads.

'Cos we saw a barn owl on telly. She wanted us to do the writing 'cos it's a little bit of work.

'Cos we were doing about colours in the classroom.

Because we're doing water vapour and how it evaporates. A week ago we did a thing with a kettle – an experiment. We put a plate on it and it steamed up and turned into water vapour.

A few children mentioned the 'products' of curricular activities:

To go on wall.

Wanted it for Mr Brown's office.

Likes to keep models, and let us show our mums. Think mums will like them.

Because she wanted everyone to make a puppet theatre like the one she made.

Others mentioned aspects of 'assessment' as the reasoning behind teacher decisions:

To see how good I write.

Don't know, but she wants to see how we can read.

To see if we were good at maths.

Just three children believed teachers had chosen curricular activities especially for their enjoyment:

Table 8.6   *Pupil perceptions of teacher intentions*

	Year 1		Year 2		Overall (%)	Total		Total	
	Girls	Boys	Girls	Boys		Boys	Girls	Year 1	Year 2
Learning	31	7	31	32	25	20	31	19	31
Required	15	36	27	18	24	27	21	26	22
Topic	15	7	19	14	14	11	17	11	17
Don't know	15	25	12	0	13	13	13	20	6
Product	15	7	4	7	8	7	10	11	5
Assessment	0	4	4	18	6	11	2	2	11
Enjoyment	4	4	4	0	3	2	4	4	2
No answer	4	11	0	11	6	11	2	7	5

Source: PACE 1 child interviews.
Sample: 54 children in Year 1 and Year 2.
Date: autumn 1990 and autumn 1991.

> 'Cos I like it.
> Because I liked it.

We analysed these data by gender and pupil year and some interesting patterns were revealed (see Table 8.6). When the children were in Year 1 a greater maturity and social awareness in the girls seems to be apparent. While the girls appreciated the teacher's learning intentions, albeit in a relatively general way, the boys either had no idea of teacher intentions or simply received the activities as requirements. This gender difference was not apparent in Year 2. Indeed, the overall numbers of 'don't know' answers fell sharply as the children aged and understanding of links between curricular tasks and 'learning' or classroom 'topics' developed.

Looking at these data positively, there was a clear pattern of increasing awareness of educational purposes as the children got older. However, there were almost no answers in other than highly generalized ways. Children were not able to relate their specific work to personal learning targets (Muschamp, 1993).

8.7 CONCLUSIONS

Overall, our interviews with pupils showed that, while they enjoyed many curricular activities, they had strong preferences. Pupils liked activities that offered them interest, success, activity and fun. They disliked curriculum activities that produced boredom, difficulty, sitting, listening and writing. In expressing their concerns in terms of activity and experience the children reflected the meaning of the curriculum to them, as primary school children had also done in previous studies. It is unfortunate that, in general terms and with the possible exception of mathematics, our findings show that the core subjects of the National Curriculum were less favoured than activities such as physical education, painting and play, which give children more scope for movement and autonomy. At face value, this would seem to suggest that pupil motivation regarding the most important subjects of the curriculum was a concern and that the curriculum as a 'planned intervention' was proving inadequate to harness the energy and interest of the children in support of the learning process. Perhaps this is partly true.

However, it would be unfair to make too much of this argument about the 'failure' of the core curriculum to motivate children because it has probably always been the case. Indeed, it could be argued that the more significant finding from our pupil interviews is that there is very little evidence that the National Curriculum has made any substantial difference at all to the curriculum as it is actually experienced by pupils. Findings from previous research are not strong enough to enable us to be categorical on this, but the criteria that the children used are very consistent with previous research, and the understanding of the purposes of tasks (or lack of it) is also as expected. While we cannot say that the children have not been affected by the National Curriculum, we cannot show evidence of any dramatic effects. Pupil perceptions and experiences seem to be much the same as before its introduction. As a child once put it, 'School is school and learning is something that they do to you.'

As Blyth (1984) suggested, it seems to be development and experience that provide the prime source of criteria for children. The 'planned intervention' that is curriculum is judged in those terms and with, as Cullingford (1990) expressed it, both a strong defensiveness and a quest for 'fun'.

Chapter 9

Teachers and Classroom Pedagogy

9.1 INTRODUCTION

In Chapter 7 we offered evidence that the introduction of the National Curriculum was resulting in an increase in curriculum classification: there was an increase in the teaching of single subjects and a decrease in integrated work. We also noted teacher concerns about what they saw as the overcrowding of the curriculum with specified content, thus reducing their scope to exercise professional judgement in the selection of learning tasks, and we observed a shift in teachers' educational priorities and objectives.

We speculated that teachers might increase the extent to which they sought to control and structure pupil time and behaviour, in response to the curricular constraints and pressures they faced. This, of course, relates to another of the analytic dimensions we discussed in Chapter 3, that of the strength of the 'frame' within classrooms. Following

Bernstein (1975), a strong frame reduces 'the power of the pupil over how he [*sic*] receives knowledge' and increases 'the teacher's power in the pedagogical relationship' (Bernstein, 1975, p. 89). On the other hand, weak framing increases the options open to both teacher and pupil in the 'selection, organisation, pacing, and timing of the knowledge transmitted and received in the pedagogical relationship' (Bernstein, 1975, p. 89).

A strengthening of frame in classrooms would thus mean that there was more constraint and greater specification over the pedagogic roles of both teachers and children. There would be less scope for self-directed and flexible activity for both. However, it is also possible that the strength of curriculum classification and frame could vary independently of one another and that pedagogy could remain relatively unaffected by a tightening of curriculum content. This chapter explores this relationship empirically. As Chapter 3 suggested, a wide range of issues is involved in a consideration of whether constraint is increased and choice reduced in the classroom. These include the selection of work and tasks, the organization of classroom activities in terms of the use of space and resources, and the grouping of pupils, as well as the contexts in which teaching takes place and its timing. Many of these issues are discussed in this chapter. In the first part of the chapter we explore teacher perspectives on pedagogy and on relationships with children, and we consider the extent to which these changed, drawing upon interviews carried out in 1990 and 1992 with our larger sample of 88 teachers, and upon interviews and discussions in 1990 and 1991 with our 18 classroom study teachers. The second part of the chapter, from section 9.5 onwards, is based mainly upon the systematic observation carried out in 18 classrooms in our nine study schools. Details of the research methods are discussed in Chapter 4.

First, however, in order to establish a baseline prior to the introduction of the National Curriculum, we examine some of the research findings of the 1970s and 1980s.

9.2 HOW HAVE TEACHERS APPROACHED CLASSROOM TEACHING AND ORGANIZATION IN THE PAST?

In terms of teachers' beliefs about children's learning, the progressive movement that led up to and culminated in the Plowden Report (CACE, 1967) had a profound and long-term influence in England. For instance, the teachers in King's (1978) study of infant schools took child-centred approaches as being axiomatic, some even regarding the move to the junior school as the end of 'real' education. Key elements in these teachers' perspectives about the nature of children's learning were ideas about developmentalism, individualism, play as learning and childhood innocence. Closely related to learning through play were ideas about the importance of child interest, happiness and busyness. Similarly, Berlak and Berlak (1981) emphasized infant teachers' perspectives in terms of seeing childhood as unique and as a special case, in contrast to the alternative view of childhood as continuous and of children as mini-adults.

However, it is often the case that there is a difference between the ideals to which people aspire and the actions that turn out to be possible. This has also been true for primary school teachers. Thus many of the research studies of the 1970s and 1980s documented a gap between commitments and ideologies and practical realities in classrooms (e.g. Bennett, 1976; Bassey, 1978; DES, 1978; Galton *et al.*, 1980; Alexander, 1984). A key finding of such work was that the 'basic curriculum' of reading, writing and number continued to dominate classroom activities and that teachers' classroom control of pupil activity has been consistently tight. It appears that while affective aims have dominated the ideologies of many primary school teachers, a limited range of cognitive aims have tended to be at least as significant in their practice.

Pollard's analysis (1985) documented the practical dilemmas that teachers face in classrooms as a result of the major structural features of primary education: limited school resources, large class sizes, high proportions of pupil–teacher contact time, compulsory attendance, external curricular expectations, etc. As a result, he argued, teachers develop 'coping strategies' as they reconcile their commitments with their circumstances and their beliefs with what is possible. As Bennett and Kell (1989) elaborated, teachers face the

> difficulties and stress involved in attempting to deliver a differentiated curriculum in classes of sometimes wide age ranges, containing children with generally low levels of language and personal skills, and differential experience of school, without adequate resources and assistance, while feeling under pressure from parents to achieve progress in the basics.
>
> (Bennett and Kell, 1989, p. 25)

The chief dilemma for Key Stage 1 is undoubtedly the issue of how to reconcile beliefs about the nature of young children, and their developmental rights and needs, with the teachers' obligation to have pupils learn basic skills. Most teachers recognize this and seek to resolve it by drawing on a mixed repertoire of teaching strategies. For instance, in Ashton *et al.*'s (1975) study of the aims of primary teachers, over 90 per cent of the teachers committed themselves to what some referred to as a 'moderate' role. This was characterized by an emphasis on 'teaching the basic skills as individually as possible and encouraging and stimulating children to use them effectively and imaginatively in all other work', while allowing 'a mixture of child and teacher choice for all the remainder of the children's learning' (Ashton *et al.*, 1975, p. 48).

A similar mixed philosophy was expressed by teachers in the Oracle study (Galton *et al.*, 1980) and in the Bristaix study of primary teachers in England and France (Broadfoot *et al.*, 1987), where teachers evinced a concern for 'balancing out' competing priorities. Thus they characterized their teaching in terms such as: 'at the same time traditional and progressive', or 'a mixture of didactic and liberal, allowing children to master basic skills and then to practise them in a way they themselves have an opportunity to organize'.

In the early 1990s, when we conducted the PACE enquiries, the dilemma had become more acute for teachers. Indeed, there had been growing controversy in the media and attacks on 'trendy progressives' by government ministers. The report of the so-called 'Three Wise Men' (Alexander *et al.*, 1992) was an explicit attempt to generate a debate on pedagogy in primary schools and to confront traditional assumptions. However, many teachers believed that the injunctions to consider more subject-based forms of curricular organization and to engage in more traditionally conceived whole-class teaching were against the interests of primary school aged children. As such controversies raged, the dilemma was well put by one teacher we interviewed in 1992. She commented:

> The problem with being a primary teacher now is that there is no consensus about what we do. Parents, teachers and educationalists all want something different. There is a pressure from people outside to get back to teaching the three Rs with a centralized curriculum.

Everything I aspire to is creative, informal, child-centred: but what I worry about is making sure the children acquire the basic skills. I want to marry those two approaches – but I think I'll always feel pulled in those opposite directions.

To summarize, research conducted before the National Curriculum has shown that, despite commitments to child-centred ideas, most teachers emphasized basic skills and attempted to solve the dilemma of competing ideologies and pressures by drawing upon a mixture of teaching methods.

9.3 WHAT WERE TEACHER PERSPECTIVES ON PUPIL AUTONOMY IN THE CLASSROOM?

As one element of this debate, we were concerned in the PACE study with teacher perspectives on pupil autonomy and to what extent they felt able to put these into practice in their classrooms. In the 18 interviews with Year 1 and Year 2 teachers as part of our 1990 and 1991 classroom studies, we asked teachers their views on how much control of classroom activities infant children 'ought' to have. Once again, we found evidence of teachers conscientiously attending to the perceived needs of young children and to their responsibilities regarding their educational progress.

The majority of the teachers felt that children should have some control over learning activities for a good part of the time, although no one felt that child control was feasible or desirable all the time. In practice, most teachers allowed for some child control of activities in their classrooms, although this was balanced by their perceptions of children's need for structure. The children's needs or age were perceived as factors in making a judgement. For instance, regarding needs, the Year 1 teacher at St Anne's argued:

With the kind of children I've got, you have to have a fairly structured approach to their learning, but there should be set times of day when they have that choice and that's usually first thing in the morning, or some part of the afternoon, or the end of the morning . . . It is a structured choice. I organize the choices so that they can't just go round the class and choose anything they like. The hospital corner, for example, would be a choice if they signed up for it. Very often they choose the writing corner or the reading corner. They have choice a small part of the time depending on circumstances.

One example of the often highly structured nature of choice in Year 1 was to be found in another classroom where each group of children had nearly an hour a day of 'free choice' activity. This was a significant proportion of classroom time but choices were carefully framed. Pupils selected from 'planning cards', which had been specially drawn up for each child, listing five designated activities. These ranged from playing in the puppet theatre to writing a story or doing construction. Most of the activities had been derived from National Curriculum attainment targets and once a child had carried out an activity this was ticked off so that the following day the range of choice was four activities, then three and so on. All five activities were expected to be carried out by each child by the end of the week.

In some classrooms, the choice was much more open-ended than this. For instance, some children were free to choose the same activity a number of times during the week, although the range of choices was still carefully structured by the teacher. Such choices tended to reflect the history of resource provision in the classrooms and the practicalities of their use. For instance, some classrooms did not have provision for water and sand play, while some that did still limited pupil use because of the potential difficulties of wet or sandy floors.

One of the most common teacher strategies was to allow choice to children only when they had finished their designated 'work'. 'Choosing' was thus used as an inducement to complete tasks, and the range of activities that could be selected was often delineated on a day-by-day basis. Often this might be limited to activities that were regarded as requiring little teacher support, thus enabling the teacher to target her attention towards children who had not completed their tasks. Of course, with this arrangement, slower children only rarely got a chance to choose.

This use of choice as an inducement to complete 'work' increased as the children became older. However, a balance was still sought. Thus Year 2 teachers said:

> Children ought to have some choice, especially as they get older and more self-reliant. But I do think you need to give them a grounding to start with and then also have the opportunities open for them around the classroom so that they can choose.
>
> (Year 2 teacher at Meadway)

> I think children need enough choice to be able to give them a sense of their own importance, but not to go overboard because we have to remember that they are still children. They need to be guided and taught, but certainly there should be times when you give a child a plan and say 'you can choose', but this again needs to be thought out by the teacher as to why she's doing it and how she's doing it and not just free for all.
>
> (Year 2 teacher at Lawnside)

It was apparent from teacher interviews conducted both through the classroom studies and in the two major interview rounds that teachers had found it progressively more difficult to reconcile their belief in the value of some child choice of activity with the demands of the National Curriculum. We reviewed some of the data that bear on this in Chapter 7, where, among other things, we reported a 1990–2 increase from 20 to 55 per cent of teachers perceiving the curriculum to be overcrowded and no fewer than 85 per cent of teachers in 1992 saying that the National Curriculum had been the biggest influence on their recent pedagogic changes. Taken overall, there was a strong feeling from our findings that teachers felt they were being forced to prescribe more and more classroom activities and thereby restrict scope for pupil autonomy.

In terms of the tension between the perceived nature of six- and seven-year-olds and required educational purposes, this was seen as resulting in requirements that were both constraining and inappropriate. For instance, one teacher of a combined Year 1/Year 2 class explicitly stated that her freedom to allow child control was now more limited: 'There's no longer the freedom to go away and write a story about what you want. Even with the very young ones, free writing is now curtailed somewhat because we're doing "my family" and it's all geared to getting ready for the attainment targets.' This was perceived as a significant change: 'It didn't used to be. Before, every child would write on subjects they chose and I would be their scribe helping to express their great needs.' Another Year 2 teacher said: 'In the last two years I've had to cover as much as possible, such as science. So I've chosen more and more of what we have to do. For instance, I aim to cover the attainment targets for science and this has rather dominated.'

Lest any reader has images of 'golden days' of the past, we should remember that, despite some popular impressions, research studies of the 1970s and 1980s consistently found that actual teacher control of primary classrooms was tight and that child choice was relatively limited. However, it appears from our data that, since the subject content of the National Curriculum and the assessment procedures have been introduced, teachers have felt it necessary to take more control and direction of children's activities. They have done so largely despite their better judgement and with concern over the imposition of a degree of curriculum overload, resulting in pedagogic constraint, which they feel to be inappropriate for such young children.

Our evidence suggests that not only had the choice of learning tasks become more restricted since the introduction of the National Curriculum, but levels of teacher intervention during tasks had also increased. This is discussed in more detail in sections 9.6 and 9.8. Of course, the latter could well have been beneficial, if more subject matter teaching and encouragement were being offered so that children became more 'interested'. However, as many teachers feared, it could also have been detrimental, if so much control was being taken away from children that their motivation and commitment to school and learning was compromised. The latter concern is an issue we consider directly in Chapter 10.

9.4 HOW DID TEACHERS PERCEIVE CHANGES IN THEIR PEDAGOGY FOLLOWING THE INTRODUCTION OF THE NATIONAL CURRICULUM AND ASSESSMENT REQUIREMENTS?

In this section we draw on data from two rounds of interviews with teachers, conducted in the summers of 1990 and 1992. The data thus reflect teacher perceptions in the early stages of the implementation of the National Curriculum and at a point when its impact on classroom practice was becoming apparent. We asked about teachers' classroom practice and how this was being affected by the National Curriculum and assessment.

In particular, teachers were asked, 'How would you describe your approach to teaching?' Their responses were coded in broad categories. The result is shown in Table 9.1. One notable feature of these data is the fact that the vast majority of teachers, over 70 per cent, stated that they adopted 'mixed' teaching methods. Even in 1990, only one-fifth subscribed exclusively to forms of 'child-centred' pedagogy, a fact that somewhat belies the sensationalism about progressivism that has sometimes filled the media in recent years. One teacher, whose response was fairly typical, said:

> I try to be a co-learner with the children, I try to increase my skills and be a more reflective teacher and I try to use the principles of really looking at the children's work and following through the stages in their learning. I think I use a range of styles, depending on what I'm working on with the children. There's a tremendous range of different levels with the children and there would be a more relaxed informal style when the children are composing writing, and spellings might be a more formal situation. When the children were planning and reviewing their work, there's quite a lot of discipline so that they listen to each other. Music has its own inherent discipline and then they're playing with construction, where they might have a task to do but there will be an informal atmosphere in the classroom where they're all doing their own activities.

However, by 1992 there was a significant fall in the number of teachers declaring themselves to endorse child-centred approaches and a corresponding increase in those whose responses were coded as 'traditional' or 'formal'.

The pattern is clear, but it was made even more apparent when we coded teachers' comments made in respect of an open-ended opportunity to amplify their previous

Table 9.1　*Teacher perspectives on their approaches to classroom teaching (percentages)*

	1990	1992
Child-centred/informal	22.7	16.1
Mixed	70.5	72.0
Traditional/formal	5.7	10.8
Other	1.1	1.1
Total	100	100

Source: PACE 1 teacher interviews.
Sample: 88 teachers in 8 LEAs.
Date: summer 1990 and summer 1992.

Table 9.2　*Open-ended comments by teachers on approaches to teaching (percentages)*

	1990	1992
Group based	50.0	50.0
Class work	3.6	29.1***
Individual work	20.2	32.6***
Emphasizing basics	31	34.9
Integrated day	28.6	8.1***
Topic work	16.7	20.9

Source: PACE 1 teacher interviews.
Sample: 88 Key Stage 1 teachers in 8 LEAs.
Date: summer 1990 and summer 1992.
Note: Figures do not total to 100 per cent because of multiple coding of open-ended responses.

response. Table 9.2 presents these data. Some of these figures are dramatic. For instance, there was a fall in teachers mentioning forms of integrated day, from 29 to 8 per cent, and a rise in teachers mentioning whole-class teaching, from 4 to 29 per cent. Both these changes are highly significant statistically. The continuity in emphasis on group work and on the curriculum 'basics' is also notable, while there was no perceived decrease in the prominence of topic work. The latter finding somewhat contradicts the patterns found through our classroom observation, but this may reflect continuing attempts to provide integrated work despite the difficulty of actually doing it.

Lest the origins of such changes be doubted, over 85 per cent of the teachers interviewed in 1992 attributed them to the introduction of the National Curriculum, while 55 per cent identified new assessment requirements. Only 12 per cent spoke of other changes in school and just 3 per cent mentioned personal sources of change. The 1990 figures were very similar. The teacher quoted above cited particularly the demands made by the National Curriculum in terms of classroom management: 'I'm finding that the demand of organizing and managing the children has changed a tremendous amount. I'm trying to maximize on time.'

This perceived change in teaching approach and philosophy was also reflected in changes in classroom practice. Most teachers (87 per cent) felt that the advent of the National Curriculum had resulted in significant changes to their working day and for 38 per cent in 1990 and no less than 62 per cent in 1992 these changes were seen as major. The most important areas of change involved more time spent on assessment-related record keeping, with over 60 per cent mentioning this in both rounds of interviews, and more time spent on planning and preparation, with this being mentioned by over 40 per cent on both occasions (see Table 9.3).

Even in 1990 there was certainly evidence for the 'intensification' of teachers' work (in the sense of chronic work overload) (Lawn and Ozga, 1981; Apple, 1986), with many teachers either having to work longer hours or having to work in a more concentrated, less relaxed way in order to discharge their responsibilities. There was a general feeling of being swamped by change. 'Too much has happened too quickly' was the way many teachers put it. While they were developing new ways of working, particularly in the area of record keeping and assessment, more information would arrive that superseded existing requirements, meaning that they had wasted their time. For example, keeping up with the documentation that accompanied the National Curriculum was seen by most as 'simply overwhelming'. 'Far too much to assimilate. I have just had to give up on it for the time being,' as one teacher put it.

Many teachers expressed frustration and even anger over the amount of time that was apparently demanded by the NCC and SEAC for record keeping and assessment. There were fears that this was beginning to 'take over from teaching', that the heavy burden demanded in time and effort left too little time for planning, for responding to children, for display work, for all the things that were seen by many as 'real teaching'.

In 1992, the pressure on teachers was clearly immense, and nearly one-quarter were beginning to change their teaching methods in order to be able to cope. However, the need to spend such major amounts of time on assessment and on meetings appeared to have declined (see Table 9.3), presumably because teachers felt they had come to terms to some extent with the demands of the SATs and the National Curriculum. One teacher argued:

> I have to put in far more hours than the 1265 hours designated in order to fulfil the needs of the National Curriculum and really the 1265 hours which we're supposed to spend on things in addition to preparation and marking is really extremely questionable. Most teachers are now getting up very early in the morning and finishing very late at night. As a class teacher you need to be in school by a quarter to eight and you need to not leave school before five or six each evening and in addition to that you need to do between two and three hours of work at home and you're still not finished. I certainly spend, I would say, about five or six hours at the weekend, so the 1265 hours really does not address that at all. Because even with doing that amount of work most class teachers feel very much under stress and unable to cope with the workload.

Table 9.3 *Teachers identifying changes to their working day (percentages)*

Type of change	1990	1992
More record keeping	62.8	63.3
More assessment	33.7	18.9***
More meetings	29.1	15.6**
Change in curriculum content	34.9	41.1
Change in teaching methods	12.8	23.3**
More planning and preparation	46.5	42.2
More pressure	not coded	64.4

Source: PACE 1 teacher interviews.
Sample: 88 Key Stage 1 teachers in 8 LEAs.
Date: summer 1990 and summer 1992.
Note: Totals do not equal 100 per cent since teachers identified up to three changes.

We thus have clear signs, from teacher accounts, of tighter classroom structures, tighter teacher control and heavier workloads in response to the National Curriculum and assessment. In the next section we consider how the tightening of 'frame' and the increased pressure experienced by teachers were felt to be influencing teacher relationships with the children in their class.

9.5 HOW DID TEACHERS PERCEIVE THE CHANGES TO HAVE AFFECTED THEIR RELATIONSHIP WITH CHILDREN?

In 1990 only 31 per cent of the teachers felt that the National Curriculum had a negative effect on teachers' relationships with children. By 1992 this proportion had increased to 58 per cent, partly as a result of the impact of the introduction of national assessment, but in particular because of a perceived increase in pressure on teachers' time, leaving them both less relaxed and less able to spend time responding to children. Most teachers had strong feelings about the importance of defending their relationship with the children, feelings that were closely tied to their own sense of identity as primary teachers (Nias, 1989).

Time and again they mentioned the National Curriculum as a definite pressure on the close relationships they had formerly enjoyed with children. Contributing to this was the loss of fun and responsiveness to children in their teaching and the feeling of a need to justify everything in terms of the attainment targets. In 1990 one teacher argued:

> There isn't anything that you do now that you don't feel, 'Can you actually justify this, what educational guide are the children getting out of it, how can you tie it up with an attainment target or programme of study?' All that sort of thing. Or can you, like you used to be able to, just do it for the pure fun and enjoyment of it?

This feeling of pressure was almost universal among the teachers we interviewed. The Valley Year 1 teacher agreed:

> I think on a bad day I'm definitely more 'crabby' because I do feel under pressure all the time. When the children do something, instead of looking at it and thinking only 'Has this child tried hard, is this good for this child?' I'm thinking, 'Does it fulfil certain criteria?' And if it doesn't, my anxiety . . . shows through. I think because of the pressures at the moment I'll be more likely not to have been so nice and loving as might have been.

Closely related to this was a sense of loss of the close affective ties many teachers had developed with the children in their class. As one teacher put it:

> I think there is a tendency to be so pressurized by the demands of the National Curriculum that there isn't so much time to spend discussing emotional and personal issues with the children. It's 'Right, let's get on. Tell me about it later.' And those issues are just as important as the more academic issues . . . So many of the very nice aspects of being with the children have been lost. And I think the children feel it. I feel they feel very tired and pressurized at the end of the half term.

The feeling of stress and a loss of relaxed, enjoyable time with the children seemed, if anything, to have intensified between 1990 and 1991. As another Year 2 teacher put it, 'I'm very aware of that close contact time, that personal connection that makes the children happy and at ease with you. You don't have time for that and you can't teach an unhappy child.' As she put it, the making of a trusting relationship with young children aged between four and seven was all-important and it would be lost: 'They'll see this horrible woman who makes me do this, this and this, through the day, and that's not right.' Another teacher agreed:

> We are not so relaxed in the classroom now. Teachers are more worried, 'Are we doing enough? Are we giving children enough experiences? There is constant planning and record keeping. Some of the children in my class would be so much better off with a motherly teacher who had time to sit with them on her knee and do things with them but it's impossible now with all the pressures.

Such feelings were intensified where teachers felt there was a particularly strong conflict between the demands of the National Curriculum and the needs of the children. The Year 1 teacher at St Anne's, working in a socially disadvantaged area in the north of England, felt a conflict between

> knowing the kind of work you should be doing and which the National Curriculum encompasses and the restrictions imposed by the kind of children they are. I feel that I'm not able perhaps to take things as far as I would like, it has to be a very simple level, sometimes I'd like to take it one step further and I'm not able to do that.

In 1990 there was evidence of a strong determination among teachers not to allow the changes to destroy their relationship with the children, and this protectiveness was still strongly in evidence in teachers' responses a year later. As the Year 2 teacher at Valley put it,

> When I feel those frictions I lay off the National Curriculum. When I feel those I say, 'I don't care, we will do something completely different', and I change my tack, and I go back to being myself the 'proper' teacher and I don't care. Angela [the head] backs me up on this. When I feel those tensions come back into the classroom I stand back. I make an assessment, make a sensible judgement, and think, 'Enough's enough'

In spite of the perceived pressures, the responses of these teachers expressed a determination to try to protect their relationship with the children and to mediate the demands of the reforms to acceptable professional ends. Nevertheless, the figures suggest that, as the implementation of the reforms progressed, an increased proportion of teachers felt this relationship to be under threat.

In the sections that follow, we draw upon both teacher interviews and our observations of 18 Year 1 and Year 2 classrooms to examine directly the changes in teachers' classroom practice.

9.6 WHAT WERE THE MAIN TEACHING CONTEXTS IN THE CLASSROOMS AND HOW HAVE THESE CHANGED?

In monitoring changes in classroom practice, we were concerned particularly with the extent of whole-class, individual and group teaching. On this, we have two main sources of data. First, we have the findings of systematic observation by the PACE team in the 18 classroom studies during the autumns of 1990 and 1991. Our second data source comes from interviews with our wider sample of 88 classroom teachers, conducted in the summers of 1990 and 1992.

Table 9.4 shows the results of the systematic observation of teaching context. It is apparent that a wide range of teaching contexts are used in infant classrooms, with approximately two-fifths of the time being spent in each of whole-class interaction and individual work, and the remaining fifth being used for group work. We should emphasize in this context that our observational coding of 'whole-class interaction' included all teaching time spent together as a class: discussions and story time, for instance, as well as more didactic teaching sessions.

Interestingly, our data record a slight fall in the proportion of whole-class interaction from 1990 to 1991, though we are unable to say whether this was caused by an absolute change in teaching approach or by teacher adaption to the age of the children. It will be recalled that our 1990 observations were based on Year 1 children but that these same children were in Year 2 for our 1991 observations. It is possible that whole-class sessions are used more for induction and socialization purposes with younger children. In any event, the decrease in whole-class interaction does seem surprising, given the pressures that were mounting externally at the time.

Data from our interviews with the wider sample of teachers also raised some interesting questions about changes in teaching contexts. In both 1990 and 1992 teachers were asked to say whether they felt they were doing 'more', 'the same' or 'less' of whole-class, group or individual teaching. The results are shown in Table 9.5. This table shows the absolutely clear perception by just over a fifth of teachers in 1990 and a quarter in 1992 that they were increasing the proportions of whole-class interaction in their classrooms. While this increase was matched by a rise in groupwork in 1990, teachers believed that their use of groups had fallen back by 1992. Individual work was felt to have decreased in 1990 but had begun to stabilize by 1992.

How, then, can we account for the apparent discrepancy between what we observed as a slight fall in whole-class interaction and the repeated teacher perception that there had been a rise?

We believe that the problem is essentially methodological and that the data can, in

Table 9.4   *Main teaching contexts: (percentage of observed time: column percentages)*

	Year 1, 1990	Year 2, 1991	Difference, Year 1 to Year 2
Class interaction	39.5	35.9	−3.6
Group work	18.4	19.2	+0.8
Individual work	39.5	41.0	+1.5
Other	2.6	3.9	+1.3

Source: PACE 1 systematic observation.
Sample: 9 Year 1 and 9 Year 2 classrooms.
Date: autumn 1990 and autumn 1991.

Table 9.5   *Teacher perceptions of changes in teaching context (column percentages)*

	Whole-class teaching		Group work		Individual work	
	1990	1992	1990	1992	1990	1992
More	21.6	25.8	28.4*	9.7	9.1	9.7
Same	64.8	67.7	65.9	74.2	65.9	77.4
Less	12.5	5.4	3.4	12.9	23.9*	10.8
Other	1.1	1.1	2.3	3.2	1.1	2.1

Source: PACE 1 teacher interviews.
Sample: 88 teachers.
Date: summer 1990 and summer 1992.

fact, be reconciled. The key question is 'What is seen to count as whole-class teaching?' We believe that the main teacher reference point on this, when answering our interview question, was likely to relate to explicit whole-class teaching sessions they had specifically planned in relation to the content of a National Curriculum subject. Indeed, our field note data confirm teacher perceptions that, in the light of the demands of the National Curriculum, the extent of explicit subject-based whole-class teaching was increasing. However, our systematic observation data record a much wider range of whole-class interaction, much of which, such as 'news time', 'review time' and 'story time', is traditional and commonplace in infant classrooms. We think it unlikely that teachers were thinking of these in response to our question on whole-class teaching.

Our overall interpretation, then, is that there has been a steady increase in explicit, teacher-planned, whole-class teaching sessions while the overall number of whole-class interaction sessions has decreased. We thus need to ask, 'How are whole-class sessions actually used?' as well as, 'What proportion of whole-class sessions are there?' We believe that our data suggest that although there may have been slightly fewer whole-class interaction sessions in 1991 than in 1990, a greater proportion of them were being used for explicit teaching purposes.

In terms of teaching the curriculum, teachers were, arguably, using the available time more effectively. However, few teachers actually saw it like that, and for most the increase in whole-class teaching was something that was forced on them by the subject specification of the National Curriculum. Indeed, it was often seen as potentially damaging to social, affective and some cognitive aspects of children's learning.

A rough comparison may be made between the PACE findings and Tizard *et al.*'s (1988) study of children of the same age in London inner-city infant schools. In Tizard *et al.*'s study, Year 1 children spent 61 per cent of their time in individual work. This increased to 66 per cent of the time in Year 2. The proportion of group work in both years was relatively low. Interestingly, children had direct contact with the teacher for only 20 per cent of their time in the classroom compared with 43 per cent of the time in the PACE study in 1990 and 41 per cent in 1991. It would appear that, since the introduction of the National Curriculum, the proportion of time children spend in group work has remained low and the proportion of time children work as individuals has decreased. However, compared with earlier research, whole-class interaction has increased and the overall proportion of teacher-led situations has grown significantly.

9.7 ON WHAT CRITERIA WERE CLASSROOM GROUPS ESTABLISHED?

Although, as we have seen, the proportion of time spent by children in group work has declined, the children we observed sat in groups for most of the time in which they worked as individuals. How teachers seat children in groups for different activities and how much choice children have over their seating arrangements can be one indicator of the strength of frame within classrooms. For example, if children were grouped by attainment for more activities now than in the past and were less likely to be allowed to sit in friendship groups, this would suggest a tightening of teacher control in the pedagogical relationship, and a reduction in the power of the pupil.

We asked teachers during the 1990 and 1992 interviews what criteria they used

Table 9.6   *Types of pupil grouping declared by teachers as a basis for classroom organization*

	1990	1992
Attainment groups	79.5	82.8
Mixed-ability groups	55	72
Friendship groups	62.6	67.7
Gender groups	13.7	9.7
Age-based groups	44.3	16.1

Source: PACE 1 teacher interviews.
Sample: 88 Teachers in 8 LEAs.
Date: summer 1990 and summer 1992.
Note: Totals do not equal 100 per cent because of multiple coding of open-ended responses.

when they grouped children for different classroom activities. The results are shown in Table 9.6. In both 1990 and 1992, the results show a repertoire of grouping methods in use, with each being adopted for particular purposes. The method declared by the largest proportion of teachers, four-fifths, was attainment grouping (often inaccurately called 'ability grouping'). This was particularly used for specific curriculum activities, such as in maths, where differentiation by task was needed. However, its use often seemed to be generalized to apply to all work within subjects, such as maths and English, in which differentiation of tasks was seen as being particularly important.

One teacher described this:

> I'm having to switch more and more to ability groupings, which I don't like with such young children because I don't think it's appropriate . . . Because of the pressure to cover all the activities that they need to, it's just impossible not to formalize the work more, and I do a lot more of dividing the class into high-ability groups, middle range and lower-ability groups just to teach them a lot more formally.'

Mixed-attainment grouping and friendship grouping were also used by most teachers for at least some of the time and such groups seemed to be used where it was more possible to differentiate tasks by outcome.

The decrease in the percentage of teachers using age as a basis for grouping is interesting. Such grouping was most prevalent in small, rural schools with mixed-age classes and there was a slight decrease in the number of mixed-age classes in the 1992 sample. On the other hand, the finding could reflect greater teacher efforts, even in small schools with a wide attainment range in each class, to provide differentiation between learners in terms of attainment. The percentage of teachers using gender as a basis for grouping remained very low. Gender-based groups tended to be used for specific purposes and with awareness of equal opportunities issues.

These findings articulated closely with research on grouping before the National Curriculum, which indicated that many teachers grouped predominantly by attainment. In Bennett and Kell's (1989) study, for example, a little over one-half of the teachers grouped children by attainment. A little over one-third of teachers used age or intake, and a similar proportion claimed to use flexible grouping. One in four said they used mixed-ability groups, and one in six used friendship groups. However, the reality was a little more complex than this, since many teachers used more than one criterion; for example, grouping by both age and attainment.

This comparison suggests that while attainment grouping has long been a significant form of classroom organization, its use has increased since the introduction of the National Curriculum and assessment.

9.8 WERE DIFFERENT GROUPS OF CHILDREN BEING TAUGHT IN DIFFERENT WAYS?

Overall, the children we observed in the PACE study were the focus of teacher attention (i.e. were observed to be interacting with the teacher) for 43 per cent of the time in 1990 and 41 per cent of the time in 1991. This figure includes whole-class, group and individual teaching contexts and compares with a figure of 20 per cent for the primary children observed by Tizard *et al.* in 1988. This difference suggests that after the introduction of the National Curriculum and assessment, teachers began to intervene far more in children's activities. However, this overall figure conceals significant variations in the way teachers allocated their time with children.

The PACE systematic observation data provide some interesting insights into the judgements being used by teachers in differentiating their pedagogic provision. For instance, focusing on data of pupil observations only, we were able to compute the proportions of time in which children of different attainment levels were in contact with the teacher in each of the three main teaching contexts: whole-class, group or individual. Attainment, in this context, was based on teacher records, with particular reference to reading attainment. The results are given in Table 9.7.

As one would expect, pupil attainment made very little difference to the contact offered by teachers when pupils were observed in whole-class contexts. The teachers interacted with the children in such circumstances whatever their level of achievement. However, teacher involvement with groupwork was heavily directed towards supporting lower-attaining children. Higher-attaining children seemed to receive only half the teacher attention that was invested in supporting weaker children. Teachers again offered most individual attention to lower-attaining children but also spent time, on an individual basis, with higher attainers. Children attaining at average levels received slightly less individual attention from the teacher.

These patterns show the ways in which the teachers studied resolved the acute dilemmas they face regarding the deployment of their scarce teaching time. It appears that teachers routinely direct whole-class interaction largely at the majority of children with average levels of attainment. They then support lower attainers, in groups, who

Table 9.7 *Total pupil time in contact with teacher in class interaction, group work and individual work by pupil attainment (percentages)*

Attainment	Teaching context		
	Class	Group	Individual
Higher	30.5	7.5	3.0
Medium	28.4	9.6	2.1
Lower	29.7	15.4	3.6

Source: PACE 1 systematic observation.
Sample: 9 Year 1 classrooms.
Date: autumn 1991.

might otherwise have difficulty in making constructive progress. Finally, they provide differentiated support to particular high- and low-attaining individuals.

A typical way of working was described by the Year 1/2 teacher at Orchard:

> I talk to the children all together first on what I expect them to achieve during the day and then I generally extract a group for either maths or language and I give the other children the chance – the ones that I'm not gathering together – usually I give them the chance to choose, within those things that I talked about first thing in the morning. So, for instance, maths will generally be in their maths book and if a child says, 'Can I do maths first?', I say, 'Well, wait until after play because I want to talk to your group about what they are going on to next.' So at some stage during the week I would have expected to see all the maths groups and have taken them on to something new so that on other days in the week they can continue, perhaps getting slightly more difficult, but on the same work that they've been doing. Then, after I have worked with the children as a group, I go round from group to group, helping individuals where I am needed.

Table 9.8 elaborates these issues by showing patterns in the experience of children of differing levels of attainment, social class, gender and sociometric status in terms of their total interaction with their teacher and their total interaction with other pupils. It tells us a good deal about teacher pedagogy and, in particular, how teachers resolve the problem of to which pupils to direct their time.

Regarding social class, it is striking that pupils of manual and non-manual parental backgrounds received almost exactly equal amounts of teacher contact. However, children of manual backgrounds spent a little more time interacting with other pupils. Of course, these quantitative data say nothing about the nature of what they were doing in either case, but there is an immediately apparent balance in the distribution of teacher time. Social class made no difference.

Table 9.8 *Patterns of teacher and pupil interaction by attainment, social class, sociometric status and gender*

	Interaction	
	Total teacher interaction with pupils	Total pupil interaction with other pupils
Attainment		
Higher	41.0	29.5
Medium	40.1	29.6
Lower	48.8	24.7
Social class		
Non-manual	43.6	25.6
Manual	43.4	29.7
Sociometric status		
Very high	33.0	36.0
High	41.2	31.7
Medium	47.9	24.2
Low	49.0	20.8
Gender		
Boys	40.3	26.8
Girls	42.2	26.1

Source: PACE 1 systematic observation.
Sample: 9 Year 1 classrooms.
Date: autumn 1991.
Note: This represents the percentage of total pupil time in contact with teacher and in contact with other pupils. Therefore percentages do not add up to 100 per cent.

Similar statements could be made regarding gender, where again there are very small differences in interaction times. Interestingly, the very slightly higher figure for total teacher interaction with girls is the reverse of the pattern found with older pupils (Galton *et al.*, 1980). While the overall differences are very small, for individual pupil interaction with their teacher, girls received 25 per cent more than boys (3.9 against 2.9 per cent of teacher–pupil interaction).

Regarding the interaction patterns of children of differing attainment and socio-metric status, teachers appeared to be making clear judgements about where to direct their time among pupils. There was significantly more teacher interaction with lower-attaining children and with children of low socio-metric status. A probable consequence was that low attainment and low socio-metric status were associated with less pupil to pupil interaction.

This evidence highlights one result of the exercise of professional judgement in the deployment of time. Teachers had repeatedly told us of their commitment to meet individual pupil needs and here, it appears, we have a resulting pattern in terms of observed interaction. As one Year 1 teacher argued, 'The kind of children I have in my class can make the National Curriculum approach difficult. It requires diversifying away from the basics and they actually need a lot of help with basic skills. I have to make that my top priority and make time to work with individuals.' Another teacher said:

> Some children in my class need a lot of help. I'm very aware that working with the whole class myself – very often I have to give that over to a part-time teacher when I really need and want to do it myself, so that I can fulfil the needs of individuals . . . But in doing that you lose that joy and that two-way communication with the class which you also need to fulfil the work and activities as it were. So you lose the cohesive stance between class work, individual work and group work because you're having to fragment that all the time.

As one example of this exercise of professional judgement, the Year 1 teacher at St Anne's adopted a strategy of making sure that she introduced difficult new work to lower-attaining groups of children on Mondays, when there were other adult helpers present in the class to work with other groups. This enabled her to spend longer with lower-attaining children and to concentrate completely on their needs. On one of the days we observed her, she was working with, and moving between, two maths groups doing work with dice, while one helper (a volunteer and grandmother) worked with children constructing and painting model plates of food as part of their topic work on 'our bodies, ourselves'. Another helper, a classroom assistant, worked with children making weather charts, and one group worked alone using worksheets.

Of course, plotted patterns of aggregated data can conceal a great deal of individual variation. As an example of this, Figure 9.1 is a scattergram showing the position of each of our 54 target children in Year 2 in terms of total interaction with other pupils and with their teacher. The spread is very considerable, from one child (top right) who managed exceptionally high levels of contact with both teacher and other pupils to others (bottom left) who had low levels of contact with both. The classroom experience of such children was inevitably very different indeed.

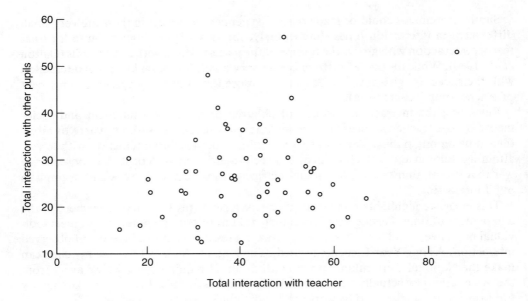

Figure 9.1   *Scattergram of total pupil and total teacher interaction (percentages).*

9.9 HOW VARIED WERE DIFFERENCES IN TEACHING CONTEXTS FOR TEACHERS AND PUPILS?

In this section, we consider differences in pedagogy in each of our nine study classrooms in 1991, taking as one indicator of difference the proportion of time in which different teaching contexts were used.

Section 9.6 showed that the predominant teaching contexts were whole-class interaction and individual work and that these were used about twice as much as forms of group work. Teachers were particularly aware of increases in explicitly planned, whole-class teaching. However, these overall aggregated figures conceal striking and significant variations in the experience of teachers and pupils in each of our nine study schools. Table 9.9 gives some idea of the range of difference, in which, in 1990, whole-class interaction varied from less than 7 per cent of the time in the small rural Orchard Primary School with its mixed-age classes to 69 per cent of the time in Lawnside Primary School, although for most schools the variation was somewhere between 30 and 50 per cent. Similarly, the proportion of time spent on children working in groups varied from 4 per cent in Greenmantle School, situated in a southern market town, to 42 per cent in Audley in the industrial North.

In 1991, the greatest variation in whole-class interaction was still between Orchard and Lawnside, but the difference between them was not so great (16 and 50 per cent respectively). The variation between most of the other schools had also fallen to between 30 and 40 per cent. The variation in group work was about the same in 1991 as in 1990, but the variation in individual work was less. This suggests that one effect of the progressive implementation of the National Curriculum might have been to move schools towards slightly greater uniformity of teaching context, although it is possible that the shift from Year 1 to Year 2 classrooms also made a difference.

Nevertheless, the divergence was still considerable, and, as we suggested in Chapter 8, this divergence in classroom organization was matched by a wide variation in the proportion of time spent on different areas of the curriculum. It is evident from Table 9.10 that those schools which spent a high proportion of their time on whole-class interaction were not necessarily using this time to concentrate on the basics. In Lawnside school, for example, where nearly 70 per cent of the time was spent on whole-class interaction, only 19 per cent of this time was actually spent on the basics, while 70 per cent of group time and 80 per cent of the time children worked as individuals was spent in this way. These data directly contradict the common stereotype of chalk and talk, whole-class teaching of the basics.

In summary, the wide variations indicated here suggest that, in these early stages in the implementation of the National Curriculum, there was still considerable diversity in children's experience in English infant and primary schools, in terms of variations

Table 9.9 *Main teaching contexts in classroom studies: percentage of observed time (row percentages)*

Teaching context	Class work interaction		Group work		Individual work	
	Year 1 (1990)	Year 2 (1991)	Year 1 (1990)	Year 2 (1991)	Year 1 (1990)	Year 2 (1991)
Greenmantle	51.1	34.4	4.3	3.1	42.6	56.3
Kenwood	20.5	27.1	20.6	43.8	51.3	29.2
St Bede's	37.7	40.0	17.0	21.7	39.6	31.7
St Anne's	34.1	32.7	24.4	3.8	41.5	57.7
Audley	31.3	29.6	41.7	24.1	27.1	46.3
Orchard	6.8	15.6	20.4	17.7	70.5	66.7
Lawnside	69.1	50.0	16.3	15.7	14.5	31.3
Valley	41.5	41.7	5.7	23.3	49.1	26.7
Meadway	50.9	43.1	20.7	15.5	28.3	37.9
Average	39.5	35.9	18.4	19.2	39.5	41.0

Source: PACE 1 systematic observation.
Sample: 9 Year 1 and 9 Year 2 classes.
Date: autumn 1990 and autumn 1991.
Note: There was also a small 'other' category of teaching context, which was used for just over 3 per cent of observations overall.

Table 9.10 *Proportion of time spent by pupils on basics (English and mathematics) in different teaching contexts, by school (percentages)*

	Whole class	Individual	Groups
St Bede's	26.0	79.0	30.8
St Anne's	17.6	96.7	75.0
Greenmantle	54.6	72.2	0.0
Kenwood	61.5	92.8	55.6
Audley	56.3	44.0	0.0
Orchard	14.3	53.3	83.4
Lawnside	18.8	80.0	70.0
Valley	16.0	72.5	42.8
Meadway	28.0	22.7	33.3

Source: PACE 1 systematic observation.
Sample: 9 Year 1 classrooms nationally.
Date: autumn 1991.

in time spent on different areas of the curriculum and on different teaching methods. A number of writers have contrasted the heterogeneity of the English child's experience in this respect with that of the typical French pupil (DES, 1991a; Sharpe, 1992; Broadfoot and Osborn, 1993). However, there was some evidence of a slight move towards greater uniformity in teaching context, possibly as the implementation of the reforms progressed.

9.10 CONCLUSION

In terms of the dimensions of change discussed in Chapter 3, there were very clear indications that the strength of frame in classrooms was increasing. Teachers were experiencing more constraint and the options open to children to select, organize, pace and time their work were considerably reduced. The teachers, in response to the pressures of the National Curriculum and assessment, appeared to be adapting by tightening their classroom control and by providing more direction to children's activities. There was apparently more frequent contact between the teacher and the children than in Tizard *et al.*'s (1988) study before the Education Reform Act and teachers perceived themselves as using more group and whole-class teaching, although our observations did not bear out the predominance of group teaching situations. More group work was becoming based on attainment levels in particular subjects as teachers sought to organize the provision of a differentiated curriculum. There was considerable variation between the schools we studied in terms of patterns of classroom organization and teaching context, but there was evidence that the variation was slightly reduced in 1991. Possibly this was indicative of the development towards greater uniformity between schools.

In terms of the debates over teaching methods in the primary school, our data suggest that, apart from the schools at either end of the spectrum, the 'balance' between different types of classroom organization suggested as desirable by Galton *et al.* (1980), Mortimore *et al.* (1988) and most recently Alexander *et al.* (1992) was already being practised by at least half the teachers in our sample. In schools that did not achieve this 'balance', teachers were often adopting coping strategies to take account of particular circumstances, as in the case of Orchard School, where the teacher found it virtually impossible to teach a mixed age group of four- to seven-year-olds as a whole class.

Chapter 10

Pupils and Classroom Pedagogy

10.1 INTRODUCTION

In this chapter we are concerned with three major issues that are related to teacher pedagogy, but we approach them with particular regard to pupil experiences and perspectives. Each of these issues relates to what is a key concern for young pupils: their teacher's use of power. Essentially, teachers have the power and authority to structure the experiences of children at school and, in so doing, to facilitate or compromise the fulfilment of pupil interests. Teachers' use of power is thus crucial to the quality of the school experience that pupils perceive. This is one reason, for instance, why pupils are so careful in 'getting to know' a new teacher at the start of a school year, why they are so skilful at monitoring teacher 'mood' and why much of their knowledge about teachers is organized defensively (Pollard, 1985). From the relatively powerless position of the individual pupil, it simply makes sense to gauge patterns in the teacher's behaviour and to be able to detect what he or she may do next. As we shall see, pupils also care deeply about what they are 'allowed to do' and about how their teacher relates with them.

The three issues on which we focus are: first, the strength of framing in classrooms, as indicated by the scope that is, or is not, offered to children for autonomous choice of activities; second, the nature of teacher–pupil relationships; third, the pattern of observed pupil activity. At the end of the chapter we relate these issues and discuss their consequences.

The ways in which behaviour is framed and maintained in classrooms are important for classroom control, but they also provide a significant element of the social context in which school learning takes place. That having been said, relationship between learning and control is complex. On the one hand there are documented advantages in pupils exercising self-directed control over the learning process (e.g. Rowland, 1987). In such circumstances they may be more highly motivated and the tasks undertaken may be self-selectively geared to existing levels of understanding and attainment. On the other hand, there are also clear advantages in there being greater teacher control over learning experiences. Teacher knowledge, experience and skills can be shared and pupil learning can be considerably extended by appropriate intervention, diagnosis, structuring and restructuring, so that pupil performance is assisted in its development (Tharp and Gallimore, 1988; Bennett and Dunne, 1992).

The second major pedagogic issue considered here concerns teacher–pupil relationships. We saw, in Chapter 6, how concerned teachers have been to sustain the quality of their relationships with pupils, despite perceived threats from the overcrowding of the National Curriculum and from assessment procedures. The data reported here provide the pupils' perspective on this issue, based on interviews in Year 1 and Year 2 with the 54 children in our sample. Recalling the analysis offered in Chapter 3, we address the issue conceptually in terms of the dimensions of the expressive, instrumental or alienated commitment that children may feel towards their teachers and we also consider the consequences that the quality of classroom relationships may have for classroom life and educational effectiveness.

The third major dimension of pedagogy on which we report concerns the nature of pupils' classroom activity. Here we document and discuss the patterns we have found in the relative balance in levels of pupil task engagement, task management, waiting and distraction, as measured for 18 different classroom settings using our systematic observation procedures. In so doing, we have regard to the limitations of this form of data-gathering but also, notwithstanding this, draw attention to the considerable strength of the patterns we discovered. We focus, in particular, on the relationships between what was coded as 'on task' and 'distracted' pupil behaviour, and between what we have termed 'potential teaching–learning time' and 'classroom management time'.

In the final major section of the chapter we investigate the relationship between our systematic observation and interview data from pupils. The result is an important qualification of over-simplified arguments, which assert the value of whole-class teaching and forms of classroom organization designed, unproblematically, to produce high levels of pupil task-engagement. Task-engaged dispositions may not, after all, be quite what they seem, and there may also be more to 'distraction' than meets the eye.

10.2 WHAT WERE PUPIL PERCEPTIONS OF CLASSROOM FRAMING AND CONTROL?

There are many ways of engaging with the issue of how behaviour is framed and maintained, for it goes back to some of the basic realities of classroom life: the goals of pupil learning and the existence of relatively large class sizes. Many years ago Waller

(1932) drew attention to what he called the 'despotism' of teachers and, even in a more enlightened era, Jackson (1968) talked of 'crowds, praise and power' as enduring features of classroom life. Such analyses reflect different teacher strategies for achieving educational goals in challenging circumstances and, one way or another, they inevitably involve the use of teacher power and authority to set structures and rules for behaviour and to establish specific goals and tasks for learning.

However, teachers know that neither the evolution of a positive and disciplined culture in a classroom nor the achievement of learning targets are attainable through their efforts alone. Thus, in primary school contexts there have been sustained efforts over many decades to evolve incorporative ways of managing classrooms, thereby leading pupils into a commitment to classroom rules and to the establishment of a social morality of expectations that can underpin educationally productive classroom interaction (Pollard, 1985; Lang, 1988). Similarly, teachers have been aware of the significance of pupil motivation on learning and of the inadequacies of simple, didactic strategies of 'chalk and talk'. Thus, despite the critique of the motivational priority that characterized some models of 'child-centred' practice, pupil perceptions and approaches to learning remain issues that cannot be ignored. From the pupil perspective, as we saw in Chapter 8 and shall see again, there are at least two particularly important aspects of pupil motivation: whether the activity itself is 'interesting' or 'boring' and the extent to which it is framed by constraint or allows for a degree of pupil autonomy.

This brings us directly to 'frame' – one of our key analytical dimensions in recording changes in primary school practices. In this context it refers to the extent to which activities are structured by power relations and expectations. Where frame is strong, then behaviour is bounded. Where it is weak, there is more scope for self-determined and autonomous activity. We attempted to monitor this issue as the National Curriculum was being introduced by identifying indications of change in classroom frame, both from teachers, as reported in Chapter 9, and from pupils.

In each of our two rounds of classroom study, in 1990 and 1991, we asked the 54 children in our longitudinal cohort, 'Do you like it best when you choose what to do or when your teacher does?' Almost two-thirds of the children, in both Year 1 and Year 2, recorded that they preferred to control their own activities. This proportion is, in itself, significant, though perhaps it might have been expected to have been even higher. The other third of children preferred their teacher to select their classroom activities. The two groups of children were asked to explain the reasons for their preferences and their responses had many resonances with the pupil views on curriculum that we discussed in Chapter 8.

Perceptions of children preferring child choice of activities

The two-thirds of children who preferred to choose activities themselves gave accounts that were coded as shown in Table 10.1. The pattern was relatively clear. The children preferred to engage, autonomously, in activities they selected and regarded as both more interesting and easier than teacher selections.

In Year 1, the 30 per cent of children who emphasized *autonomy* ('my choice') said things like:

Table 10.1   *Reasons given by pupils who preferred to choose activities themselves (percentages)*

	Year 1	Year 2	Overall
Because it's easier to do	8	14	11
Because it's more interesting	17	8	13
Because it's my choice	30	39	35
Because it's good for me	2	0	1
Don't know	8	2	5
No answer	2	0	1
Total percentage	67	63	65

Source: PACE 1 child interview data.
Sample: 54 Year 1 and 54 Year 2 children.
Date: autumn 1990 and autumn 1991.
Note: These are percentages of choices made by the whole cohort in each year.

> I like to choose my very best things I like doing.
>
> Because you can do what you want.
>
> Because you don't have to wait.
>
> 'Cos you can choose to play.

Among the comments of the 39 per cent emphasizing autonomy in Year 2 were the following:

> I like to choose which games we have and who you are with.
>
> We can't get on with what we want when she chooses. 'Cos she sometimes gives us something that isn't very good, 'cos we can't make something good out of it. I'd like a spaceship that drops down toy bombs or a car with guns that shoot out.
>
> I feel I can do whatever I want and you don't have to do what you don't like.
>
> Because sometimes Miss gives us jobs I don't like, don't want to do or am not very good at . . . because it might be too hard.
>
> Because we can do anything we like. It's better.
>
> Miss don't know what I like best.

The 13 per cent who appreciated scope to choose *interesting* things to do, in Year 1, said:

> Because Miss gives us boring things.
>
> 'Cos you can make things.
>
> 'Cos I can choose nicer things.
>
> 'Cos I like it. More fun. I play with dough.
>
> I think it might be because I like playing.
>
> 'Cos you can get at the Polydroms and you can stick 'em together.

In Year 2, children said very similar things. For instance:

> Because you do good things like painting and puppets. It's fun.
>
> 'Cos I can play with me mates.
>
> Because then I can choose Clever Sticks or Polydrons and I like playing with toys.

A further of 11 per cent of children overall drew attention to the greater *ease* of pupil-selected activities or the greater difficulty of teacher-directed tasks. They said things such as:

> She just gives us writing to do and it's really hard. She gives us a lot and I get really tired.
>
> Because I don't want to do hard things.
>
> Because we can choose easy work – not hard work.
>
> Because she might just say, 'Go and draw a picture', like one of those [Tudor] houses and it's hard to do.
>
> Because if I don't like it I might get it wrong and then I won't like it.

Two-thirds of children thus appeared to appreciate opportunities to take decisions, to follow and develop their own ideas, to be creative, to have fun and to 'do things' that were not too difficult. As we saw in Chapter 8, they wanted some success. Their concern for the intrinsic value of activity was also contrasted with their view of many teacher-directed activities as being 'boring' and as 'things we have to do first'. These criteria articulate very closely with those represented in Figure 8.1 regarding curriculum and this fact reaffirms their significance to children.

The differences from Year 1 to Year 2 are suggestive of pupils becoming more aware of a prime need to cope with classroom requirements that might, themselves, outweigh the intrinsic value of activities. This possibility of these children gradually adopting strategies for coping with school and 'playing the system' as they mature within it is suggested by the decrease in pupil concern with interest and the increase in references to making choices autonomously and simply making things easier. This could be interpreted as reflecting the development of a form of instrumentalism as pupils strive, one way or another, to satisfy the more structured tasks that teachers reported setting since the introduction of the National Curriculum (see Chapters 7 and 9).

Perceptions of children preferring teacher choice of activities

The third of children who preferred their teacher to select classroom activitie. for them were also asked to give the reasons for their preference, and the results were also coded and tabulated (see Table 10.2). Then main reason given for valuing teacher choice was consistent in both Year 1 and Year 2: teachers were simply regarded as providing more interesting activities.

Table 10.2 *Reasons given by pupils who preferred their teacher to choose activities (percentages)*

	Year 1	Year 2	Overall
Because it's easier to do	0	2	1
Because it's more interesting	19	24	22
Because it's my choice	0	0	0
Because it's good for me	10	4	7
Don't know	0	2	1
No answer	1	2	1
Total percentage	30	34	32

Source: PACE 1 child interview data.
Sample: 54 Year 1 and 54 Year 2 children.
Date: autumn 1990 and autumn 1991.
Note: These are percentages of choices made by the whole cohort in each year.

On this issue of *interesting* activities, the children said things such as:

> I like it when the teacher chooses 'cos she's nice and chooses good things.
>
> She lets us do good work, colouring, playing on the computer, playing in the Wendy House, construction, Lego.
>
> 'Cos she has better ideas. We haven't been taught.
>
> You do more things when Miss chooses.
>
> 'Cos sometimes we pick out the boring things, the teacher picks out the better things.
>
> When we go home at night, she sorts something out. It's usually good.
>
> She does fun things.
>
> Sometimes I like a surprise for what I'm doing.

Some 10 per cent of Year 1 children took an explicitly deferential view of teacher judgement. They favoured teacher selection of activities on the grounds that it simply was the teacher's decision and clarified requirements.

> Well she's the teacher, so if she chooses we know what to do.
>
> 'Cos she's the teacher and she's bigger.
>
> Because we won't know what we're doing if the teacher doesn't tell us.

However, in Year 2 this certainty was less evident.

The preference of almost a quarter of Year 2 children for teacher-led activities because of the interest they derived from such work is a very encouraging finding for teachers, many of whom have, as we saw in Chapter 6, put great efforts in recent years into developing both their subject knowledge and the quality of curriculum provision. However, as we indicated earlier, the growing pupil search for 'easier' activities may also reflect pupil recognition of the ways in which learning tasks progressively challenge them, on a day-by-day basis, as they move through school. Interestingly, we could find no pattern in these results by pupil attainment or gender.

We thus have results that document children's clear preference for autonomy, interest and ease in the selection of classroom activities. Although a significant minority of children appreciated the interest of teacher-led activities, there were also signs of children, as they got older, adopting more instrumental strategies to accommodate the progressive challenges they faced in school.

Pupil perceptions of teacher control

Having considered child preferences, we also wanted to consider what, in their view, actually happened in their classrooms. We therefore asked them: 'Do you choose what you do at school or does your teacher choose for you most of the time?' Not unexpectedly, as Table 10.3 shows, the children indicated a very high degree of teacher control – almost 70 per cent across the two years.

The results here are very striking in overall terms, with only 7 per cent of children suggesting that they had significant degrees of choice. This figure, of course, directly contrasts with the image of infant classrooms as arenas for 'free play'. Table 10.3 also suggests that children, like their teachers (see Chapter 9), perceived a tightening of teacher control and direction as they moved from Year 1 in 1990 to Year 2 in 1991. Of

Table 10.3 *Children's perspective of who selects tasks at school (percentages)*

	Year 1	Year 2	Overall
Teacher	59	80	69
Children	13	2	7
Both	26	13	19
No data	2	6	4

Source: PACE 1 child interview data.
Sample: 54 Year 1 and 54 Year 2 children.
Date: autumn 1990 and autumn 1991.

course, we cannot be sure of the extent to which this apparent tightening of frame is related to adaptions in pedagogy as the children grew older or to growing pressures of the National Curriculum over the period, but the comments of teachers, reported in Chapter 7, suggest that curriculum pressures were considerable. Our 1991 data thus show that no fewer than four-fifths of Year 2 children recognized their experience of classroom life as being framed by tight teacher control, with only 13 per cent drawing attention to joint decision-making.

As we have seen from the earlier parts of this section and from the discussions of pupils' views of curriculum in Chapter 8, the children were not universally appreciative of this degree of teacher control and frame around their activities. As many of them saw it, teacher control restricted their autonomy, posed more challenging activities than they desired and often required them to do things that were usually less interesting than they would have selected themselves. In a word, despite important exceptions, teacher-framed work was likely to be more 'boring'.

However, whatever their views and preferences, all the children in the sample perceived the necessity of 'doing what the teacher says' while at school. We know this from their answers to the question we put to them: 'Do you have to do what your teacher says?' Over the two years, 94 per cent of children's answers confirmed the paramount significance of teacher decisions. A few more aware children, particularly in Year 2, recorded that it all depended on the activity and situation, but no children claimed that what their teacher said did not matter. Sometimes the pupils were explicit about the ways in which teacher power might be used, as the following answers to our question show:

Otherwise she gets angry and might send you out of the class.

'Cos if you don't you'll have to go down to [headteacher].

'Cos if we don't she says we'll get told off.

Because if you don't she gets cross and tells you off and you might feel worried.

Or you'll get told off. If someone is very naughty they have to stand by the wall inside.

Yes, and if you don't do what you're told you have to stand in the book corner and you're not allowed to leave or talk.

Here we see pupil concerns with being shown up, told off, worried and isolated from their peers. Following the analysis of Pollard (1985), these can be interpreted as concerns over the threat to 'self'. The children feared being drawn individually out of the relatively safe anonymity of the class and having their dignity threatened.

Returning to Jackson (1968) and his identification of crowds, praise and power as facts of classroom life, we thus have to say that the children in this study were very much aware of the power of their teachers. The children knew what they preferred in terms of autonomy, and in terms of making their classroom lives more interesting and less difficult, but they accepted that it was teachers who structured and framed their classroom activities and experiences. In this respect there were no clear differences in our post-National Curriculum findings from those available before 1988. It seems that pupils have always had to take account of teacher power and control in classrooms – and they still do.

10.3 HOW DID PUPILS SEE THEIR RELATIONSHIPS WITH THEIR TEACHERS?

An area central to the PACE research was the question of whether the imposition of external requirements on teachers as embodied in the National Curriculum and assessment procedures would affect the relationships between teachers and children.

In particular, we wanted to investigate whether the close personal relationships, to which primary school teachers have been so strongly committed in the past, would be comprised by the impact of external pressures. If this were the case, we reasoned, both teacher and pupil perceptions and actions were likely to become more instrumental or, perhaps, even alienated. In terms of the analytical dimensions reviewed in Chapter 3, we thus sought to track the nature of, and change in, the expressive–instrumental–alienated dimension of classroom interpersonal relationships.

As we saw in Chapter 9, when asked if they felt that the quality of teacher–pupil relations had been affected by the introduction of the National Curriculum, 31 per cent of the 88 teachers interviewed in 1990 said that there had been a change for the worse and that their relationship with children was affected adversely by pressures on teaching time or by feelings of stress on the part of the teachers. Many felt that contact with children had become more formal and artificial. Considering data from our 1992 interviews, we found a significant rise, to 58 per cent, in the number of teachers perceiving a deterioration in teacher–pupil relationships. However, though this deterioration was resisted and regretted, there was no weakening in teacher commitment to close and caring relationships with pupils. There did not seem to be a movement by teachers towards instrumentalism.

When we conducted our interviews with the children in our study, in 1991 and 1992, we asked them directly about relationships. First we enquired, 'How do you get on with your teacher?' This was followed up with the question, 'What do you like best about your teacher?' The children's responses did not convey the sense of the worry and foreboding felt by the teachers, but they mapped almost exactly on to the teachers' concerns and also revealed some interesting patterns of response.

In the first place, for the children in Year 1 and Year 2, the quality of classroom relationships was very strongly attested. As Table 10.4 shows, only 3 per cent of all the children's answers were coded as indicating negative responses to the question, 'How do you get on with your teacher?' Most of the children, 53 per cent, made positive statements about their relationship with their teacher, and 41 per cent of responses were coded as 'neutral': 'quite well', 'all right', 'OK'. Certainly, a finding of only 3 per cent of answers in the negative is a powerful affirmation of the success of infant teachers in maintaining high-quality relationships with their pupils.

However, there were some other interesting patterns that are worth noting. First,

Table 10.4 *Year 1 and Year 2 pupils' perceptions of their relationships with their teacher (percentages)*

	Year 1	Year 2	Overall
Positive	57	48	53
Neutral	35	46	41
Negative	2	4	3
Don't know	2	0	1
No data	4	2	3

Source: PACE 1 child interview data.
Sample: 54 Year 1 and 54 Year 2 children.
Date: autumn 1990 and autumn 1991.

Table 10.5 *Boys' and girls' perceptions of their relationships with their teacher (percentages)*

	Boys	Girls	Overall
Positive	43	63	53
Neutral	52	29	41
Negative	2	4	3
Don't know	0	2	1
No data	4	2	3

Source: PACE 1 child interview data.
Sample: 54 Year 1 and 54 Year 2 children.
Date: autumn 1990 and autumn 1991.

Table 10.6 *Children's perceptions of their relationships with their teacher, by attainment (percentages)*

	High	Attainment			Low	
	1	2	3	4	5	Total
Positive	12	14	15	5	7	53
Neutral	6	6	12	11	6	41
Negative	0	1	0	0	2	3
Don't know	0	0	1	0	0	1
No data	0	0	1	1	1	3
Total	18	20	29	17	17	100

Source: PACE 1 child interview data.
Sample: 54 Year 1 and 54 Year 2 children.
Date: autumn 1990 and autumn 1991.

referring back to Table 10.4, a slight trend away from positive replies and towards more 'neutral' statements can be seen. Table 10.5 develops this detail by showing the overall distribution of perceptions of boys and girls. It can be seen that boys were considerably less appreciative than girls. Of the latter, no fewer than 63 per cent expressed positive feelings about their teachers.

The final table in this set, Table 10.6, shows the same aggregated data by pupil attainment. Here we can see that there appears to be a tendency for higher-attaining children to be more positive about relationships with their teacher than lower attaining children.

The significance of these variations, by age, sex and attainment, is, of course, that they suggest the gradual emergence of differentiated pupil perspectives. As developed though child culture and further school experiences, these could evolve to contribute to more explicit differences in pupil motivation, attitudes to learning and attainment. This is something that will be investigated further in future phases of the PACE research.

As we saw above, to elicit their perspectives and reasoning a little more, the children were also asked, 'What do you like best about your teacher?' Five major categories were used to code the children's responses.

Interaction was recorded for 34 per cent of all pupil responses. These were directly concerned with actions of the teacher towards, or with, the child or children. For instance:

> When she says something nice, like 'Well done, Sarah.'
>
> Bestest is that she likes doing things with us. When I can't do it, she writes it for me – helps me.
>
> When she doesn't shout. That's when I like her.
>
> When she's not mad.
>
> She's kind and she lets us go to the toilet when we want to.

Interest was used, for 29 per cent of all responses, to categorize comments that referred to the perceived quality of content or activity offered by the teacher. Thus:

> When she does good work with us.
>
> The way she reads.
>
> I like her stories.
>
> When she gives you work you like.
>
> When she comes and she's doing things with us, like when she had a big table and we have all things to taste and we dip papers in and it goes different colours.

Personal was a code used to classify pupil statements referring to some teacher characteristic of appearance, temperament, dress, etc. It was used for 13 per cent of all comments. For instance:

> I like her clothes and when she dresses up.
>
> It's the way she talks. She's got a nice voice.
>
> Well, she looks nice.
>
> He's got a beard.
>
> He's handsome. I love him.

Choice, used for 9 per cent of all comments, described pupil references to the ways in which their teacher provided them with opportunities to choose activities:

> When she lets us play games and read books and go out to play.
>
> If she says we can choose.
>
> 'Cos she lets us do painting.
>
> Because she lets me play.
>
> When she lets us go over to dinners and we can sit by somebody.

Finally, *ease* was recorded for 4 per cent of statements and was used to categorize reference to teachers reducing the challenges of schoolwork. Thus:

> She gives easy work.
>
> When she lets us play games and read books and go out to play.

Table 10.7 *Child criteria for liking teachers (percentages)*

	Year 1	Year 2	Overall
Personal	11	15	13
Interest	33	24	29
Ease	6	2	4
Choice	11	7	9
Interaction	24	44	34
Don't know	9	4	6
No data	6	4	5

Source: PACE 1 child interview data.
Sample: 54 Year 1 and 54 Year 2 children.
Date: autumn 1990 and autumn 1991.

Table 10.8 *Boys' and girls' criteria for liking teachers (percentages)*

	Boys	Girls	Overall
Personal	7	19	13
Interest	41	15	29
Ease	4	4	4
Choice	9	10	9
Interaction	27	42	34
Don't know	7	6	6
No data	5	4	5

Source: PACE 1 child interview data.
Sample: 54 Year 1 and 54 Year 2 children.
Date: autumn 1990 and autumn 1991.

As with children's overall perceptions of relationships, there were some important patterns in the reasons given by the children when in Year 1 and Year 2 and by boys and girls. Regarding pupil year, Table 10.7 shows the distribution of categories of things the children liked best about their teachers. There is significant move here in the proportion of children mentioning the nature of pupil–teacher interaction, though the criterion of the interest of teachers' curricular provision seemed less important.

Table 10.8 shows that while girls focused on the nature of their interaction with their teacher and on personal factors, boys were far more likely to prioritize the interest, or otherwise, of the curriculum and of the activities that the teacher offered. Having choice, a reflection of the value of autonomy to children, remained important to both boys and girls.

Of course, such patterns in children's concerns are not unexpected. They are very similar, on the one hand, to findings reported by other research studies such as those of Davies (1982), Pollard (1985) and Goodnow and Burns (1985). On the other hand, they resonate with other PACE findings, reported both in Chapter 8, on children's curricular priorities, and earlier in the present chapter. It may be recalled from Chapter 8 that among the pupil criteria for evaluating curricular activities were ease and success, interest, fun, activity and autonomy. In many respects, our findings on pupil perceptions on relationships with teachers echo these curricular concerns. Earlier in the present chapter we also found that children valued selecting their own school activities – even though they felt that this was rarely allowed. They liked having autonomy, choosing more interesting things to do and making their classroom experiences easier.

As we also saw, there were some signs of the children, as they got older, becoming a little more 'canny' regarding the requirements of their teachers and a little more aware of the exercise of teacher power. The data on teacher–pupil relationships reinforces this impression. Certainly as Year 2 children in 1991, the cohort, particularly the boys, were less positive about their relationships with teachers than they had been in 1991. The overall impression from this may well be that the boys in particular were becoming aware of the contested character of classroom life, and of the tension between their desire to 'have fun' and 'do interesting things' and their teacher's concerns with order and learning.

However, we should make clear that, in terms of influences on teacher–pupil relationships, our data provide little evidence that we can specifically attribute to the National Curriculum or assessment procedures. This seems to confirm the success of teachers in their commitment, reported in Chapter 9, to ensure that relationships did not deteriorate despite the increased pressure to which they felt they were subjected. Pupil experience in this respect again seems to have been one of relative continuity.

What, following this analysis of what pupils said, did they actually appear to be doing?

10.4 WHAT PUPIL BEHAVIOUR WAS OBSERVED IN THE CLASSROOMS?

As described in Chapter 4, as part of our classroom studies we classified pupils' classroom behaviour into key categories and used time-sampled systematic observation to measure the proportions of each. In this approach, the observer codes the pupil activity at each sampling point, thus building up a systematic record of researcher judgements of pupil activity (Croll, 1986). We used four pupil activity categories – 'task-engaged', 'task management', 'distracted' and 'waiting for teacher' – categories that, though important and well established, also require relatively high levels of researcher inference or judgement.

Evidence from research studies of the 1970s and 1980s that have adopted this approach to studying pupil behaviour has consistently indicated that, for about 60 per cent of their time, young children were judged to be directly involved in their work (e.g. Galton *et al.*, 1980; Tizard *et al.*, 1988). Findings from the PACE study show very similar results, as Table 10.9 shows.

Table 10.9   *Main types of pupil activity in the classroom (percentages)*

	Year 1 (1990)	Year 2 (1991)
Task-engaged	56.9	59.5
Task management	11.8	13.5
Distracted	19.3	21.5
Waiting for teacher	8.0	5.6
Other	4.0	0.0

Source: PACE 1 systematic observation.
Sample: 9 Year 1 and 9 Year 2 classes.
Date: autumn 1990 and autumn 1991.

Despite their different ages, the children in the PACE project were judged to be 'task-engaged' for roughly the same amount of time as the Key Stage 2 children studied by Galton *et al.* (1980). They were also deemed to be 'managing tasks' and 'distracted' for roughly similar amounts of time. More time was spent by the PACE children in 'waiting for the teacher', and this probably reflects the younger age of the children. A similar comparison with slightly adapted data from the Tizard *et al.* study of infant children yields results that are not drastically different, although the Tizard *et al.* children seemed to be coded as distracted slightly less often.

Overall, the results are fairly consistent. Children in English primary schools are likely to be regarded as task-engaged for about 60 per cent of their classroom time. They may be seen as distracted for up to 20 per cent of the time and are likely to be organizing themselves to complete the task or waiting for the teacher for the remaining 20 per cent of the time. The aggregated pupil 'time on task', in getting organized or working, is just over 70 per cent of classroom time.

10.5 DID THE CLASSROOMS SEEM TO PRODUCE VERY DIFFERENT LEVELS OF PUPIL TASK ENGAGEMENT?

The observation data produced interesting variations in levels of pupil task engagement, and in the following two sections we shall discuss some of the factors associated with different levels of time-on-task across classrooms. However, these results and their possible implications need to be treated with some caution. Clearly the amount of time pupils spend task-engaged is interesting and important educationally. Equally clearly, however, it does not in itself tell us anything about the amount or quality of learning going on. This has been well put by Karweit (1984), who wrote that 'Time is a necessary but not sufficient condition for learning.' Time-on-task cannot be used as a surrogate measure for classroom effectiveness and the analysis here cannot tell us how pupil learning actually takes place or which classrooms produced the 'best' learning outcomes. Nevertheless, we do have some interesting and challenging findings about patterns of variations in a major feature of classroom life.

Figure 10.1 charts our results for each of the four categories of pupil activity in each of the 18 classrooms in which data were collected. Looked at another way, the figure shows our classification of the activity of the same target children, in Years 1 and 2 of their school careers, within nine primary schools.

The classrooms in Figure 10.1 have been ordered on the basis of descending percentages of recorded pupil task engagement. This creates a dramatic visual impression of one of our key findings of classroom variation. Expressing exactly the same data in more aggregated, statistical terms yields the rank order correlations contained in Table 10.10.

In discussing classroom variation we will use particular combinations of the four variables of observed pupil activity to produce three indicators: 'classroom management time', 'teaching and learning time' and 'time on task'.

Classroom management time

This indicator is based on the combined pupil time spent in task management and waiting for the teacher. Our use of this combination of variables is based on the argument

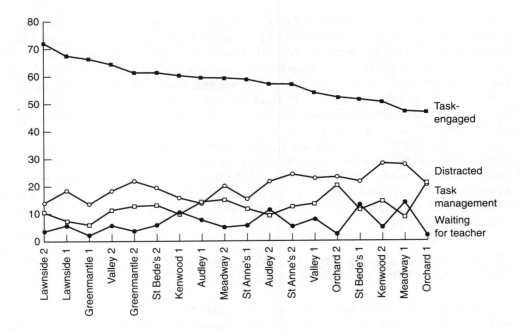

Source: PACE 1 systematic observation.
Sample: 9 Year 1 and 9 Year 2 classes.
Date: autumn 1990 and autumn 1991.

Figure 10.1   *Extent of classroom variation in achieving pupil task engagement.*

Table 10.10   *Pupil activity in the classroom (correlations)*

	Pupil task-engaged	Task management	Waiting for teacher	Distracted
Pupil task-engaged	1.00			
Task management	−0.56	1.00		
Waiting for teacher	−0.38	−0.35	1.00	
Distracted	−0.75	0.33	0.28	1.00

Source: PACE 1 systematic observation.
Sample: 9 Year 1 and 9 Year 2 classes.
Date: autumn 1990 and autumn 1991.

that such data will record pupils who are more, or less, dependent on teacher guidance, depending on the routines, procedures and overall management system that exist in their classroom.

Our first finding of note is that there is a tendency for task management and waiting for teacher to vary together. Where task management is high, waiting for teacher tends to be low, and vice versa. This pattern must be slightly qualified, for both variables were low for a few classrooms (see the data on the left of Figure 10.1), classrooms that also had relatively low levels of distraction and high levels of task engagement. Overall figures for classroom management time in Year 1 classrooms were also slightly higher than our Year 2 findings, perhaps reflecting greater time taken by younger children in learning classroom procedures. Notwithstanding these slight variations, over all the classrooms, task management was coded for almost 13 per cent of pupil observations and waiting for teacher for just under 7 per cent, a total of almost 20 per cent.

This classroom management figure of 20 per cent of observed pupil time is important. While it can evidently be reduced in some circumstances, we believe that it is realistic at present to accept that this is the sort of proportion of time that is likely to be spent by pupils on classroom management, *whatever* the teacher strategy. Perhaps an approximate commitment of 20 per cent of pupil time is simply a necessary time commitment, given the range of class sizes and task, group and resource organization to be found in English primary schools.

Of course, having noted the overall 20 per cent figure for classroom management, we must look at its composition. What is the ratio of 'waiting for teacher' to 'task management' that may be undertaken without the teacher? This has implications for both use of teacher time and the development of pupil independence.

Teaching and learning time

The use of teaching and learning time is our second indicator of classroom variation, and is arguably the most significant. We define teaching and learning time as the time that remains once classroom management issues have been dealt with. Putting this another way, if we allow 20 per cent of observed pupil time for classroom management of one sort or another, how do pupils use the remaining 80 per cent of time?

The codes that relate to teaching and learning time are 'task-engaged' and 'distracted', and clearly they are likely to map against each other in some way. Children who are not task-engaged could well be distracted, and distracted children will certainly not be task-engaged. However, in our comparisons of classrooms we were not expecting as strong a pattern as the one we found. As both Figure 10.1 and the correlations in Table 10.10 show, there is a very considerable difference in pupil activity within the classrooms and a very strong relationship between task engagement and distraction.

Classes that have high levels of pupil task engagement do tend to have relatively low levels of pupil time used in waiting for the teacher and in task management. Proportionately, however, as we would expect, they have even lower levels of pupil distraction. Conversely, classes with relatively low levels of task engagement tend to have much higher levels of distraction. The correlation on the latter relationship, −0.75, is very strong indeed. These variables are not, of course, independent of one another, for if more time is spent on-task then there is less time for other activities. However, the correlations show which of the tasks co-vary with task engagement.

Thus, in terms of the question 'how do pupils in different classrooms use the 80 per cent of classroom time that is available for teaching and learning?', the answer has to acknowledge huge variations in the level of task engagement rather than distraction. Interestingly, the extreme cases are Lawnside Primary School, serving a relatively affluent commuter village near a large Midlands city, with its 'Year 2 class figure of 72 per cent of observed pupil time on task engagement and only 14 per cent of time coded as distracted, compared with the Year 1 class at inner-city Meadway Primary, serving a community with severe socio-economic problems, where task engagement was down to 47 per cent and distraction was up to 28 per cent, twice the Lawnside figure.

Time on task

A further, and more commonly used, way of exploring the relationship of these variables is to monitor the total 'time on task'. Thus the time in which pupils are 'task-engaged' and involved in 'task management' is added and compared. Table 10.11 shows the results of this procedure, classroom by classroom, for the two rounds of PACE data-gathering.

There is some variation here from year to year and between classes in the same year. The extremes are again the over 80 per cent 'on-task' activity of Year 2 pupils at the village school of Lawnside and the figure of less than 60 per cent recorded for pupil 'on-task' activity at inner-city Meadway. These cases having been noted, the degree of consistency is perhaps surprising, with almost all the other 16 classrooms producing pupil on-task figures of between 65 and 75 per cent. It seems that, despite what one may occasionally read in some newspapers, in most classrooms at Key Stage 1 pupils work on-task for the bulk of their time. The real question seems to be not whether the children are on-task in itself, but whether on-task activity is educationally productive. Certainly some classes, such as that studied in both years (though with different teachers) at the small, rural Orchard Primary, had unexceptional figures for time on task overall, but unusually high levels of task management concealed within them.

The averages of time on task for all classes are once again worth considering. For Year 1 the figure is just under 69 per cent but for Year 2 classes there is a rise to 73 per cent. Further phases of the PACE research will enable us to monitor this possible trend of increasing task focus as children get older.

There was also substantial variation between the classrooms, and between the average percentage of pupil time devoted to forms of classroom management for each year. Thus, for instance, classrooms at Lawnside, with the highest recorded figure of whole-class interaction (50 per cent), produced significantly lower classroom management figures for each year than those at, say, the small, rural Orchard Primary which, with mixed-aged classes, had the highest figure for individualized work (67 per cent).

10.6 WHAT PATTERNS OF TEACHING WERE ASSOCIATED WITH PUPIL TASK ENGAGEMENT?

We looked at how total time on task varied according to different teaching contexts and some interesting relationships emerged. The issue was investigated by calculating correlations between the four main categories of pupil activity and the three main categories of teaching context. Table 10.12 conveys the results. This is a fascinating and challenging table. It shows that classrooms where high levels of class interaction were recorded are also likely to have been coded with relatively high levels of pupil task engagement, low levels of pupil task management and fairly low levels of pupil distraction. Classrooms with high levels of individual work are likely to have relatively low levels of task engagement and waiting for the teacher, but higher levels of pupil time taken through task management or distraction. Group work falls between these two patterns on each variable. These results echo those reported by Croll and Moses (1988), based on 32 junior-age classrooms.

Of course, time on task is not in itself an indicator that learning is taking place,

Table 10.11 *Total pupil time on task (percentages)*

	Lawnside	Valley	Greenmantle	St Bede's	Meadway	Ardley	St Anne's	Orchard	Kenwood	Average
1990, Year 1	74.9	67.8	72.4	63.2	56.7	73.7	71.1	68.4	70.1	68.7
1991, Year 2	82.6	75.7	74.2	74.4	74.5	66.6	69.6	73.2	65.8	73.0

Source: PACE 1 systematic observation.
Sample: 9 Year 1 and 9 Year 2 classes.
Date: autumn 1990 and autumn 1991.

Table 10.12   *Patterns of teaching associated with pupil task engagement (correlations)*

	Pupil task-engaged	Task management	Waiting for teacher	Distracted
Class interaction	0.57	−0.74	0.09	−0.21
Group work	−0.23	0.21	0.20	0.03
Individual work	−0.42	0.58	−0.24	0.20

Source: PACE 1 systematic observation.
Sample: 9 Year 1 and 9 Year 2 classes.
Date: autumn 1990 and autumn 1991.

although it may well be a pre-condition for it. Indeed, a number of earlier studies have indicated a positive association between time on task and pupil performance (Brophy and Evertson, 1976; Soar, 1977; Stallings, 1980). Southgate *et al.* (1975) found that teachers of pupils who made the greatest degree of progress in maths, language and reading tended to make use of whole-class or group instruction, whereas in classrooms where there was a high level of individual attention children tended to spend less time concerned with the task. The ORACLE study (Galton *et al.*, 1980), which attempted to identify teaching styles most closely associated with pupil progress, named one group of teachers as 'infrequent changers'. These teachers engaged in a high level of whole-class interaction not, as the stereotype would have it, in order to drill pupils, but to provide a high level of challenging questions and statements. Such teachers also used praise more often than other teachers and encouraged a positive climate in their classrooms. In particular, they were able to switch their organizational strategy to take account of particular circumstances in the classroom, for example from individual to whole-class work, in response to their judgements of the children's needs.

10.7 HOW DID PUPIL PERCEPTIONS OF TEACHERS RELATE TO CLASSROOM VARIATIONS?

At first sight, from an adult perspective and despite our cautions on interpretation, Figure 10.1 and our other findings appear to show that the range of classroom effectiveness is considerable and that more effective classrooms are characterized by greater proportions of whole-class teaching and by more efficient classroom management. We wanted to relate such impressions to pupil experiences and perspectives.

We investigated for a pattern of pupil perspectives by sorting the 18 classrooms from our two years of study into two groups of nine classrooms each. The first group of nine were those in which we had recorded the higher levels of pupil task engagement, and the remaining classrooms had lower levels. Our pupil interview data were then reanalysed with the data from higher and lower task engagement classrooms being treated separately.

One question that was analysed in this way was that in which we had asked the children what they liked best about their teacher. It may be recalled from section 10.3 that the largest proportion of children's answers to this question, 34 per cent, had made reference to the nature of teacher action and the effects of it. We coded such answers as *interaction*. Many of the answers showed acute awareness of teacher power and of the potential threat it could pose to pupils if they were seen to be failing to comply with

Table 10.13 *Pupil reasons for liking their teacher in classes of higher and lower levels of pupil task engagement (percentages)*

	Higher	Lower	Overall
Personal	11	16	13
Interest	22	36	29
Ease	2	5	4
Choice	7	11	9
Interaction	45	22	34
Don't know	7	5	6
No data	5	4	5

Source: PACE 1 child interview data.
Sample: 54 Year 1 and 54 Year 2 children.
Date: autumn 1990 and autumn 1991.

teacher requirements. Children thus 'liked her when she is nice to us', or thought 'she is best when she does not shout'. The second largest coding category, at 29 per cent overall, was *interest*. Most of the pupil statements coded in this way related to the perceived value or pleasures of activities that teachers provided. Children noted that 'she reads good stories', or that 'it's quite interesting when he gives us an experiment to do'. Of the other codings, *personal* related to personality or physical characteristics of the teacher, *ease* to the difficulty of the work that was required and *choice* to the degree of autonomy that was allowed.

Table 10.13 shows the results of plotting these codings of pupil reasons for liking their teachers in the nine classrooms with higher levels of observed task engagement and the nine classrooms with lower observed levels. The patterns here are very noticeable.

Pupils in classrooms with higher levels of task engagement, which we also know to mean classrooms that tend to have high levels of whole-class interaction, evaluated their teachers primarily in terms of how they interacted with them. No fewer than 45 per cent of answers from children in these classrooms were of this type. The children's answers, showing particular awareness of teacher power and of its potential use, are perhaps to be expected if the frame in such classrooms is strong. Expectations of pupils may thus be relatively specific and, in the public setting of whole-class contexts, compliance is relatively easily monitored.

Pupils in classrooms with lower levels of task engagement, and lower levels of whole-class interaction, tended to think of their teachers in more diverse ways, but with particular attention to the interest of the curricular activities that were provided by them. Pupil criteria had a stronger focus on the quality of curriculum activities, with reference, in particular, to what they intrinsically offered in terms of enjoyment and experience. They were also more inclined to make reference to personal characteristics of their teachers and to comment on the ease or difficulty of work and on the degree of autonomy they enjoyed.

We carried out a similar analysis focusing on pupils' perceptions of curriculum subjects, reconsidering the children's views reported in Chapter 8. The results of this are reported in Table 10.14. Here we see another facet of the same pattern being repeated. Children in the classes with higher recorded levels of task engagement and whole-class interaction more aware of the need for success and were concerned to evaluate the relative difficulty of activities. They seemed to be a little more sure of their evaluations

Table 10.14　*Pupil criteria for evaluating curriculum subjects, by level of task engagement (percentages)*

	Higher	Lower	Overall
Fun	12	18	15
Activity	12	11	12
Interest	20	27	23
Autonomy	5	3	4
Education	5	2	4
Success/ease	33	19	26
Don't know	12	19	16

Source: PACE 1 child interview data.
Sample: 54 Year 1 and 54 Year 2 children.
Date: autumn 1990 and autumn 1991.

of curricular activities (there are fewer 'don't know's) and they seemed to expect less classroom 'fun'. In classrooms where task engagement and whole-class interaction were lower, the children were more inclined to evaluate the interest and fun of curriculum activities, but also tended to be more uncertain in their views of curricular activities. Perhaps of particular note, they also seemed to be less concerned with achieving success.

In one sense then, pupil experience in the classrooms with lower task engagement seemed to produce pupil views that, compared with the classrooms with high levels of task engagement, were broader and more focused on intrinsic aspects of classroom life and curriculum experience. Such pupils also seemed to be more relaxed about their learning – less sure of their curriculum evaluations and less concerned with success, but more aware of the intrinsic interest of the curriculum activities they experienced, of the personal qualities of their teachers and of 'having fun' at school.

10.8 CONCLUSION

The findings reported in this chapter require careful interpretation and some caution. Pupils, we have seen, would like more control in classrooms, though they do not really expect to have it. Their answers to our questions on classroom control and on relationships with their teachers tended to reaffirm their concern to experience interesting classroom activities, thus avoiding boredom. However, their awareness of the extent of teacher control and power was considerable. In this, they also repeated the major themes of their views of curricular activities, as reported in Chapter 8.

In terms of the analytic dimensions we discussed in Chapter 3, pupils recognized constraint but preferred autonomy; they recognized teachers' rights to impose requirements but preferred negotiation; they were very aware of the strength of frame in different classroom contexts and of the ways in which this influenced their activities; they showed signs of the emergence of differentiated responses with varied strategies for action and with different degrees of commitment to teachers' classroom goals.

We have also reported findings that there was a considerable range in levels of apparent task engagement in different classrooms, according to our systematic observations, and that pupil perceptions varied in patterned ways. In terms of the analytical dimensions we introduced in Chapter 3, the classrooms in which higher levels of task engagement were observed appeared to be more concerned to teach established knowledge than to provide conditions in which pupils could construct their own. Pupil perceptions implied that teachers in such classrooms tended to be more categoric than provisional in their assessments. However, they also seemed to be more constraining and tended to produce more instrumental attitudes on the part of the children. From the pupil perspective, they were less 'fun' and less 'interesting'.

We need to be cautious about these results and they will be investigated further in later phases of the PACE research, but they do raise some important issues about the priorities of infant schooling for children. For instance, is it possible that the majority of parents, who, as Hughes *et al.* (1990) found, prioritize social aims for their young children, would actually prefer their children to attend the ostensibly 'less effective' classrooms because of the reduced pressure that seems to be indicated and the greater intrinsic satisfaction of the experience that is suggested? On the other hand, if it is essential to focus children's attention on learning objectives and provide a tight frame around their efforts, as seems to be provided in the apparently 'more effective' classrooms, should we be concerned by the indications that the children seem to be more aware of the power of the teacher in evaluating their work extrinsically rather than concerned about the intrinsic educational goals to which teacher efforts are supposedly directed? In other words, is tight teacher control appropriate for six- and seven-year-olds, whether it be inspired by government, 'wise men' or others?

Of course, teachers, curriculum providers and educationalists are not simply charged with making life enjoyable for children, though childhood remains a unique phase of life, of value in its own right. The point is to strike some sort of balance between the classroom structuring that is necessary if teachers are to offer children appropriate support in their learning and the provision of psychological space and opportunity for children to learn through more self-directed experiment and experience. Much psychological research suggests that for successful learning to take place, whether the teacher or the pupil initiates the activity, it is important that the learner retains a degree of control so that new knowledge and understanding gained can be incorporated into pre-existing schemata and frameworks (Gage and Berliner, 1988; Tharp and Gallimore, 1988).

Motivation remains vital in this whole discussion and our findings have some important messages to offer. First, to those who address curriculum content while ignoring pupil motivation, it simply asserts their short-sightedness. More constructively, it confirms the views of many teachers that classroom control or whole-class teaching are unlikely to be sufficient to produce high-quality learning gains. Certainly, as we have seen, they can produce pupil awareness of the need to comply with teacher requirements, but the connection with learning has to come through an engagement with and interest in the curriculum itself. However, the potential is there, for a significant minority of children do value teachers as a source of 'making classroom life interesting'. Nevertheless, there is arguably much more that could be done.

Once more, then, while affirming the importance of teacher–pupil relationships in providing positive social contexts in which learning can take place, we are back to the need for teachers to have a rich resource of subject knowledge and a wide repertoire of pedagogic strategies to convert their expertise into productive pupil activity.

Chapter 11

Teacher Assessment

11.1 INTRODUCTION

This chapter and the next are particularly concerned with the scope and impact of the assessment initiatives that have been brought about by the 1988 Education Reform Act. Highly visible to all sectors of society – be they teachers or consumers – the requirements of the national assessment programme must be rated as one of the most controversial of the Government initiatives. The high-profile debates about technique and manageability that characterized the introduction of standardized assessment captured, as far as education was concerned, an unprecedented degree of media attention. Rather less generally visible, but arguably just as important, were the significant numbers of new obligations that were placed on teachers in relation to making, recording and reporting assessments more generally.

In what follows we shall briefly review the evidence on how the teachers in our study saw assessment before the impact of National Curriculum assessment. We will then explore the nature and significance of the changes that have impacted on them in this respect.

As in the other chapters of this book that deal with the impact of various different aspects of the legislation, our attempt to explain the changes in teachers' assessment practice that this chapter documents will be informed by the key themes of power, values and understanding. More specifically, these themes translate into issues concerning what assessment is (understanding), how it may most profitably be used to promote learning (values) and who should decide on the purpose, nature and use of assessment (power).

As indicated in Chapter 3, we shall argue that the principal dimension of change in relation to assessment, which brings together many of the tensions concerning understanding, values and power, is the shift from provisional to categoric assessment, from assessments that are essentially intuitive and idiosyncratic to assessments that are explicit and based on a common language of achievement.

11.2 HOW DID TEACHERS APPROACH ASSESSMENT BEFORE THE EDUCATION REFORM ACT?

Until the advent of the 1988 Education Reform Act relatively little research had been conducted on assessment in primary schools and little had been written for teachers to support their professional practice. Why was there such an apparent lack of interest in primary school assessment?

Certainly, part of the explanation lies in the fact that with the demise of the 11 plus in most areas in the 1960s, most primary schools no longer had to grapple with formal assessment requirements. Not only did they no longer have to prepare children for formal tests, they were not required to provide formal written reports for parents. Indeed, one of the effects of post-Plowden, child-centred, ideologies was to provide a rationale for a very different approach to pupil assessment. Thus, to motivate children and as a basis for communicating with parents, assessment was seen as a much more intuitive, holistic and informed procedure. Previously, the teacher would have been likely to communicate with pupils through a statement of marks awarded for work in different subjects and would have used the same explicit form of communication to report to parents. However, with the advent of more child-centred ideologies such evaluative insights were increasingly communicated to pupils and their parents in the form of descriptive comments referenced to the teacher's overall assessment of the child's intellectual capability, behaviour and application.

As Sharp and Green (1975) argued in their classic study, such holistic evaluative judgements were further related to the known personal circumstances of the child, especially ethnicity and home background, to provide the basic information for an individualized pedagogy. As we saw in Chapter 6, the PACE study has confirmed the findings of previous studies (e.g. Ashton *et al.*, 1975; Broadfoot and Osborn, 1993), which showed that English primary teachers' professional ideologies are centred typically on providing learning experiences that meet the emotional, as well as the intellectual, needs and interests of the individual child. This ability to interpret pupil behaviour in relation to existing assessments of a pupil's strengths and weaknesses, needs and interests, and to make pedagogic decisions accordingly, has arguably become a central element of professional competence in the contemporary English primary classroom.

This broad background to the current programme of change highlights a number of points that are helpful in interpreting the progress and significance of assessment developments in primary schools. First, we can note that primary teachers' existing views of and practices concerning assessment are explicitly *ideological*, reflecting the broader professional ideology held by the teacher. This, of course, as we saw in Chapter 6, embraces their approach to curriculum and pedagogy as well. Second, it is apparent that the teaching of primary age children is not *inevitably* associated with a particular ideological approach. This is made clear by the experience of countries in which both teaching and assessment are much more formal in content than has been the case in England. For instance, it is significant that the French Government's current concern to make teachers more responsive to the differing learning needs of children is manifest in a nationally imposed comprehensive programme of diagnostic assessment.

In this chapter, we explore further some of the issues raised above. We report findings concerning how the teachers in our study saw the role of assessment, how they used it and what they perceived to be its effects on children. Many of these findings are drawn from conversations and observations with the teachers involved in our detailed classroom studies. Others are drawn from interviews with teachers in our larger sample of 48 schools.

11.3 HOW DID TEACHERS SEE ASSESSMENT AT THE TIME OF OUR STUDY?

When asked what role they felt assessment ought to play in infant classrooms, teachers' responses were structured around three main dimensions: frequency, purpose and mode (see Table 11.1).

In terms of *frequency*, all the teachers who took part in our detailed classroom studies stressed the need for assessment (and associated feedback) to be continuous and immediate – part of the on-going dialogue of teaching. Many of the teachers adopted a constructivist view of learning and talked of the continuous, intuitive, diagnostically orientated mental process they 'had always used'.

It's an integral part of the process of teaching.

I think that it should be diagnostic, I think it should be the teacher's way of carrying the child from A to B, noting whether you have to go from A to A1, A2, A3 before you get to B. Note whether you can skip over C because the child is good and go on to D and to record that somewhere, whether it be an internal school record informally with other colleagues that can help you and then later on to pass that information on to the next teacher, to discuss with parents how they can help if you feel that something external might be influencing what's happening in school, but purely diagnostically because the children are assessed externally. They have their reading tests, their maths test and I think that's sufficient.

Table 11.1 *Mode, purpose and frequency of assessment*

	Assessment to support the construction of knowledge	Assessment to monitor the acquisition of established knowledge
Mode	Covert/intuitive	Overt/explicit
Purpose	Encouragement/guidance	Accountability
Frequency	Constant	Intermittent

In terms of *purpose*, the emphasis was on needing to assess in order to make pedagogic decisions. 'We've always been assessing. As teachers we need to assess in order to know where to go next . . . now it's written down on paper you feel more constrained.' This clear emphasis on assessment to inform teaching decisions was associated with the antipathy felt by many teachers towards National Curriculum assessment. Their essentially informal, holistic approach was contrasted with what was perceived to be the reductionist requirements of 'ticking boxes' associated with National Curriculum assessment. The latter was seen as making assumptions about the 'established' nature of knowledge, with which many teachers could not agree (see the discussion of assessment dimensions in section 3.5).

The *mode* of assessment most often mentioned was a mental record. Perhaps the most extreme representation of this approach was those teachers who were unable to describe their approach to assessment.

> I think we just take that for granted – I don't know that I've ever questioned that aspect of it.

> I'd have said [assessment shouldn't have] a very big role, mainly because you've got so many other things to cope with; assessment needs to be something that should come later.

Implicit in these responses concerning the three headings of frequency, purpose and mode is a continuum of practice. At one end are those teachers for whom assessment is almost entirely an unexplicated, almost unconscious, integral part of the process of decision-making on which their teaching is based. It is implicit in their work. At the other end of the continuum are those teachers who are increasingly explicitly making a conscious and active distinction between this constant intuitive evaluation and feedback relationship and the quite separate activity of recording evidence for later use in reporting and accountability.

Interviews with Year 2 teachers in 1991 produced a very similar picture to those conducted in 1990, when our cohort of target pupils was in Year 1. However, the same strong stress on holistic, intuitive, informal monitoring was increasingly contrasted with the formal, explicit, externally imposed, detached assessment which for them was associated with the National Curriculum. One other noticeable difference of emphasis was the addition of an *affective* element in the identification of assessment purposes. Several teachers mentioned the role of assessment as a source of encouragement for pupils as well as of guidance for themselves. For instance:

> Every time a child brings a piece of work up I do make sure that I read it, read it with them, or they read it to me and then if there's anything there that is to do with language, to do with spelling, to do with organization, I'll draw it out of them then and there. I mean, spellings hit me immediately, I notice them, straight away and if I can use something that's a howling mistake with all of the children, for instance the spelling of 'ou' sounds we were doing this week. So many were putting the spelling of 'ow' or whatever, then I'll draw that out for the whole class. But I suppose in time – I'm not sure – I don't often accept the piece of work as it is, I'll always try and make some constructive comment about that piece of work. Either 'Yes, that's lovely handwriting, that's very neat, you've really worked hard on that' or 'Can you see what mistake you've made with this?' So there is an assessment going on with every piece of work.

In teachers' minds there would appear to be a clear distinction between assessment that is quite explicitly carried out to promote the learner's confidence and motivation, by providing *reinforcement* and *enjoyment* for the child, and assessment for *diagnostic* purposes. Such diagnosis of progress made may be further divided into *general* curriculum evaluation, for example collecting up a list of words that the class *as a whole* is spelling wrongly and setting them as the spellings to be learnt for the week, and *individual* curriculum evaluation, which might lead to teaching of the specific words that a particular child was finding difficult.

Another difference noticeable in the 1991 responses was the growing feeling of assessment pressure reported by teachers as the combined effects of the children growing older and the increasing implementation of national assessment made themselves felt. This was well described by one teacher, who used a 'tick box'. This was a box into which the children put their work when they had finished it and/or at the end of the session. The teacher then checked the work later.

> I have a cursory glance at it, and if I've noted 'Oh dear that is wrong' then I will deal with that child. If it's right, then I give them a little praise and then it's on to the next task. If it's really good, I'll try and spend a minute (well it's not a minute, I would reckon it's about fifteen seconds if you actually timed it) of praise, but then it goes in the tick box. At one time I would read through every essay with the child, every story and make the discussions. I'd try and do that with each child once a week, you know, read through their story with them – correct punctuation, discuss punctuation, etc. – and now the work goes in the box and I have to look at it at home. Each night I take the box home and I assess what I see. Now I would have done that anyway with children, but *with* them, and discuss it with them . . . But I can't now because the tasks that I've set myself to do have taken time away from that. So the child hasn't got that reflective feedback on their work; I'm going to somehow try and do a reflective period where I gather all the files together and I actually look through them with them. I'm going to try and fit that in, I don't know when, but I'd like to try, so that we can get, perhaps once a week if I did three files, and we look through them and we could reflect that way on, you know, the past half-term's work.

Like many other respondents, this teacher was being forced to move from her preferred professional approach in which assessment involved constant monitoring coupled with immediate feedback to the child, to a situation in which she felt she had 'lost that sitting back and looking time'. She felt that assessment was now more time-consuming but less valuable because its emphasis – on the greater externalization of information – was different.

It was thus possible to identify a number of contrasting features in the assessment practices operated in the primary schools we studied – features that articulated with the constructed and established dimensions of knowledge and learning, which we first discussed in Chapter 3.

Of course, in one sense assessment is an integral part of the second-by-second process of teacher decision-making in classrooms. These decisions are informed by concerns such as the management of the classroom, discipline, keeping children's attention, intellectual extension and the need to encourage effort and motivation, and then filtered through each teachers' specific set of judgements about the current state of achievement for each child. There was some evidence that this detailed, intuitive assessment process, which largely occurred in the past without the aid of an explicit language of objectives, was being facilitated by the provision of the detailed learning targets embodied in the National Curriculum because of the provision of a language for thinking about and communicating such decisions. As one teacher put it,

> If they're doing specific activities as part of the National Curriculum work, if I've perhaps asked them, for example, to write a story about something to do some sequencing work

in story form, then I'd obviously be trying to assess whether they're achieving writing simple words on their own or whether they are beginning to write in sentences, or sequencing their story in a logical way, so I'm making those sorts of assessments as we go along, so that I know the kind of work to give them next and the kind of help they're going to need to move on to the next stage.

This comment is much more structured in terms of specific curriculum targets than most teachers' comments about their assessment. In fact, assessment was typically described in a rather general way; for example, correcting mistakes, completing the work set following instructions or demonstrating certain work-related social skills. However, it is worth emphasizing that the issue of *what* is assessed came across as much less important than the 'how' and 'why' of assessment in teachers' responses.

11.4 HOW DID TEACHERS RESPOND TO THE NEW CLASSROOM ASSESSMENT REQUIREMENTS?

The PACE study of the impact of national assessment began in mid-1990, when the first SATs for Key Stage 1 were about to be piloted and teachers were just beginning to implement assessment in relation to National Curriculum attainment targets. Interview data generated at this stage showed that many of the teachers' reactions were based on both their experience of the National Curriculum to date and their anticipation of the changes to come. When they were asked, 'How do you feel the needs of your pupils relate to the requirements of the National Curriculum?', teachers' spontaneous comments in 1990 included 24 per cent who felt the teacher assessment procedures were useful and relevant, against 76 per cent who felt that it was the assessment procedures in particular that were unrealistic and time-consuming.

In view of the contrast between the assessment requirements of the National Curriculum and the preferred approach to assessment that characterized our teachers, it is not surprising that changes in assessment and record keeping combined to produce a large source of changes in classroom practices. In 1992 these changes were mentioned by 44 per cent of teachers – as against the content of the curriculum, which was mentioned by 58 per cent. Although the physical constraints of the environment, the size of the class and pupil characteristics were identified as the major constraints on teaching approaches, in 1990 in the early stages in national assessment implementation, 22 per cent of teachers identified assessment as a source of constraint on their teaching approach, and this rose to 25 per cent in 1992.

Of the changes teachers had experienced, more record keeping had far and away the most significant impact, with 60 per cent of teachers remarking on the way it had changed their work. Meanwhile an increase in assessment (33 per cent) and changes in curriculum content (34 per cent) were perceived as broadly equal sources of change. However, by 1992, these feelings had changed to emphasize changes in teaching methods (45 per cent) and curriculum content (40 per cent) rather than assessment (18 per cent). The emphasis appeared to change with the implementation phases of the legislation and with the ebb and flow of public debate. More generally, although nearly 47 per cent of teachers were broadly positive about the changes they were making in their own classrooms in relation to the National Curriculum, 30 per cent disliked those associated with assessment.

Table 11.2 *Emphasis and recent changes felt by teachers concerning different types of assessment (row percentages)*

Type of assessment	Year	Do you use these forms of assessment?			Has your use of these forms of assessment changed recently?		
		Yes	A little	No	More	No change	Less
Standardized tests	1990	15	11	73	3	93	3
	1992	24	22	52	12	82	3
Marking written work	1990	61	30	8	8	92	0
	1992	91	7*	0	9	88	3
Pupil self-assessment	1990	32	28	39	14	86	0
	1992	44	28	27	15	77	8
Listening to children	1990	80	14	6	22	64	14
	1992	87	4	9	11	80	8
Discussion/ review	1990	82	11	7	27	71	3
	1992	74	13	12	11	85	4

Source: PACE 1 teacher interviews.
Sample: 88 teachers in each year.
Date: summer 1990 and summer 1992.

In an attempt to identify the precise nature of these changes, we asked teachers in our larger sample to describe the approaches to assessment that they typically used and any changes in this respect of which they were conscious. From Table 11.2 it appeared that in 1990, not surprisingly considering the age group, very few schools were using standardized tests. Marking of written work, by contrast, was frequently practised, particularly by 1992, with the emphasis on doing it *with* the child, often with some tick, 'smiley face' or message to provide personal reinforcement and encouragement. This collaborative approach was also in evidence in the use by 32 per cent of teachers in 1990 and 44 per cent in 1992 of some form of pupil self-assessment, which typically involved the children with the teacher or with each other discussing their work and assessing its quality. In a few cases the use of self-assessment was more formalized. One school, for example, had a school policy of children self-assessing their topic work and undertaking an annual self-assessment.

Listening to children was, not surprisingly, frequently practised, though the impact of the National Curriculum on this seems to have been variable. Some teachers in 1990 felt they had less time for this very important area than before, others that the obligation to formalize the assessment of children's listening and speaking had transformed listening and speaking from being simply an assessment vehicle into an assessment focus. In some cases this was felt to be good because it justified and systematized something that had always been done; in other cases teachers found such assessment very difficult and resented it.

Discussion and review were widely practised, both with individuals and with the class as a whole. One example involved children being invited to talk about their work to the class at the end of a topic. Another was for the children to plan daily activities with the teacher, set targets and review whether these had been achieved at the end of the day. Some respondents mentioned explicitly that standards had improved as a result of this approach.

In 1990 many teachers planned to implement more changes in the future, with 22 per cent mentioning in this respect such assessment procedures as developing the skills of listening to children more conscientiously. Changes in methods of recording achievement were anticipated by 17 per cent of teachers. Reference was also made to assessing more curriculum areas separately from each other than hitherto, to assessing personal and social dimensions and to cross-curricular assessment.

Some respondents felt that their teaching had changed in response to assessment requirements. Becoming clearer about teaching objectives was mentioned, as was the need to pose problems for children at different levels of achievement. There was some evidence of the impact of new assessment practices on relationships, with teachers giving more attention to talking with children and their parents. This was partly to help gather more information but was also associated with teachers using the assessment process to clarify learning goals with children, to provide reinforcement and encouragement and to set individual learning targets. A very formalized example of this was in relation to one LEA's primary language record, which required teachers to interview every child and their parents regularly so that a contract between teacher and parents could be drawn up and used as the basis for on-going comment by both. However, some teachers were unhappy with this kind of formalization, feeling that, as one teacher put it,

> Teachers get the feel of children and just know things. It's not always necessary to assess formally . . . it should be on-going without tests . . . just general . . . Teachers should be assessing and have always continually assessed to know what to do next and when to move into new work. It's the breaking down of subjects that makes a huge workload.

The tension between what can be seen both as encouragement to greater structure, discipline and accountability in assessment under the legislation and as its manifestation as undesirable, time-consuming, bureaucratic paper-pushing was quite marked. It was a tension that characterized many other aspects of the Education Reform Act's provision, since it reflected the changing balance of power between teachers and the Government. By far the most commonly perceived pressure, predictably, was that of time. For one respondent, assessment that used to take place at the end of a term or year had been replaced by regular assessments of different things for different groups throughout the year. Another found she had to set aside one week at the end of each half-term for assessment. Others mentioned the need to cut corners; for example, their attempts to formalize observation of particular tasks.

There was thus some evidence at the beginning of the project in 1990 of teachers beginning to use assessment creatively to support learning according to the diagnostic and formative purposes of the Government's Task Group on Assessment and Testing (TGAT) Report (DES, 1988). Teachers were stimulated to experiment with creative new approaches to assessment as it moved increasingly centre stage in professional development and as in-service training programmes were mounted by local education authorities. Such approaches were often characterized by collaborative approaches to assessment involving pupils and parents, and by the use of a wide range of techniques for gathering and storing evidence of attainment. At the same time, such developments did not appear to reflect widespread enthusiasm for change, set as they were against a background of essentially reluctant acquiescence and generally low morale.

11.5 HOW DID TEACHERS RESPOND TO RECORD KEEPING REQUIREMENTS?

Many of the changes in record keeping practice echoed those identified in relation to assessment techniques. The virtually unanimous view among teachers that record keeping had increased was variously explained by the need to develop and try out different methods and forms, the need for careful curriculum planning and evaluation to ensure full coverage of the appropriate attainment targets, and the extension of records to cover subjects, such as science, not hitherto the subject of records.

In 1990 the picture that emerged was of teachers spending a considerable amount of time devising and completing their own records or completing records imposed on them from outside, such as from their LEA. Much of this work was carried out in teachers' own time and against a background of anxiety or even panic about how to do it, guilt about not doing it well enough, cynicism about its potential value for pupils' learning and resentment about being made to feel inadequate. The words of one respondent ably summarized this feeling: 'All these changes make you feel that unless you're good at documentation in the National Curriculum, you can't be a very good teacher.'

Equally striking was the enormous variety of records being used. Subject records were mainly centred on science, maths and English, with more than one record being used for some subjects, such as an 'at a glance' record and a more detailed 'broken down' record in maths or an oracy, reading and general record in English. A number of respondents mentioned their use, or anticipated use, of 'profiles' and records of achievement, particularly in terms of keeping children's work for later review and discussion with them and their parents.

The theme of time recurred consistently in the responses:

> I could be doing it all the time.
> It stops you spending time teaching.
> 'You have to spend your own time dealing with it.
> We're making a big effort to keep it up.
> I feel guilty . . . I should do more but I've no more time.

The concern was undoubtedly exacerbated by a general lack of *confidence* among teachers that they were doing what would be required centrally in terms of recording or what would be demanded of them by parents, and by the lack of value they perceived the records to have.

> But staff are still not recording in enough detail to meet the requirements. We have a reading record book and individual records to take home, brief evaluation of individuals in the weekly planning book and each child has a pupil profile book.
>
> Well, if children learn the National Curriculum in terms of following improved attainment targets and the levels . . . if I'd been doing it I'd know exactly what they'd been doing but they don't. And no amount of writing it down like that will actually tell me.
>
> We always have assessed – now we're filling in tick sheets.

While the conduct of such assessments may have become easier with the passage of time and growing familiarity, this seems to have done nothing to reduce teachers' resentment and frustration at the amount of time they were having to spend on procedures for which

Table 11.3   *Changes in the amount of time spent on record keeping (percentages)*

Change	1990	1992
A lot	81.0	90.0
A little	8.0	7.0
No change	1.0	2.0
Expected to change	10.0	0.0

Source: PACE 1 teacher interviews.
Sample: 88 teachers in each year.
Date: summer 1990 and summer 1992.

Table 11.4   *Nature of changes in record keeping (percentages)*

	1990	1992
More written recording	99.0	98.0
Less written recording	0.0	0.0
More direct work with pupils	11.0	9.0
Less direct work with pupils	2.0	1.0
More work with colleagues	30.0	9.0
Positive feelings about assessment/record keeping	8.0	3.0
Negative feelings about assessment/record keeping	56.0	66.0
Mentions records of achievement	27.0	24.0
Other	20.0	0.0

Source: PACE 1 teacher interviews.
Sample: 88 teachers in each year.
Date: summer 1990 and summer 1992.

they did not see a value. As Table 11.3 sets out, in both 1990 and 1992 virtually all teachers reported a huge increase in the time spent on record keeping and a growing number reported negative feelings about assessment and record keeping. A further question elicited the nature of these changes (Table 11.4).

The key to understanding these feelings does not entirely appear to be concern about parental pressure or even worry about the direct effects of assessment on pupils. Although more than half the teachers interviewed in 1992 thought that the National Curriculum was exerting a negative influence on teacher–pupil relations – a figure almost double that of two years earlier – very few teachers (9 per cent) identified assessment directly as a factor in this respect. Equally, almost as many teachers identified an increased emphasis on partnership with parents as reported an increase in the requirement for assessment information.

Rather, the major source of teachers' resentment is hinted at by the response to a question that required teachers to identify their own strengths as a teacher. Whereas 61 per cent mentioned curriculum-related skills in this respect in 1992, only 2 per cent mentioned assessment. While many curriculum-related skills may in practice include many of the intuitive and individualized assessment decisions referred to above, it is clear that very few teachers regarded the overt and deliberate assessment that was required by the introduction of the National Curriculum as something that was part of their own professional competence.

Equally revealing in this respect were teachers' 1990 replies to an open-ended question ('What does professional responsibility mean for you as a teacher or head teacher?') that had been included in an initial postal questionnaire to all teachers in the sample. Although responsibility in relation to assessment and evaluation was mentioned spontaneously by a relatively small proportion of the sample (16 per cent) as compared to, for example, relationships with colleagues (47 per cent) and teaching approach (39 per cent), this represents a significant increase on the answers to a similar question, which was asked as part of the Bristaix project in 1985. In that study only 7 per cent of English primary school teachers included assessment as an explicit element in their conception of their professional responsibility.

So far, this chapter has addressed questions concerning teachers' responses to the new assessment and recording obligations that the Education Reform Act imposed. In summary, the picture that emerged over the three years of the project showed much greater emphasis on formal assessment and record keeping; some considerable resentment at the time demands and the perceived unnecessary formalization of much assessment work; fears about the potential impact of intrusive assessment and recording procedures on teaching–learning processes; and concerns about relationships with parents and the pupils themselves. At the same time there was some evidence of the beginning of a more positive phase of development in the use of assessment, as teachers' growing confidence and knowledge allowed them to mediate external requirements towards more professionally acceptable ends.

11.6 WHAT DID PUPILS UNDERSTAND ABOUT ASSESSMENT?

To explore only from the teacher's point of view the significance of the momentous changes that have been taking place in infant classrooms would be to miss the opportunity to explore the even more important question of the impact of such developments on pupils. How infant teachers' preferred intuitive approach to assessment affected pupils' learning, and the significance of increasingly explicit assessment and reporting procedures in this respect, are questions that are of central importance in any attempt to research the significance of the 1988 Education Reform Act.

Unfortunately, however, whereas a considerable body of research exists concerning the apparent impact of different pedagogic and curriculum strategies in primary classrooms, there is a lack of equivalent base-line research in relation to assessment. We simply do not know how different assessment practices impact on children's learning in primary classrooms. Moreover, we lack a conceptual framework that would help to identify the key variables with which to address this issue. Thus, before we turn to an examination of the possible effects of National Curriculum assessment it is appropriate to examine in a little more detail what our data had to say about pupils' awareness of, and reaction to, assessment.

Given that, as we have seen, classroom assessment in primary schools has rarely been explicit, it was not possible to enquire directly of such young pupils in a meaningful way. Rather we asked a series of more indirect questions of the 54 pupils whom we observed as part of our detailed classroom studies in 1990 and again in 1991. These questions were designed to address the more tangible sources of pleasure or anxiety of which a pupil might be aware in relation to assessment interactions such as 'Do you like it when your teacher asks to look at your book?' The result of this question is shown in Table 11.5.

Table 11.5 *Responses of pupils to the question 'do you like it when your teacher asks to look at your book?'* (*percentages*)

	Positive	Negative	Mixed	Neutral
Year 1	57.4	22.2	14.8	5.6
Year 2	51.9	20.4	20.4	7.4

Source: PACE 1 child interviews.
Sample: 9 Year 1 and 9 Year 2 classes.
Date: autumn 1990 and autumn 1991.

In both 1990 and 1992, over half the children gave positive answers to the question. Among the main reasons children gave for feeling 'good' were so that they could go on to something else, because they got a reward – a smiley face or a sticker – or because they felt pride and satisfaction. As some of them put it,

I feel good because I can get it over with and go on to something else.

It's good because I've done good work and she's pleased with me and I get a sticker like this.

I feel OK – proud of myself.

Because I can find out if I've done it right.

Yes, 'cos she might mark all of them right. When she ticks them, I feel like doing three more pages.

The main negative reasons given were not wanting to do the task again or fears of being told off or not being praised:

Because I'll never be super.

I doesn't want the teacher to look at it.

In case I have to do it again.

I worry in case it's wrong.

The mixed responses expressed sentiments such as 'I like the teacher to look at my work if it's good but not if it's bad.' Significantly, these pupils appeared unable to predict what the outcome was likely to be on any given occasion. Thus their responses combined both pleasure at having the teacher's attention and anxiety because the work might be wrong. Most children clearly liked, and actively sought, teacher praise. Indeed, they seemed to depend on it to regulate their own pace of learning and appeared to have little capacity to judge this for themselves. There thus appeared to be a tension for many pupils between wanting attention in order to receive praise and to get the necessary curriculum guidance, and wanting to avoid possible censure for not following instructions or having to repeat tasks:

Sometimes, because sometimes I rush a bit and sometimes I take my time. I like it when I've done it really neat and tidy and keep within the lines.

Quite happy because sometimes she sends us to other teachers and they give us smiley faces and stars.

Sometimes I do and sometimes I don't . . . Because it's not very good sometimes, but sometimes it's quite good . . . When it's good, I feel quite nice and when it's not good I feel sad. I don't want to get shouted at.

Yes, when I done it wrong, I feel upset and when I done it right, I feel happy.

There was no apparent difference between the schools studied in this respect or between boys and girls.

When asked, 'Does it matter if you don't do things the way your teacher wants them?', the children responded in two different ways. Some cited educational reasons why it mattered, such as 'Otherwise you won't learn anything'. Others cited extrinsic reasons, such as the need to avoid getting told off! However, in both years, 70 per cent of children recognized the need to follow the teacher's requirements and instructions. The majority cited educational reasons for this: 'Yes, it matters – she tells instructions. If you don't follow you don't learn.' A significant number referred to potential teacher disapproval: 'Yes, otherwise you get told off.' The reaction of this group to the question thus depended somewhat on whether they thought the teacher would be cross – perhaps because they had been messing about – or would understand and be tolerant of mistakes:

> Yes. If you do it wrong, you have to start all over again and it wastes time and we get told off.
>
> No, she rubs it out and she says, 'I know you listened quite well, but you got it wrong.' Once the whole class got it wrong.

From the previous discussion of teachers' attitudes to assessment, we may deduce that the ways in which teachers react to individual pupils in these circumstances would have been governed by their assessment of what was likely to be most constructive and appropriate in leading to better work from each individual pupil.

A few children responded to the question in a way that reflected very clear views of themselves as learners, and their relationship with the teacher as one in which they accepted their teacher's power unconditionally. For example:

> I haven't tried it [not doing things the way the teacher wants them] so I don't know what it's like.
>
> I always do it right.

In summary, it appeared that children perceived the assessment interaction of the classroom in terms of three main issues:

- task management – knowing what to do and/or not being found out if the task was incorrectly done;
- affect – pleasure at receiving praise and pain at being told off;
- intellectual – being told what educational tasks to engage in next.

This analysis of children's understanding of assessment purposes is in line with the analysis of Mavrommatis (1993) concerning assessment in Greek primary classrooms, in which he identifies *teachers'* use of assessment as spanning three main dimensions: the psychological (affect), the intellectual (cognitive guidance) and the managerial (behaviour).

Interestingly, children's understanding of these various facets of assessment were also reflected in their interpretation of why some children do better than others. The children were asked: 'Why do some children do better at school work than others?' Their answers were coded and analysed and, as Table 11.6 shows, there was a considerable imbalance in the reasons given for some children doing better than others at school work!

Examples of the kind of response given for each category are:

Table 11.6 *Responses of pupils to the question 'why do some children do better at school work than others?' (percentages)*

Reasons given	
Age	12.7
Effort	45.1
Ability	18.6
Skill	13.7
Don't know	9.8

Source: PACE 1 child interviews.
Sample: 54 children in Year 1 and in Year 2.
Date: autumn 1990 and autumn 1991.

Age:	Because they're younger.
	They have been there longer.
Effort:	They don't mess about.
	Because they get on with their work and don't mess about or nothing.
	They don't say 'Miss, Miss', they just get on.
	They just try harder.
Ability:	Because they think in their minds.
	Because they've got more clever brains.
Skill:	'Cos they do gooder pictures than the others.
	Some just do round circles for eyes and nose and half a square for body.
	Tidiness 'cos they can do it neater.
	Some do big writing and some do nice writing.

It seemed from their responses that many children had begun to develop a perception of teachers' assessment criteria. Pupils were particularly aware of the importance of 'effort', with no fewer than 45 per cent mentioning its importance.

These responses echoed the teachers' evaluative criteria that Pollard (1985) identified in terms of three broad domains of 'productivity', 'behaviour' and 'individual responsibility'. Relating to productivity and efficiency at school work the evaluative criteria he identified were:

Effort:	Let's make a really big effort today.
Perseverance:	Try a bit longer.
Neatness:	That's a nice page.
Regularity:	Is that your best work?
Speed:	Has anyone finished yet?

Relating to behaviour and social relationships were:

Self-control:	Stop being silly.
Obedience:	Did you hear what I said?
Politeness:	That's not a very nice thing to do.
Quietness:	Silence now.
Truth:	Let's have it straight now.
Respect for authority:	Hands up if you want something.

Relating to individualism and competitiveness were:

Achievement: Have you got that right?
Individualism: Do it yourself.
Hierarchy: Who got ten out of ten?
Self-reliance: Go and find out.

It may be significant that, in talking about reasons for achievement, some children mentioned actual learning *behaviour* while others referred to circumstantial characteristics over which pupils have no control, such as age, language and gender. While it is not possible to make a great deal of this distinction at the present time, it is possible that these explanations were linked to individual pupil's learning attributions and thus could be significant in influencing their future learning. In future stages of the PACE study we shall be able to pursue this further.

A third aspect of assessment activity that we explored with the children concerned their attitude to rewards. When they were asked, 'What happens if someone does their work really well?', pupils' responses were coded to produce the analysis shown in Table 11.7. Not surprisingly, the most explicit rewards for good work, such as praise and symbolic rewards, were the ones most likely to be remarked upon by the children. However, it was interesting that boys were more likely to stress symbolic rewards, such as ticks, stars and smiley faces, than girls and that girls were more aware of praise.

Table 11.7 *Responses of pupils to the question 'what happens when someone does their work really well?'* *(percentages)*

	1990		1991		Overall
	Boys	Girls	Boys	Girls	
Praise	28.6	25.0	21.4	50.0	31.2
Symbolic reward	50.0	32.2	60.8	35.8	44.7
Material reward	7.2	10.8	7.2	10.8	9.0
Choice	10.8	10.8	3.6	7.2	8.1
Nothing	0.0	3.6	0.0	0.0	0.9
Don't know	8.6	8.6	3.6	3.6	6.1

Source: PACE 1 child interviews.
Sample: 54 children in Year 1 and in Year 2.
Date: autumn 1990 and autumn 1991.

Certainly relevant to this question is the bitter envy expressed by some of the children in discussing teachers' rewards. It provides clear testimony to the potentially negative, as well as the positive, affective impact of assessment, even when it is not directly addressed to a particular child:

I feel like *I* want to do it – I feel like taking their work away from them.

I get angry 'cos I want a star too.

You feel jealous.

You show it to the class. I get jealous; they stand up and get clapped sometimes.

She shows us it and she goes 'look at this work – it's wonderful'.

While our evidence is too scanty at present to support any firm conclusions in this respect, it does suggest that the more explicit the assessment procedures used, the more differentiation between pupils will be made explicit. This is likely to affect pupils' motivation and self-esteem.

11.7 HOW DID THE CLASSROOM ASSESSMENT REQUIREMENTS OF THE EDUCATION REFORM ACT IMPACT ON PUPILS?

Our data suggest that the advent of National Curriculum assessment, with its emphasis on explicit learning targets and overt assessment criteria, is transforming the assessment culture and its associated language. Although the children themselves are too young for it to be possible yet to make any such comparison from their point of view, some testimony to this is provided by interviews with teachers in our classroom study schools. Asked if they thought the National Curriculum and its assessment were raising children's awareness of differences in achievement, most teachers thought that children, even at the infant school, had always been aware of differences in their levels of achievement. However, teachers felt that young children were unconcerned about such differences because they were not aware of their meaning and significance in the way that older children would be. Although there was some feeling among teachers that SATs, in particular, would make even infants more aware in this respect, teachers largely felt they could protect children from such pressure through praise for efforts made and by recognizing alternative achievements. The majority of the teachers questioned did not feel that National Curriculum assessment had yet significantly changed the classroom climate. However, most teachers felt that the constraints of reporting children's achieve-ment in the controlled format of the new requirements would prevent them from showing a genuinely individual and hence diagnostic picture of a child's different achievements. Only one teacher described the benefits of having a clearer structure on which to base curriculum coverage, diagnosis and progression.

Asked about their strategies for minimizing such effects, teachers mentioned the use of praise for alternative achievements, planning the curriculum to embrace children's particular perceived talents, adjusting tasks to facilitate pupil success and explaining differences in attainment by giving non-threatening reasons, such as age. The use of these strategies was reflected in the pupils' explanations discussed earlier. One teacher mentioned grouping by 'ability' so that the differences were not obvious – at least within the groups. However, it is significant that teachers did not always find it easy to articulate their strategies in this respect. For some, their responses to individual pupils appeared to be part of more intuitive behaviour in which assessment activity was implicit.

Although it is too early in our longitudinal study to characterize the impact of new assessment procedures on pupils, the above data do enable us to be a little clearer about the key dimensions of assessment activity in primary classrooms. Assessment activity may usefully be regarded as a form of language that allows for the communication of evaluative messages between teacher and pupil. It thus contributes to a given classroom's culture, in which particular symbolic forms are imbued with evaluative meaning for those interacting within it. We may hypothesize that pupils' capacity first to *understand* the way in which such cultures operate and subsequently to learn to *operate* successfully within it is likely to influence their future success as pupils (Filer, 1994).

11.8   CONCLUSION

In this chapter we have suggested that, in the infant classroom prior to the 1988 Education Reform Act, the particular value system informing teachers' evaluations of pupils and their work was likely to have been unclear both to the teacher herself and to her pupils. For many teachers this value system was typically bound up with their more general professional ideology about the task of teaching and about how children learn.

As far as assessment is concerned, we have seen that this ideology was structured in terms of teachers' understanding of the *mode*, *purpose* and *frequency* of assessment. For teachers who could be described as having constructivist views of knowledge and learning, such understanding has been characterized as an approach to assessment that was intuitive and continuous with the central purpose of providing instructional feedback and encouragement. The requirement to make a major change in this understanding, which the Education Reform Act has brought, involved teachers developing their assessment repertoire considerably. As well as the diagnostic and formative assessment activity in which they had always engaged, teachers were now required to undertake summative and evaluative assessment, which emphasized the explicit categorization of pupils' achievement.

The dislike of many teachers for this requirement was not simply because it meant an increase in their workload or required skills that they did not feel they had. Rather their resistance was rooted in an objection to the use of the coercive power of the law to impose on teachers the obligation to operationalize a different set of understandings concerning the role of assessment in primary schooling. This conflict of understanding in turn reflected a fundamental challenge to the values typically held by primary school teachers concerning how children can best be helped to learn, and the particular role of assessment in this respect (see the discussion of dimensions in section 3.5).

We have suggested in this chapter that before the advent of national assessment requirements, assessment was typically not a separate domain of activity but part of a broad web of professional strategies. We have described how these strategies are constantly being manipulated by teachers in the light of their on-going judgements about appropriate interventions to meet the intellectual, emotional or behavioural needs either of individual pupils or of the class as a whole. As teachers have begun to respond, in various ways, to the challenge of formalizing the assessment process, it is becoming clear that a more refined model of the relationship between educational ideology and teachers' assessment practice is needed.

Of particular interest here is the model of MacCallum *et al.* (1993), which identifies three distinct types of teacher approach to assessment within the National Curriculum. MacCallum *et al.* contrast 'critical intuitives' whose child-centred approach leads them to concentrate on the 'whole child' in their assessment; the 'evidence gatherers' for whom assessment is largely a periodic, summative activity to provide an evidential record of judgements made; and the 'systematic planners', more or less overt in their approach to assessment, who deconstruct the issue of achievement from any interpretive context.

The spectrum of increasingly deliberate and explicit data-gathering and interpretation on the part of teachers as identified by MacCallum *et al.* accords with the findings reported in this chapter concerning the salience of timing, purpose and mode as defining variables in assessment practice (see Table 11.1). Perhaps more difficult to represent are the differences in understanding concerning how children learn and the nature of knowledge. Such conceptions incorporate a complex mixture of more or less clearly thought-through views concerning how pedagogy, classroom organization, curriculum materials and, not least, assessment should be arranged to facilitate learning. At one extreme is what we introduced in Chapter 2 as the 'elementary' ideological tradition in primary education, with its conception of education as the initiation of children into a corpus of established knowledge. This ideology is readily associated with both didactic pedagogy and the carrot and stick approach to assessment, with its emphasis on competition and sanctions. At the other extreme is the developmental ideological tradition, with its conception of education as the provision of a curriculum ladder individual to each child. Teacher intervention is designed to support learners in constructing progressively higher levels of knowledge and understanding.

Most teachers' ideology is likely to be a mixture of these different elements, and their practice will be informed by a mixture of pragmatism and habit as well as educational philosophy. By the same token, assessment practice is likely to reflect a similar mixture of influences. The value of such models is thus not to provide for the 'mapping' of individual practice but rather to reinforce the importance of the relationship between teachers' views and practice of assessment and their more general professional understanding. It is only with such an appreciation that the true significance of the conflict between the Government and teachers, to which the imposition of national assessment has led, can fully be understood. In terms of each of our analytic themes of power, values and understanding, the challenge of national assessment could hardly be more fundamental.

In this chapter and the next, we describe the ways in which teachers are adjusting to these requirements and incorporating them into both their ideologies and their practices. In reporting these changes the most significant question in terms of the overall purpose of the PACE study must be the extent to which teachers were finding it possible to integrate national assessment requirements within their professional practice. Did this reflect a change in their educational values and understandings? Or did it reflect a change in the values and understandings implicit in national assessment itself, as these were originally conceived, in the process of its realization in the classroom? On the answer to this question will rest not only the outcomes we may predict from the imposition of national assessment *per se*. Given that the assessment requirements of the Education Reform Act arguably represent the most explicit expression of the ideology on which it is based and the most powerful mechanism for imposing this ideology on schools and teachers, the fate of the whole reform initiative is likely to depend on the way in which national assessment comes to be realized in practice. It is at the apex of the power struggle between the Government and the teaching profession.

At present there is little to suggest that there has been any significant change in the values informing the classroom assessment culture since the Education Reform Act. We must anticipate, however, that the pressures of the educational market, in which assessment information is the currency, may well bring about changes such as an increased emphasis on achievements that can be formally demonstrated and recorded and an associated increase in the emphasis given to competition.

With this in mind we turn to the final element in our research, which has been, and remains, one of the most controversial of all the provisions of the 1988 Education Reform Act.

Chapter 12

The Challenge of Standardized Assessment

12.1 INTRODUCTION

As the preceding chapters of this book have shown, the changing balance of power between the various stakeholders in education is associated with very different understandings among these groups concerning the definition of educational quality and the most effective ways of achieving it. We have described how the changes we have studied are rooted in a very different set of social and educational values from those which have formed the basis for professional practice in English primary schools in recent decades.

Thus our analysis of both how teachers *felt* about the changes they were experiencing and the scale and character of the changes that were actually being realized in classroom practice is permeated by our three central analytic themes of power, values and understanding. Within these broad themes the various dimensions of change, which were identified in Chapter 3, typically centre on long-standing debates concerning educational priorities, and philosophies and the manifestation of these in different approaches to pedagogy, curriculum and school organization.

However, one of the power struggles in education of the early 1990s was particularly active. Whereas most other aspects of primary school provision had been subject to sustained and detailed scrutiny on the part of researchers, teachers and trainers, so that a very considerable range of literature existed to inform the debate about priorities and practice, the imposition of national assessment as part of the 1988 Act's requirements was much more than a change *within* existing practice. In requiring teachers to implement externally derived tests, and in imposing on them externally determined requirements for recording and reporting children's progress and achievement, standardized national assessment represented what was arguably the most novel, the most coercive and the most difficult part of the 1988 Act's provisions to implement.

Whereas, as we saw in Chapter 11, 'assessment' for primary teachers and their pupils had typically meant the informal, continuous and often intuitive process of monitoring pupils' performance and making interpretations on which to base subsequent teaching activity, national assessment procedures required them to formalize this process into one based on the explicit collection and labelling of evidence, on explicit acts of assessment and on categoric reporting of children's achievements in terms of a national scale. It is in relation to this dimension of change – from implicit and provisional assessment to explicit and categoric assessment – that the central arguments of our study are most clearly demonstrated. We found that teachers sought various ways to 'protect' their pupils where the provisions of the Act were in conflict with their professional judgement. Indeed, we found that in trying to fulfil the new obligations being placed upon them, teachers coped with an almost overwhelming burden of work, and that many of the assumptions inherent in the Act's provisions were misconceived or impractical because they were not grounded in existing practice and classroom constraints. Perhaps most important of all, we found that the ideology of dedication to children, of the commitment to doing their best for every child socially and emotionally as well as academically, which was the defining characteristic of the teachers in our study, provided the foundation for a professionalism that was not easily commanded or changed. Thus the formal assessment and reporting requirements of the Education Reform Act, which culminated in the publication of league tables of relative school performance, represented the biggest single challenge to the understanding, values and the professional power of English primary school teachers. Their boycott of the reporting of the 1993 Key Stage 1 SATs was a rare example of collective and sustained teacher resistance to the Act's provisions. As such it was the clearest possible demonstration that the formal standardized assessment required by the Government provided a focus for the issues that were at stake for primary schools in this reform.

In what follows, we first explore the reasons behind this conflict and document the ways in which teachers responded to standardized assessment requirements during the 1991 and 1992 testing rounds. Second, by means of observational data and the results of pupil interviews, we examine the impact and significance of such requirements.

These findings are based on visits to nine schools for two days during the administration of SATs in 1991 and again in 1992, together with questionnaire findings from our larger sample of 48 schools gathered at the end of the relevant summer term in each of the two years. Further data concerning the impact of the SATs were provided by means of interviews with the teachers observed and a sample of the children in each of their classrooms. Readers should note that, for this part of our study, the pupil groups studied in 1991 and 1992 were both Year 2 pupils (see Chapter 4 for further details). In what follows it will be apparent that, although there were some significant changes between 1991 and 1992, at the more fundamental level the issues remained essentially the same.

12.2 HOW MANAGEABLE DID TEACHERS FIND THE SATs?

The 1990 pilot

The first experience of SATs was the pilot conducted by three different development consortia in summer 1990. In this study a 2 per cent sample of children was used, drawn from a sample of schools across the country. It soon became apparent that the developers had grossly overestimated the amount of testing they could reasonably expect teachers to carry out. While the teachers were rushed off their feet and worked extraordinary hours, children who were not carrying out assessment tasks tended to be given occupational work. A vivid impression of the effects was provided by Torrance (1991) in an article drawn from letters sent to him by teachers who had been involved in the pilot. Among the things the teachers reported were the following:

> It was an onslaught of new activity after new activity . . . eventually we were just 'getting through'.

> [The children] could not understand it when they were left to get on with all these strange new tasks, sometimes as many as four a day, without the usual support and explanation.

Other respondents cited children's behaviour and work deteriorating through lack of teacher attention:

> Conducting SATs goes against everything else that happens in school and is as far removed from good primary practice as it is possible to get. We are constantly helping and encouraging children. . . . Then suddenly for half a term all this changes. They have a problem and we can't help them.

The anger and concerns embodied in these statements reflected what were proven to be enduring concerns among teachers in subsequent years about the effects of the testing on children, and the fact that teachers felt required to act in ways they regarded as unprofessional, damaging and in conflict with their personal commitments and beliefs.

National testing at Key Stage 1

The 1990 pilot SATs were followed by full-scale testing of all children in 1991. A great deal has been written about both teachers' experiences with these SATs (DES, 1991b, 1992; Shorrocks *et al.*, 1992) and the results of children in relation to the tasks (SEAC, 1991b, c; DES, 1991c). As a result of these findings some aspects of the SAT tasks and conditions were altered for the 1992 Key Stage 1 testing programme.

The 1991 *Handbook of Guidance* for SATs issued by SEAC suggested that 'the SAT is designed to be used by a single teacher with the resources normally available in schools' (SEAC, 1991a, p. 12). Most SATs were indeed based on activities frequently seen in infant classrooms and the resources needed were usually easily available. The great exception was time. Although SATs had been widely piloted, most teachers found that the tasks took far longer than the estimates in the *Handbook*. To give individual children and small groups the close attention needed for careful assessment, much extra support and help were needed, and unaided teachers usually found it very difficult to manage both the SAT group and the rest of the class. Virtually all the teachers we questioned reported that in 1991 the SATs caused major disruption to normal classroom practice, preventing the pursuit of normal Year 2 activities. At least half the 1991 sample felt that SATs were unmanageable.

In 1992, as Tables 12.1 and 12.2 show, the SATs were generally found to be a great deal more manageable, with the majority of teachers appreciating the combination of a smaller number of tasks to be undertaken combined with the much longer period allowed to complete them. However, SATs remained disruptive to normal classroom practice.

In 1991 the average time required for SATs was estimated at between 82 and 90 hours for planning, collecting resources, doing the assessments, marking and recording the results. Carrying out the assessments took on average 52 hours, rather than the 30 envisaged by SEAC (NUT, 1991). In some cases teachers reported that the SATs took up five weeks of three-quarters of the timetable (NPC-SW, 1991), rather than the three weeks of half a timetable envisaged by SEAC. In addition, work for the rest of the class had to be prepared and planned as usual in consultation with support staff, and many class teachers felt it necessary to go through children's work in their absence. The extra workload was coupled with the additional exhaustion reported by teachers, resulting from working intensively with small groups, constantly probing, questioning and spurring the children to their greatest efforts, as well as recording. Overall it proved to be extremely exhausting for teachers.

Table 12.1   *Manageability of teacher assessment and SATs (percentages)*

	1991	1992
Teacher assessment		
Very manageable	16.0	6.0
Fairly manageable	59.0	85.0
Not at all manageable	24.0	8.0
SATs		
Very manageable	3.0	16.0
Fairly manageable	48.0	73.0
Not at all manageable	49.0	11.0
	$n = 67$	$n = 47$

Source: PACE 1 SAT teacher questionnaires.
Sample: 48 schools in 8 LEAs.
Date: summer 1991 and summer 1992.

Table 12.2   *Degree of disruption to classroom practice when undertaking SATs (percentages)*

	1991	1992
Teacher assessment		
No disruption at all	27.0	35.0
Some minimal disruption	55.0	44.0
A fair amount of disruption	18.0	21.0
SATs		
No disruption at all	2.0	2.0
Some minimal disruption	12.0	33.0
A fair amount of disruption	86.0	65.0
	$n = 67$	$n = 47$

Source: PACE 1 SAT teacher questionnaires.
Sample: 48 schools in 8 LEAs.
Date: summer 1991 and summer 1992.

Significance of school support

The degree of manageability and overall teacher stress experienced by individual teachers in both the years in question is in part at least a reflection of the degree of support received from the rest of the school by the teacher undertaking SATs.

In both 1991 and 1992 all Year 2 teachers in the PACE survey were involved in carrying out the SATs themselves, with just under half in both years being helped by the headteacher or another colleague undertaking some of the assessment. Most of the Year 2 classrooms, when studied, had SATs taking place in them (88 per cent in 1991; 83 per cent in 1992), though most schools were also able to use a separate place, such as a library or staffroom. Only 19 per cent of teachers in 1991 and 16 per cent of teachers in 1992 had no other help in the classroom while the SATs were taking place. The vast majority of classrooms had the support of a supply teacher, a classroom assistant, a student, a parent or a colleague helping with the other children in the class, so that in most cases the class was able to carry on with at least some of the normal programme of work. However, in 1991 in particular, nearly half the classes, according to their teachers, also did relatively mundane 'holding activities' specially assigned for the SAT period.

These support arrangements were often in themselves a source of anxiety. Year 2 teachers were uncomfortably aware of the effect their needs were having on the rest of the school. In one rural school a teaching headteacher gave up all of her own non-contact time to release the Year 2 teacher. Elsewhere, all the other teachers gave up their ancillary help. They willingly cooperated but the knock-on effect was marked, and some headteachers wondered how they would possibly manage if no major changes were made when Key Stage 2 assessment began. Where, more rarely, support teaching was expensively bought in, this raised questions in the minds of teachers about the use of scarce resources, and the tendency for teachers to see the SATs as a waste of time exacerbated their frustration.

It became apparent that the availability or otherwise of classroom support during the SAT tests had a marked effect on children's ability to perform well in the tasks. The salience of this issue varied with the nature of the task. For example, children engaged in making a game (Maths 1, Part B, 1991) were able to spend some time without close supervision while drawing and colouring their games. However, exploring floating and sinking (Science 1, Part B), which became a notorious example of unmanageability in the 1991 SATs, made heavy and virtually constant demands on the teacher's time and attention. This was quite possible when the SAT was carried out in a separate room or when the rest of the class was otherwise supervised, but it was extremely difficult for teachers who had to supervise the SAT and the rest of the class at the same time.

There is a strong likelihood of children's performance being affected by such very considerable variations in circumstance. Indeed, although the conduct of SATs in the classroom surrounded by other children doing normal tasks had the benefit of normalcy, our field notes showed a clear relationship between pupil attentiveness and the location where the SATs took place. The possibility of interference from other children appeared to reduce SAT children's concentration and hence performance.

Teachers' sense of stress was, in many cases, exacerbated by their awareness of not being able to provide appropriately for all the children in the class while working with those involved in the SAT. Teachers' worries in this respect were evident whether they had vertically or horizontally grouped classes. Those with a single year group in their class were weighed down by the sheer number of children who had to be assessed but those with a mixed-age class constantly worried about whether the non-SAT children were being neglected, in spite of their best efforts to avoid this.

Constraints on nominal classroom practice

Although it had been claimed that the SAT activities could be woven into a teacher's planned curriculum, providing learning experiences in themselves, this contradicted the requirements that teachers must avoid giving children direct help and 'asking questions that lead the child to the correct response'. Teachers found this an unnatural way of working and felt that the children could not understand the change in their practice. As one teacher remarked, 'I really find it so frustrating being unable to help them when they don't understand.' At another school the teacher had to rebuke two children, Mark and Tracy, who had begun to discuss their work: 'Mark, Tracy, if I have to tell you not to talk again, I may get angry.' This strange departure from normal classroom practice produced in the children a puzzled and slightly hurt reaction.

Teachers disliked having to change the practices which the children expected. Thus, another teacher was heard to say: 'No, go away Paul. I don't want you to see this.' Later she commented: 'He looked at me as if I'd gone mad.' Torrance (1991) reported that in consequence teachers often felt deskilled because pre-specified tasks and the observation of pre-specified outcomes were fundamentally against the commitment to responsiveness to pupil needs that has underpinned work in infant classrooms.

In many cases the reading SATs were particularly noticeable in this respect. Even if the SAT was presented as a 'normal' reading task, the odd circumstances, namely reading a special book to a teacher in a special room, alone, the teacher refusing to help when a child got stuck, no discussion between teacher and child, made it likely that the children would sense that this was an extraordinary situation, even if they did not know that it was a test.

Nevertheless, as we shall see, such was the combination of teacher effort and the limited awareness of these young children that many children were unaware of the extent of testing.

12.3 HOW STANDARDIZED WERE THE SATs THEMSELVES?

Issues concerning the manageability of SATs were closely related to the reliability and validity of the information they generated, since variability in the organization in which SATs took place meant that children were given different contexts in which to show their level of achievement. These factors alone would be sufficient to challenge the assumption contained in the official 1991 SAT *Handbook of Guidance* that 'because all other teachers of Year 2 children will be using the same SAT the results will be more standardized than your own continuous assessments' (SEAC, 1991a, p. 4).

In addition to these variations, our data identified a range of sources of variability within the operation of the tasks themselves, many of which were the result of differences in classroom circumstances or of teachers' strategies to minimize pupils' anxiety or awareness of failure. These are also likely to have affected children's ability to demonstrate their achievement. We consider the following below:

- variations in the testing situation;
- providing support and making judgements;
- reducing children's awareness of assessment;
- the effect of pupil anxiety;
- lack of clarity in assessment criteria;
- deciding which level to award;
- the influence of other pupils.

As a preliminary to our discussion, we offer, in Table 12.3, a summary of the very different assessment conditions that we noted while the same SAT was carried out in three schools.

Table 12.3   *Standardized assessment: a comparison of conditions*

Variables	Meadway	Greenside	Valley
SAT location and physical conditions	Corner of classroom. Ample space, sink, water.	Corner of classroom, Crowed, cramped, no water, no sink.	Separate room, ample space, water, sinks, etc.
Number of SAT/ non-SAT children	20/0	11/15	13/9
Support in classroom	None while observed	Ancillary takes rest of class	Head takes whole class one day each week, pays for extra supply cover, enabling SAT groups to be removed from class
Effect of support for Year 2 teacher on rest of school	None	Other classes lose most of usual ancillary support	Teaching head loses usual non-contact day each week: all admin in own time. Usual parent volunteer removed from SAT class after complaint from other parent
Non-SAT children	Usual work: teacher tries to cope during SAT	Work planned with ancillary: discussed each day	Work prepared by class teacher, carried out in her absence

Variations in the testing situation

One obvious source of potential variation concerns the person who conducts the tests, since children are likely to be more at ease with someone they know. The stage of SAT administration was also significant, in that teachers were variously tense, confident and relaxed, or bored, depending on how many times they had administered the SAT. However, perhaps the most significant issue in this respect was whether or not the teacher made the reality of testing explicit to the children and what consequences this decision may have had. In some cases the SAT was presented as a game, in others as a learning activity, and in a few as a test. In many classrooms, if an observer had not known what was going on he or she would not have realized that some children were involved in an assessment activity.

In one classroom in 1992 the teacher was so concerned about the impact of the Maths 3 SAT in particular, involving the pressure of both timing and categoric, right or wrong answers, that she was prepared to undertake testing the children on a one-to-one basis in a class of 30 even though this caused major administrative problems. It is an illustration of the strength of the teacher's commitment to protect the children from anxiety and from a feeling of failure that she was prepared to engage in such a lengthy period of testing, in which there was relatively little teaching for the rest of the class.

It was particularly noticeable in the more explicit testing materials of 1992 that the categoric nature of some of the SATs, notably the maths test, produced a greater tension and anxiety in the children and a greater awareness of failure, which some teachers took great pains to counteract by a variety of subterfuges. On almost all occasions when such SATs were observed, activities were presented as 'fun' or as part of normal classroom life, which both observation and later interviews with children suggested were accepted as such.

Teachers' strategies for avoiding stress in children included making no overt reference to, or demonstration of, assessment in their presence. Children were not usually dismissed from a group if they were clearly finding the task too difficult but were allowed to continue with teacher assistance, which meant that they would not be considered to have reached the level on which they worked.

Sometimes they were told that they had worked extremely well but that they looked tired and 'could leave this work for now'. One teacher even wondered whether her children's relaxed attitude to the SATs was conducive to their producing the best work of which they were capable, or whether some awareness of being tested might have lent an edge to their performance. The rather unorthodox implementation of the Maths 3 SATs in one school in 1992 bears out this argument to some extent. The teacher said: 'We're going to start off nice and easy so Ben won't get his worried face, and Amy won't get her frown' (funny expressions on the teacher's face). 'To help you, you'll have these sheets.' He read out: '4 + 2 Ugh! (pulled a face, encouraging the children to 'have a go') 2 + 3 Ugh!' The teacher said:

> They're very easy. As soon as you've finished, turn over your paper and take out your puzzle book. You won't need to look at anyone else's because they're *so* easy. Don't worry if you get left behind. It's only a bit of fun and we'll have another competition later. So, remember the rules: no looking at anyone else's, no showing anyone else. When you've finished I'll come round and give team points.

After conducting the SAT, the teacher concluded with: 'I think I made that too easy. I'm going to have to give out lots of house points. If you like that puzzle, shall we try that again on Monday with some harder sums?' Children: 'Yes, yes.'

While this teacher successfully presented the Maths 3 SAT as a game or competition, which the children appeared to enjoy, the other Year 2 teacher in the same school took a different approach. She carried out the same SAT in a straightforward way, more like a 'mental arithmetic' test. She commented that the children tightened up a lot, sat back in their seats, drawing in their breath, and appeared rather stressed. 'It was so unlike the way we normally work', she commented. This lack of standardization in the presentation of SATs, even within one school, was not unusual.

Providing support and making judgements

Such presentational differences were more than matched by differences in the amount of help given and time allowed to pupils. Some children received much more help than others in the same classroom; some teachers gave more help and were more generous in their interpretation of the criteria than others. For example, despite the strict instructions surrounding the Maths 3 1992 test, in which the context for testing and the criteria of performance were unambiguously defined, we observed many variations in the way in which teachers actually introduced and judged the SATs. Some were very flexible in the timing allowed for doing the sums; others allowed children more than one attempt at the task, or provided aids in the form of flash cards. Some allowed children to count on their fingers or to shout out answers, even though this was explicitly against the official guidelines.

Similarly in 1991, in one classroom where the floating and sinking SAT was being undertaken, different weights were recorded and accepted for the same object from different children. It was not clear whether the wrong answers were caused by weighing errors, counting errors, distractions from other children or unreliable equipment, and since the teacher was working with the whole class, she had little opportunity to observe this. She accepted the answers as satisfactory even though they varied considerably.

Conversely, in some cases, the teacher may have given less help than she was allowed to offer. For instance, at one school a teacher's anguish was recorded in the field notes made by members of the research team:

> The teacher seemed quite upset as she looked at each completed Maths sheet. She named children who 'can do it' but feels they've 'got muddled up or something'. There was speculation:
>
> 'Oh dear, I think they can get one wrong but I'll have to check. It means I won't have many Level 2s. They'll all be Level 1s. I think I may have done it wrong.'
>
> The teacher checked the Teacher Book for procedures and discovered that she should have helped the children to write in a first example of the task. This was the one, where the children have to give change, that has caught out most children.
>   In the staffroom for coffee, the teacher studied the Teachers' Book to check for further details. She decided that she would ask individual children to think about their answers to Maths 3 in the afternoon 'to see if the penny drops. Well, they can do it, I know – but they haven't done it and I should have helped them more, so we'll see if they can do it now.'
>   There was a lot of sympathy. One teacher commented: 'What is it all for?' Other teachers replied: 'It's for the parents. It doesn't help us at all.'

The teacher in this example was not trying to cheat; she simply wanted the test to reflect validly what she felt the children could do. Feeling that it did not, she was prepared to manipulate the situation. The field notes record then reads: 'The teacher had spent the afternoon checking children who had "not understood what to do in the morning". She judged that six children had been able to pass Level 2 in fact – because they had succeeded when the example was explained.'

Our field notes record several examples of teachers giving differential degrees of help to different children and groups or interpreting performance in ways not explicitly permitted by the regulations because they felt that the child in question was truly worthy of a particular level. As one teacher explained, 'I just rubbed it [the answer] all out because there's no way he isn't a Level 2.'

Teachers' judgement as to how much help is acceptable and appropriate in the context of the SAT regulations is an interesting illustration of the overlay of professional behaviour in what is supposed to be a standardized testing situation. It would seem to be a fundamental issue, in any such attempt to provide more authentic testing, whether sources of variability in the testing context, such as those described above, can ever be removed (Abbott, 1994).

Reducing children's awareness of assessment

Teachers were anxious to make the assessment tasks as stress-free as possible for children and drew on their professionalism and judgement to do so, in particular by providing extensive encouragement.

On several occasions we observed SATs being administered as a game or competition. For instance, one teacher approached the assessment of Maths 3 in the following way in 1992:

> We've all got to start together to make it fair, so put your name on it, but don't start yet. To help you, you can use a number line or counters. It's only a bit of fun to make up some points. When I count to three you can start – but no one must see yours. Otherwise it won't be a fair competition. Don't forget the counters if you need them.

The teacher circulated round the tables and offered comments:

> I told you they were easy. Don't forget the top are take-aways and the bottom adds.

Rosie had already finished and taken out her puzzle.

> David, ssh!

To Rosie:

> Good girl. She's got her paper turned over so I know she's finished. Let's see which table comes first. If it were Rainbow Table it would be good because there's someone from every team on their table.

Rosie had finished but Heather, Clare and John worked on.

> OK, Yellow Team is finished and that's 20 points to them. Which team will be next? Oh, yes, we're only waiting for Michael on that table now.

To John:

> Don't forget, the ones on the bottom are take-aways, *not* add-ups.

> How are we doing now? A couple more minutes then, there'll be a chance to win some more points with another game. One more to go – will Red Team get third? No, it's Blue Team who are finished. Well done, Blue Team. Ten more points for Blue Team. All right, close your puzzle books. Now, the next one you'll have to be really speedy so switch your brains on.

Teacher efforts to reduce pupil awareness and anxiety of assessment were skilful, creative and well intentioned – but they did not always contribute to standardization.

The effect of pupil anxiety

In other cases, however, it was not possible for teachers either to allay children's anxiety or to reduce the awareness of a testing situation. In some cases, this was because the children were already anxious, and aware of what was involved, before the testing situation. In one example, a girl finished her work after very prolonged deliberation and gave her assessment sheet to the teacher. Some time afterwards the teacher casually asked her the three subtraction sums she had wrong. The child answered correctly. The teacher discussed this: should she consider that the child can meet the attainment target or not?

Anxiety was particularly marked in some Maths SATs involving mental arithmetic, where children were under pressure to get the right answer in a given time, and in the reading SAT, despite teachers' best efforts to allay their fears. For instance, a field note of a reading SAT recorded the following episode:

> A boy, Sam, arrived. The teacher gave him a chance to look at the books and choose which he wanted to read. He leafed quickly through the books while the teacher completed her records for the previous child. In the end he picked 'Dogger' but was unable to tell her what the book was called. Other children previously tested did not get a choice of books. Sam read for several minutes with prompting for some words. He got stuck on 'brother' and the teacher gave him lots of help such as asking him:
>
> *Teacher*: 'What have you got at home? Is it a sister?'
>
> *Sam*: 'No, a boy.'
>
> *Teacher*: 'So if he's not your sister, what is he?'
>
> *Sam*: 'Brother.'
>
> The teacher gave a lot of prompting. Sam continued to read. There was also a lot of noise from children in the toilets outside. The teacher let him read for a long time while she filled in her records. She gave him several chances to work out words, more than she had given the previous pupil. She seemed to be leaving some gaps in her record to give him a better chance. Eventually he went out. The teacher explained that Sam knew this was a test. He must have talked about it at home because he had asked her why he had to do all these tests. The teacher said he usually reads far better than this and was getting stuck on very simple words. She felt he was very anxious or else 'being silly because he knew it was something special'.

Lack of clarity in assessment criteria

Such causes of real differences in pupil performance were more than matched by inadequacies in the specification of assessment criteria to record achievements at given levels. Specifically, each level seemed to include an extraordinarily broad range of attainment. For example, in a classroom studied in 1991, one group needed an hour to complete Science 1, Part B (the SAT was estimated to require only about an hour even if children also completed Part C, Level 3).

A first group were seen by their teacher as the 'most able'. She stayed with them for about ten minutes, carefully explaining the first part of the activity, and then moved about the classroom, returning to give help and reminders at each new phase, using the hand lens, weighing, etc. The children worked with concentration and care, needing only brief interventions until they were individually questioned. However, none of them achieved two of the Level 3 criteria, so they did not move on to Part C and all were assessed at Level 2.

A second group in the same class needed much more help and more detailed instructions. When the teacher moved away, they all waited for her to return before making the next step and they constantly asked and told one another what to do. After 40 minutes, most of this group had completed only one line on the recording chart. They continued for well over another hour in the afternoon and by that time their teacher had decided to sit with them and to guide them through each new step. The official *Handbook of Guidance* stressed that 'there is no time limit for an activity; some children, some groups will take longer.' Thus the teacher felt that she had no alternative but to assess the second group also at Level 2, although she felt very uneasy about it. In this case the Level 2 assessment range, between those just achieving Level 2 and those just missing Level 3, potentially a two-year gap in real achievement, seemed to encompass children of such widely different achievement as to be almost meaningless.

Deciding which level to award

As we have seen, the lack of clarity in assessment criteria produced some highly questionable results, and this was compounded by the difficulty then posed for teachers in judging the standard of work that was appropriate for each level. While levels were intended by TGAT to be criterion-referenced, the reality of their interpretation was sometimes more pragmatic or normative.

It is pertinent to stress here that teachers' constructive interpretation of the testing rules did *not* appear to be caused by a desire to raise their results in a high stakes context – to produce a better position for their school in league tables, for instance. On the contrary, several teachers expressed their concern at giving children what might be flattering scores, which would cause a problem for their colleagues in subsequent years.

> I don't really want Level 3s – I mean, I know their parents will be delighted but they only go up to 4 by the end [of primary school] then.
>
> I'm trying to be very careful in assigning levels to children, but children perform so variably and they seem to forget so much during the summer holiday. If I say that Mary has achieved Level 3 for Maths and next year she doesn't perform so well, how will her next teacher feel? We've always had such good relationships here, the last thing we want is friction over assessment.

The precise interpretation of level appeared to be a difficult problem. For instance, in 1991, in the SAT that involved making a game, one child who was considered to be 'able' was not able to answer all the questions posed to him by a teacher on his very complicated game, and so was not given a Level 3. A second child, who was regarded as a lower achiever, had produced a much simpler game and, probably because of this, was able to answer all the questions on it. The result was that he was given a Level 3, whereas a teacher assessment would probably have produced the opposite result for the two children.

Many teachers reported that children could be assessed as being at the same SAT level, even when the teacher felt they were really at very different levels of development. 'Well, he's managed all of these so I must record him as Level 3 but he's not really a Level 3 child.' Most teachers appeared have a view of their pupils' achievement that was not affected by the evidence provided by SATs.

In answer to the question, 'Do you feel that the SATs give an accurate picture of the child's level of achievement?', the following responses by two teachers were typical:

> Yes, I do actually think it's accurate, yes. But it gave the picture that you expect it to give, because I think you in many ways work it out so that it does. For instance, those three children on Maths 3 that didn't reach Level 2 and I reassessed them, I reassessed them because I felt certain that they were Level 2. I haven't reassessed two other children that in my heart of hearts I didn't feel were Level 2. So I think that it gave the result that you expect it to give.

> I would say it's not always accurate. Simply because I see children sometimes just scraping up to the next level, just by the bare minimum, when really I feel that they've got there just by that little bit of luck and I know they certainly couldn't be stretched further, and that really the lower level was a true reflection of them. And again, the other way around, there's some times when for some silly reason a child does something which, you know, in fact was unfortunate. Because I had somebody sitting with me, one of our sort of moderators was there, she supported me in what I did. Because there's one little girl who I knew had made a mistake, simply because being the little girl she is, a day-dreamer, she had missed what I'd said and completely went off at a tangent. And I knew from conversations previously that she knew the particular answer to the question involved.

This tension between awarding levels based on the sometimes arbitrary application of criteria, as against the teacher's judgement of the pupil's level based on lengthy observation, was also the basis for many difficulties in the moderation process and thus in achieving consistent standard-setting between schools (James and Connor, 1993). For instance, in 1991 our observations included the case of one girl whose knowledge and understanding of maths were felt by her teacher to be very good, but whose natural mode of work was slow and careful. Maths 3, Part B, required children to add and subtract to ten without any obvious counting or computation. Her teacher was sure that the girl was not counting; she answered correctly but hesitantly. The moderator on this occasion insisted that answers should be given before a count of three and that this particular girl was too slow in responding to reach Level 2. What was being assessed here? Mathematical ability, reaction time, speaking style or confidence?

Many teachers perceived moderation as a pressure and, while some looked to the moderator for advice and guidance to clarify how the SAT was supposed to be being conducted, in some cases there was conflict between the application of judgements by the moderator and the teacher's own professional knowledge of the child, which led her to want to make more interpretative judgements. Nevertheless, the majority of the teachers observed said that they had been surprised to find that some children achieved higher levels than they had anticipated. In 1991, 60 per cent of teachers said they had learned some new things from the conduct of SATs, although this dropped to 35 per cent in 1992.

Intuitive judgements about levels were also likely to lead to decisions about which children should attempt Level 3 SATs. Not surprisingly, these decisions were usually a product of professional judgement combined with a desire to protect the children from the possibility of failure. For example, one teacher chose to enter for Level 3 all children who had achieved Level 2 and those who, in her judgement, ought to have achieved it. Other teachers allowed the whole class to try Level 3 in order to avoid any sense of differential achievement among the children.

In none of the classrooms observed was there evidence of deliberate strategies being used to raise scores for reporting and 'league table' purposes. Teachers' worries over SAT results, and their anxiety that children should do well, appeared to be bound up much more with their own sense of professional competence being at stake than with fear of the effect of poor results on themselves or the school.

The influence of other pupils

So far we have discussed a range of factors that reduced the reliability of SAT results, including the choice of SAT, its timing, the skills involved, the teacher's approach to it and general classroom conditions. To this list we must add the effect of other pupils on those being assessed. In addition to the obvious problems of interruptions from other children, there was evidence of slower and less confident children becoming anxious as other children in the group finished more quickly or were more obviously successful than themselves.

This issue was particularly marked in one classroom, where, unusually, two Year 2 classes were being assessed in parallel. SAT children from both classes were tested in one classroom by their respective teachers, while the rest of both classes were taken in another classroom by a supply teacher. One teacher in the assessment classroom was using mixed attainment groups and the other was using groups broadly grouped by attainment. This provided an interesting situation in which to observe the effects of differential attainment on pupils undergoing SATs. In the group mixed broadly according to perceived attainment, the children seemed very happy with the SAT experience and were quite unconcerned by the Maths 3 task observed. By contrast, several children in the mixed attainment group, doing the same Maths 3 task, showed acute signs of anxiety.

Some teachers reported problems with children copying, especially where they had been trained to work collaboratively: 'There have been several instances when I've noticed that children have *changed* their answers or have written down what they've seen somebody else write down because they know it's important, they're so desperate to get the right answer.'

Inevitably there was a significant degree of what might be termed 'passive practising', or the children's ability to watch and learn from their colleagues' earlier attempts at particular tasks. In one classroom, for example, the teacher interspersed non-SAT children among her Maths 3 group in order to stop the latter copying from each other, so giving a not inconsiderable advantage to these children who were able to observe the task in advance.

A example, cited in the 1991 NUT survey, concerns a boy who was asked in one test whether he thought a pineapple would sink or float. The child answered that it would float. When the teacher asked why he thought this he explained: 'Because it's been floating all the week.' This last point highlights the inevitably social nature of the testing situation, especially with children who are too young and inexperienced to appreciate the significance of instructions designed to minimize collaboration, such as 'do your own work'.

The contrast between the social relations required by at least some of the SATs and those normal in infant classrooms focuses attention on the impact of SATs on the children. We had hypothesized at the onset of the project that this impact might take two main forms. First, pupils might feel stress at experiencing a strange and perhaps tense working situation, plus pressure from parents; second, they might become more aware of their relative achievement and abilities following this more categoric assessment. It was expected that this might have effects on their image of themselves as learners. The actual impact on pupils of SATs is discussed in the next section.

12.4 HOW DID PUPILS RESPOND TO SAT TESTING?

In presenting here a picture of how children responded to SATs in 1991 and 1992 we have drawn on 203 interviews with children in our nine field work schools, on data from interviews with their teachers and on questionnaire responses from teachers in the larger sample of 48 schools.

As we saw earlier in this chapter, teachers were initially very concerned that SATs would be damaging to pupils – particularly at the time of the pilot in 1990. However, the PACE data showed these concerns, while present, to be somewhat less dominant once the SATs had been experienced. Thus, while our 1991 teacher questionnaire on assessment showed figures of 31 per cent reporting that anxiety was felt by some children, the 1992 figure was 14 per cent. Over the two years together, two-thirds of teachers reported that children showed 'no special reaction' to the SATs, while an average of 58 per cent reported pupils to have 'enjoyed' doing them.

In our judgement such findings reflect the success of teachers in actively mediating the potentially adverse effects of the assessments, as reported in previous sections of this chapter. Teachers, as we have seen, went to quite extraordinary lengths to present SATs in ways that would mitigate pupil vulnerability or sense of failure. This was reflected in our interviews with pupils about the SATs in which they had just participated. The figures for 1991 and 1992 were almost identical: 74 per cent of children spoke positively about their SAT experiences, 18 per cent had mixed views and only 8 per cent expressed negative feelings.

These pupil views reflect again the criteria we reviewed in Chapter 8 on pupils' perceptions of the curriculum. Pupils wanted classroom life to provide them with success, fun, interest, autonomy and activity. However, in the context of a test of their knowledge or capabilities, as SATs were, the question of success was particularly prominent. For instance, among the 26 per cent of pupil comments coded as negative or mixed were the following:

A bit hard because I didn't know what the answers were. Miss didn't tell us. But I liked having a go.

OK. I was enjoying it. Didn't enjoy the writing down 'cos it was difficult and I didn't know how to do the second part.

I had this funny feeling in my stomach. I get that feeling when I'm going down hills in the fairground and when I'm doing spellings. When I finished I went 'Whew!'

I like doing stories, but not that much. Because you have to do a lot of work to do it. Like you're doing so many, of words and it's like that you've got to write and do your work quickly and there's a lot you have to do.

I felt nervous doing it – didn't want to make a fool of myself spilling pegs and didn't want the boys to laugh at me. I felt quite happy because I was chosen to play the game.

> Not much fun. I liked seeing what was floating and sinking better. 'Cos this time we had to stay sitting and I like moving and getting up and going to other tables and doing things.

As is readily apparent, such statements from pupils indicate some anxiety, but they do not provide evidence of great stress.

In further confirmation of this broad pattern, most teachers felt that the majority of children were either unaware of being tested (72 per cent in 1991; 71 per cent in 1992) or were too young to understand the significance of it. The exceptions reported to us included a number of children whose parents' concern had been communicated to their children, as in the following example of a boy named John.

John's teacher commented on his evident anxiety. She explained that his mother helped in the reception/Year 1 class several times a week and joined the staff at break, etc. 'She's very well aware of what's going on and she's making him anxious. He's under a lot of pressure and it's not helping him. She's been promising him treats and trips at half term and so on if he does well.' Our field notes of John being assessed on the reading SAT recorded that he came into a small, quiet room to read to the teacher. He began reading very fluently. The teacher then began recording his success. However, as soon as she started filling in the checklist John faltered, paused, but then continued. He read quite well but occasionally halted at words such as 'trouble' and 'embarrassed'. As he went on, this happened more often. He seemed to lose confidence when the teacher didn't respond by helping him as she usually did. Soon he was reading far less fluently than he had been at the beginning. The abnormal situation, with the teacher not supporting him when he failed to read words, seemed to deepen his anxiety.

Here we have an illustration of the downward spiral of performance caused by a lack of expected and familiar feedback, coupled with awareness and anticipation of the testing situation. This actually affected the child's ability to perform and resulted both in child stress and in a lower assessment than might otherwise have been achieved.

It would be wrong to convey an impression of parental anxiety as a major source of pupil stress. Certainly, 61 per cent of all children interviewed reported that their parents would be 'interested in how they had got on', but there were very few signs of this being more than the routine interest of parents in their children's activities and progress at school.

Thus, although a small proportion of children showed mild signs of stress, the majority of the teachers who responded to our questionnaire suggested that most children took the SAT tasks in their stride as just another classroom job. Many experienced considerable enjoyment in doing the SATs.

We wanted to explore the extent to which these seven-year-old children were aware of the assessment process that was going on. To do this, having observed them engaging in a SAT, we asked them: 'Why do you think your teacher asked you to do that?' The pattern of answers is shown in Table 12.4.

Overall, a fifth of the children simply declared that they did not know why the teacher had asked them to engage in the activity that had been used for assessment purposes – and we suspect that proportions of at least this level would be true for almost any classroom activity. Young children do not routinely expect to know the reasons for the classroom requirements to which they are subject. However, as the figures show, they were willing to offer sensible, but generalized, reasons in terms of 'learning', future

Table 12.4   *Pupil perception of teacher intentions for SATs (percentages)*

	1991	1992	Both years
Don't know	25.5	17.9	21.8
For assessment	28.7	17.9	23.4
For learning now	22.3	46.1	34.2
For the future	6.3	3.1	4.8
For content coverage	7.4	6.3	6.9
For transfer to juniors	2.1	4.7	6.1
For a game	2.1	3.9	3.0

Source: PACE 1 SAT pupil interviews.
Sample: 216 Year 2 children.
Date: summer 1991 and summer 1992.

development, content coverage, transfer to the juniors or for the fun of a game. Among the statements made under these categories were the following:

For learning

She wanted us to learn other books because when you're older we can read them better.

To learn about things that sink and to learn about grams and weights and to see if we could manage to write all the things down.

Because we always want to learn things like times tables and that and she asks us to do things like that.

'Cos he wanted us to learn, Miss. Like to do our shoelaces properly and our ties properly. When you are 18 and you get a job and you have to wear a tie, you can't say, 'Mum, will you do it for me?'

For future development

To help us learn because when you're grown up someone might ask you it and you might not know it.

To help me along when I get further in the future, so when I grow up I won't be thinking what I have to do and I'll know it straight away. My dad has to learn things 'cos he doesn't know how to speak Japanese like my mum and we are going to Japan soon.

'Cos, if you want to grow up to be a teacher you can learn to do it and if you've got children of your own you can learn them.

For content coverage

Because we've been doing sums a lot: we used to not have much maths, but we have a lot now.

Just to help to do the pond really.

So we could learn much more about floating and sinking; what could float and what could sink.

I don't know – we were doing work on materials and Miss wanted to know which would melt.

For transfer to the juniors

'Cos she wants us to learn and to get well for when we go up into the juniors 'cos that's when you have to start double writing.

So when we're in that [junior] class we'll know how to do it – say we do something similar to it, it might be the same – and if we don't do it – when we go in the next class – kerboom! Out! We won't be able to do it.

Miss wants us to do the activity because she wants everybody to know everything before they go up.

For the fun of the game
Because we like doing games and she thought we'd like to do some more – nice for us.

No he was trying to make us feel better and happy. He was making a game.

Because he wants to see which team will get the most house points. The winning team gets lollipops and goes to the library first.

It was a really good game. Miss could give it to a game-making company – they could sell it to a shop.

Regarding more explicit *awareness of assessment*, the children's comments included the following:

It was one of our tests. We're doing tests now and nearly everything we do is a test. It's to see which Level we got on – 1, 2 or 3 – and to see how good we are and what we'll be like in the next class.

Because we'll have tests soon and I think she wants to see what we remember before our proper test. We'll have a proper test in a few weeks and those will be quite hard, because we've been at school for a long time.

Because we're having tests, like we've got to learn how to read and nobody is allowed to tell you no words. Emma is the best reader – she tells me words like wheel-barrow.

'Cos it was a science test. To see if we can draw things and men will look at it and they will see if you're clever enough to go into the big school and do writing there and sums there.

It's part of our tests, to see what Level you're on – 1, 2 or 3. Three is best, then 2, then 1 is the horriblest. *Why does Miss need to know your levels?* I don't know, she keeps it a secret.

The proportions of these comments, as shown in Table 12.4, are particularly interesting. The 1991 assessments were the first full round of SATs and before they took place many teachers were particularly worried about their effects. Pupils were both more aware of assessment itself than in 1992 (29 against 18 per cent), and more uncertain of other explanations for the unusual classroom activities they were experiencing (26 per cent 'don't knows' against 18 per cent). By 1992 the SATs had been somewhat scaled down in their demands and teachers had become more united and explicit in the educational explanations they offered to pupils. This, we believe, was reflected in the high figure of 46 per cent of pupils in 1992 reporting that the purpose of the SAT activities was to assist their learning. As if confirming this dominant perception, almost 90 per cent of children, in both years, stated confidently that they *had* learned something from the SAT activities and 'might get on better next time'.

In summary, it could be argued that the assessment awareness of seven-year-olds decreased from 1991 to 1992. There was less uncertainty and less explicit assessment awareness; almost half the children attributed SAT activities directly to learning objectives. These data provide a picture of children who typically had only a very general awareness of assessment – what it is, how it works and what its significance is. In this context, SATs were no exception.

12.5 CONCLUSION

In sum, we can say that in 1992, as in 1991, there were enormous variations in the manageability, the conduct and the interpretation of SATs. Variation was caused both by differences in the opportunities provided for children to perform at their best and by the interpretations of that performance by the teachers. A considerable part of this variation was also caused by the determination of teachers both to normalize assessment as much as possible and to minimize any possible adverse effect it might have on pupils. In this, as our data from pupils showed, teachers were generally very successful, though at considerable personal cost.

The original blueprint for national assessment, which was set out in the 1988 TGAT Report, identified four different purposes for national assessment: diagnostic assessment to identify individual pupil's strengths and weaknesses; formative assessment to give feedback and encouragement; summative assessment to report on a given pupil's attainment at a given stage of schooling; and evaluative assessment to provide aggregated information about the overall level of pupil achievement in any particular school, as a basis for comparing one school with another. It is immediately clear from our findings, and other research, that the SATs of 1991 and 1992 did not provide very well for any of these purposes. They were not frequent enough, or sufficiently integrated into the normal routines and curricular emphases of a given classroom, to provide guidance for pupils and teachers about appropriate individual learning targets. Nor were they reliable or detailed enough to provide summative and evaluative information that could be confidently trusted by teachers, parents and the public, even if this were desirable. Indeed, our data suggest that in the context of English primary education, in which child-centred commitments are still central, it is not likely to be possible to devise assessment tasks or tests that will not be subject to very considerable contextual effects. Teacher concern with potentially harmful effects on pupils of 'inappropriate' assessment is very strong. However, even if this were not so, there are many other problematic contextual factors (Filer, 1994).

For teachers, the central issue was the extent to which SATs could be *integrated* with teaching, or might be adapted to form part of teacher assessment. Opposition focused on aspects of assessment over which teachers had no control: the spurious categorizations by levels that SATs produced; the inappropriate use of assessment results to inform competition between parents and between schools; the inappropriate timing and organization of SATs with associated undesirable effects on the curriculum; the unfairness of certain SATs for certain children; arbitrary procedures of aggregation and moderation; and the lack of genuine formative value as a consequence of all these impositions.

The strength of this distinction in teachers' minds between formative and summative assessment, one of the dimensions identified in Chapter 3, was clearly underlined by the fact that, despite the often overwhelming problems of implementation they had experienced, it was only in 1993 that Key Stage 1 teachers' unhappiness finally transformed itself into concerted resistance. Even then, action was initiated by secondary school teachers of English protesting at inappropriate assessments at the end of Key Stage 3 (age 14). It was fuelled by a teacher union winning an historic court case over the unreasonable workloads caused by assessment procedures, and then by other teacher associations, including the headteachers, mounting a strong case against the proposed use of assessment data for league tables in a 'market' for educational provision. This ultimately proved to be the most unacceptable aspect of standardized assessment and reporting.

As suggested at the beginning of this chapter, the use of assessment data to categorize pupils and to report comparative achievement provided the clearest possible illustration of the different educational understandings and values that underlay the tension between the Government and the profession in the early 1990s. Indeed, the strength of feeling manifest in the struggle over the use of the assessment provided telling evidence of the nature of the power struggle that was taking place in English education.

Chapter 13

Change in English Primary Schools

13.1 INTRODUCTION

This book is wide-ranging and complex, reflecting the phenomena and period of change we have studied in this first phase of the PACE project. In this chapter we therefore attempt to trace the major themes of the book and to highlight some of their implications. To do this we first, in section 13.2, review salient findings from each chapter in relatively simple and descriptive terms. In section 13.3 we consider the broad impact of change in terms of our themes of values, understanding and power, and the analytical framework concerning 'dimensions of change' that was first introduced in Chapter 3. Finally, in section 13.4, we address the implications of this study for the future of educational policies and primary school practices.

13.2 THE SALIENT FINDINGS AND ARGUMENTS OF THE BOOK

Echoes of the past

The Education Reform Act was not a one-off piece of legislation and should be understood historically. We traced the history of the elementary school tradition and the developmental tradition, each with its own values and assumptions about knowledge and learning. Both also influenced recent changes and struggles between teachers and the Government. Similarly, we need to understand the origins of teacher professionalism and to note that a new form of professionalism had been emerging in the 1980s based on 'practical theorizing'. This contributed to, was threatened by and provided a source of mediation and resistance to recent educational changes.

The Educational Reform Act followed a long-running critique of primary education and among other influences reflected the implications of New Right thinking on the role of markets in improving educational standards.

School change

The introduction of the National Curriculum was only one of many changes that affected schools and headteachers. There were direct effects on curriculum provision and assessment procedures, but there were also indirect effects on staffing, organization, teaching methods and management.

As the immediate pressures and concerns on headteachers and classroom teachers grew and began to diverge, there was a growth of managerialism and a movement towards more directive change, although many schools still tried to retain collegial participation. There has been a growth of collegiality.

A large number of schools adopted strategies to mediate and incorporate the National Curriculum and assessment into their previous practices, but there were also some shifts to compliance at the expense of previous practices. There was a strong association between directive management and the extent of change from previous practices.

Teachers' perspectives on their professional role

There were fears that the ERA would deskill teachers and that they would be reduced from being professionals exercising judgement to become classroom technicians. However, teachers, in both 1990 and 1992, held strong personal value commitments and felt morally accountable to their pupils and colleagues. Their sense of external accountability had increased considerably since Broadfoot and Osborn's 1985 research, so that, overall, they felt accountable in many, often conflicting, directions.

Many teachers felt that their role had changed since the ERA through increased bureaucracy and central direction. The job was felt to be more stressful and spontaneity in work with children decreased. Teachers' sense of fulfilment from their work reduced but they increasingly developed, and valued, collaborative relationships with other colleagues. Relationships with parents continued much as before, though there was concern about the effects of publication of assessment data.

In 1990, half the teachers in our study were pessimistic about the future of primary education and felt that work and stress levels were unsustainable. In 1992, most teachers felt that constraint would increase and professional autonomy be reduced. Many expected fulfilment to continue to decline. Older teachers were more depressed than younger ones. Teachers in inner-city schools felt the National Curriculum to be particularly inappropriate for their pupils' needs.

Overall, teachers' work intensified, but many teachers were unwilling to give up their expressive commitment to pupils and their 'extended' view of their professional role. New, external models of accountability were accepted but teachers retained their previous, internalized sense of commitment. There were diverse strategic responses. These ranged from compliance, through incorporation, active mediation and resistance, to retreatism. During our study, most teachers seemed to favour incorporation, but the 1993 action against assessment was one of resistance.

Teachers and the curriculum

Teachers initially accepted the National Curriculum in principle, but they were suspicious of the assessment proposals. In 1990 teachers prioritized children's happiness and then basic skills, but this priority was inverted in 1992. The basics continued to be given great emphasis, but music and art may have suffered and teachers felt their control of the classroom curriculum had tightened as overload became apparent. Having experienced the National Curriculum implementation, teachers began to feel that it was too much, too soon, that it was constraining and that it did not allow for responses to pupils' particular learning needs.

Classroom observation showed the dominance of the core curriculum, particularly of English and maths. Foundation subjects were squeezed in many schools, making the achievement of curriculum breadth difficult. From 1990 to 1991 there was a considerable move away from combining subjects in pupils' classroom tasks and towards tasks based on single subjects. Teachers' classroom planning became much more precise and more collegial, with awareness of progression, differentiation and coherence. Teachers used a teaching repertoire, particularly with the core subjects with which they were most familiar. There were significant changes in teachers' curriculum practices. But, although they worked very hard to implement the National Curriculum, teachers had serious reservations about it.

Pupils and the curriculum

Previous studies have shown pupils' concern with 'what they have to do' rather than with curriculum subjects *per se*. They often also wish to avoid risk. We found that pupils perceived curriculum coverage fairly accurately, though they overestimated the amount of physical education. They preferred to engage in physical education, painting and home corner play but particularly disliked writing, maths and science.

Important pupil criteria for judging curriculum subjects were ease and success, interest, fun, activity and autonomy. These related to pupil fulfilment in terms of both pupil and teacher sources of power in classrooms.

Pupils found it difficult to understand or explain specific teacher intentions in setting classroom tasks, other than in generalized ways, though this developed a little when the children were in Year 2.

Teachers and pedagogy

Previous research has shown that, despite commitments to child-centred ideas, most teachers have emphasized basic skills and drawn on a mixture of teaching methods. Teachers in our study felt that pupils should have some classroom autonomy within a clear organizational structure. However, they felt that because of the National

Curriculum they were increasingly having to direct pupil activities. Most teachers reported that they used 'mixed' teaching methods, but the proportion emphasizing more traditional methods, including whole-class teaching, increased from 1990 to 1992. This change, often unwelcome, was attributed to the pressure of National Curriculum requirements.

Observation showed that whole-class interaction of various sorts and individual teaching were each used about twice as much as forms of group work. Teachers were particularly aware of increases in explicitly planned, whole-class teaching. Classroom groups were formed on various criteria, with attainment grouping being used by 80 per cent of teachers to provide differentiation. Teachers used specific teaching strategies to meet the needs of children of different attainments. High- and low-attaining individuals and low-attaining groups received specific attention.

Teacher contact with pupils seemed to be much higher overall than that found in previous research. Teachers directed more of their classroom time to work with low attaining children and children of low sociometric status. There were considerable differences from class to class, and within classes, in the proportions of time spent in whole-class interaction, group and individual work.

Overall, teacher control tightened and teacher direction of pupil activities increased.

Pupils and pedagogy

Most pupils liked classroom autonomy but were very aware of, and generally accepted, teacher power. There were some indications of older pupils acting more strategically and instrumentally in classrooms. However, pupils generally liked their teachers and pupil–teacher relationships did not worsen over the period of study.

There was great variation in classroom task engagement and 'apparent classroom effectiveness', and these were associated with the proportion of whole-class teaching and the pedagogic frame. However, there were also indications from pupil perspectives that classrooms deemed 'less effective' on these measures were more fun and more interesting, and enabled children to construct understanding, rather than have it imposed.

Teacher assessment

Teachers' views of assessment reflected their existing professional ideologies. Thus teachers tended to favour formative, provisional and implicit assessment, rather than summative forms of explicit and categoric assessment.

National Curriculum assessment procedures were regarded as unrealistic and time-consuming. There were fears that they would adversely affect relationships. Initially, record keeping was reported as having a great influence on changing practices, and as bein a heavy workload. Forms of assessment were varied, with listening, discussion and marking prominent.

Pupils valued teacher praise and feared 'doing things wrong'. While some pupils understood teacher assessment criteria such as neatness and effort, many others did not. Children were very aware of differential attainments and of the use of teacher praise.

Classroom values such as productivity, behaviour and individualism persist and were reflected as implicit assessment criteria.

Standardized assessment

The 1991 SATs consumed a great deal of classroom time and school support was significant in terms of resources, pupil performance and teacher stress. However, the SATs constrained and distorted normal classroom practice.

SATs were implemented in variable ways, producing different assessment contexts in which children were to demonstrate attainment. Variations related to teacher stimulus, explication and presentation. Pupil anxiety sometimes depressed performance. Assessment criteria were difficult to interpret and teachers interpreted 'levelness' in various ways.

Overall, there were enormous variations, with interpretation relating to pre-existing teacher ideologies and practices. Teachers did not believe that SATs justified the time spent on them, and it is doubtful whether SAT data can be regarded as being either valid or reliable.

13.3 ANALYTICAL THEMES: VALUES, UNDERSTANDING AND POWER

As the introduction to this book sets out, the goal of the PACE study goes well beyond simply describing the changes that have taken place in primary schools following the Education Reform Act. Our aim is also to contribute more generally to collective understanding concerning the nature of education and how to provide for it most effectively. Thus, in each of the various aspects of our enquiry – as these are reported in the different chapters of this book and summarized above – we have sought not only to document but also to interpret the nature of these changes and to consider their significance for the future of English primary education.

Three analytic themes emerged as central to our attempt at interpretation, and in Chapter 3 we identified these themes as *values*, *understanding* and *power*. We now revisit them to structure the conclusions from our study.

Values

Values lie at the heart of all educational decisions. At their most general, these concern the broad commitments that inform educational and social aims and the moral foundations of educational provision.

Such values are fundamental to decisions about curriculum, teaching approaches and the sorts of outcomes that are intended from educational processes. Messages about educational values are either given explicitly in statements of educational aims or implied by decisions about curriculum, assessment and pedagogy. The feelings and perspectives of teachers and children about their experiences in schools also reflect value positions. Teachers' conceptions about what it is to be a teacher and about the nature of the teaching profession are the cornerstones of their professional ideologies and are inevitably heavily value laden. Children's responses to classroom situations may also be considered in value terms as they begin to absorb the beliefs and commitments of their families, culture and society. Value considerations may thus be used to describe the changing orientations of participants to educational situations and to explain their feelings and perspectives.

In Chapter 2 we sketched out the historical background to the debate about the nature of English primary schooling, and the way in which changing social, economic and political movements, trends and struggles have impacted on issues concerning the nature and content of that provision. We described the long-established traditions of elementary schooling in England and Wales, which are rooted in the mass state educational provision of the nineteenth century, and fed by concerns over social order and the perceived need for international competitiveness. This tradition emphasizes the inculcation of basic skills and a moral order through tight central control of curriculum and assessment arrangements, and hence of teachers and schools. By contrast, the equally long-standing 'developmental' tradition is rooted in the work of major educational philosophers, such as Rousseau and Dewey, and of influential practitioners, such as Maria Montessori and Charlotte Mason. It emphasizes the importance of responding to the needs and interests of the individual child and of helping him or her to 'develop' to his or her full potential. As we saw in Chapter 3, these differences in values have resonances with the analysis of 'education codes' that has been so powerfully advanced by Bernstein (1975, 1990).

Into this long-running debate came a new market ideology in education, which, as in other parts of state provision, brought with it an emphasis on competition and consumerism. Policies rooted in this philosophy have starkly polarized the values of most teachers against those of the Government. However, of all the sectors of the education profession, it is arguably primary teachers who have experienced these tensions the most sharply, for they had most thoroughly embraced the implication of the developmental tradition. In addition, the emergent professionalism that had been developing in the 1980s was strongly supportive of collaboration between schools, teachers and pupils as a form of learning and collective development. The contrast in value positions could hardly have been more stark.

Teachers initially supported the National Curriculum because of the entitlement to broad and structured experiences that it offered. In this sense, it embodied egalitarian values. Such values had been reflected in relatively undifferentiated curriculum provision in primary schools. However, the National Curriculum and assessment procedures emphasized the need for curriculum differentiation for different pupils. Governmental and parental concern for academic standards reinforced this, but teachers were nervous about its effects, particularly if it led towards forms of streaming or setting.

Understanding

Understanding is a concept that highlights the representation of what is to count as educationally valid knowledge. Linked to this are assumptions about the nature of teaching and of teachers' roles, and about various more specific features of practice, such as assessment. The issues that are at the heart of this book lie in the contrast between an understanding of education as the inculcation of established knowledge and its definition as a process of helping learners to construct their own insights and understanding.

Knowledge has traditionally been viewed as an established body of fact that, with associated skills and attitudes, can and should be taught. This view was articulated by the right-wing pressure groups that contributed to the Education Reform Act and was reflected in the subject specification and much of the content of the National Curriculum. An alternative, Piagetian perspective, placing emphasis on the ways in which learners construct knowledge from experience, was superseded in the emergent professionalism of the 1980s by a new approach. This approach, influenced by Vygotskian psychologists, informed several curriculum development projects. It drew attention to the importance of experience *and* instruction, and to the nature of the social context in which learning takes place and the support that needs to be available from more knowledgeable others. Both these theories of learning and of the curriculum were reflected in National Curriculum documents. Indeed, their uneasy coexistence was the basis for a good deal of the controversy that surrounded the generation of the different subject curricula.

The net effect of this was that, while teachers had been gradually evolving one view of knowledge and learning through the 1980s, much of the National Curriculum, and certainly its assessment procedures, required them to act in ways that derive from quite different assumptions. While the former emphasized the teacher's professional skills, judgement and understanding in promoting learning, the latter tended to devalue the professional pedagogic skills of the teacher by implying that the 'delivery' of the curriculum was largely unproblematic. This was well illustrated in the Government's 1993 proposal that non-graduate teachers should be accepted for work with young pupils.

Differing ways of understanding knowledge and learning also have implications for different perspectives on *curriculum organization* and teaching method. Over the period of the research reported here, considerable pressure was applied to schools to get them to consider introducing more subject specialist teaching, rather than using forms of integrated topic work. As Chapter 7 describes, this pressure had a strong effect, though it was regretted by many teachers. Similarly, we have seen how classroom pedagogy has been changing as new ways of understanding teaching and new educational priorities are put forward.

Understanding of the purpose and capacity of *assessment* also relates to views of knowledge and learning. Government attention in the early 1990s focused on standardized testing in the hope of providing attainment information for parents and for published school league tables. This strategy assumed that it was both possible and desirable to treat assessments as providing reliable categoric evidence. Teachers had a rather different view, as Chapters 11 and 12 describe. Thus teachers saw the ways in which teacher assessment could feed, formatively, into teaching–learning processes, and many embraced this as part of their professional repertoire. Assessment information was treated as provisional evidence, reflecting the continuous learning process. The gap in understanding between teachers and government on this specific issue is very considerable, but it stands as an indicator of a far wider range of differences in perception. This brings us to the issue of power.

Power

Issues of power pervade any consideration of the introduction of educational reform in the early 1990s. Like other major changes, the introduction of the National Curriculum not only involved the direct application of power, but also revealed power relationships that in other times had been hidden or so taken for granted that little attention had been paid to them (Lukes, 1974).

The most obvious power struggles involved in the introduction of the National Curriculum were those between central government imposing or requesting changes and the educational service (LEAs, schools, teachers) implementing, mediating or resisting them. The changes introduced in the 1988 legislation were widely interpreted as a shift in the relations of power between central government, local providers of education and the teaching profession. However, as well as demonstrating power over the educational system at governmental and policy-making level, the changes associated with the legislation had implications for the operation of power within schools. Thus there were changes in the implementation of relationships between governors, heads, teachers and parents. Changes in school practices also affect classroom practices and, as we have seen, the relative power of teachers and pupils to influence classroom events has begun to change as teachers attempt to 'deliver' the National Curriculum.

However, while power is typically conceived as a means of *control* and a source of constraint, it may also be manifest in more positive ways. Changes may, in principle, also be *empowering*: for instance, if they allow people to work together in more effective pursuit of agreed goals. Unfortunately, there have been few signs of this over the period of our study.

Headteachers in particular faced enormous pressures at the internal–external interface of their schools. They became directly accountable to governors for implementing central policies, but they did not always agree with these or feel that it was possible to deliver them. Having formerly had considerable autonomy in their role, they now felt immensely constrained. In response to this, some headteachers used their power in more managerial ways.

We described how classroom teachers were often required to act in ways with which they fundamentally disagreed and which they considered to be educationally unsound. This was particularly true in relation to the perceived overloading of the curriculum, the pressure for change in pupil–teacher relationships and what was regarded as the inappropriateness of summative assessment procedures.

Teacher responses to this broad but consistent trend varied between compliance, mediation and resistance. Initially, many welcomed the National Curriculum and sought to incorporate it into existing practices. Some drew very constructively on the 'practical theorizing' that had underpinned the emergent professionalism of the 1980s. They attempted to maximize positive aspects of change, such as formative assessment, curriculum progression, the use of subject knowledge and whole-school planning. In so doing, they were, in a sense, recreating their source of professional power in 'expertise'. Other teachers simply tried to survive in the context of rapidly imposed and changing requirements. Workloads, stress levels and demoralization became very high and teachers began to consider forms of collective action to assert a countervailing power to that of the Government. The most telling example of this was provided in 1993, when resistance over assessment requirements led to reporting procedures being boycotted in many schools.

The pressure on headteachers, teachers and pupils was reflected in changes in classroom practices. As we describe in Chapter 7 in particular, teachers used their power over pupils in that context to tighten classroom organization and to increase direction of pupil tasks.

There can be no doubt that, overall, the trends for headteachers, teachers and pupils in terms of power were all in the direction of increased constraint.

13.4 DIMENSIONS OF CHANGE REVISITED

In initially identifying these broad themes of power, values and understanding, Chapter 3 provided an analytic framework that links the complex mass of specific changes springing from the 1988 Education Reform Act to the enduring issues and concerns surrounding primary school provision more generally. Our three themes were thus reflected in the 14 'dimensions of change' that were discussed in Chapter 3 and are summarized in Figure 13.1.

These dimensions of change provide for analysis in a number of different ways. First, the dimensions can be used to summarize the characteristics of changes that have taken place. Second, they provide a means of distilling more general understandings about particular features of English primary education. Finally, the dimensions map on to

School organization and management

school-based development – negotiated change – imposed change

compliance – mediation – resistance

top-down management – managed participation – collegial management

individualism – collegiality

subject specialists – subject generalists

Teacher professionalism

expressive commitment – instrumentalism – alienation

restricted professionalism – extended professionalism

autonomy – constraint

Teachers' classroom practice and pupil experience

strong classification of curriculum knowledge – weak classification of curriculum knowledge

broad curriculum content – narrow curriculum content

established knowledge – constructed knowledge

strong pedagogic frame – weak pedagogic frame

formative assessment – summative assessment

strong categorization – weak categorization

Figure 13.1 *Dimensions of change: a summary.*

existing theories and research in education, thus allowing us to articulate middle-range analyses in more generalizable frameworks. The dimensions cluster around three key aspects of educational provision and change: school-level organization and management; teacher professionalism; and teachers' classroom practice and pupil experience.

School change

At the whole-school level, our understanding of the changes required under the Education Reform Act led us to anticipate that the analytic themes of values, understanding and power would find expression in the different ways in which schools responded to externally imposed change and the nature of the resistance, if any, generated by such impositions. We anticipated that headteachers' different ways of managing change would be particularly important in this respect.

Essentially our data showed that, although most primary schools had participative or collegial approaches to management, there was a trend towards more directive, top-down management. This was particularly associated with changes away from established school practices in favour of greater adaptation and compliance with new requirements.

Teacher professionalism

Regarding teacher professionalism, we focused in Chapter 3 on three dimensions: views of knowledge and learning as established or constructed; external constraint and autonomy; and commitment to restricted or extended forms of professionalism. Our overall findings on these dimensions are represented in Figure 13.2.

The bottom left-hand corner of Figure 13.2 represents the main elements of the professional perspective of English primary teachers before 1988, in its emphasis on a child-centred, constructed curriculum largely under the control of the teacher. However, in Chapter 6 we reported how teachers feared the erosion of this power to exercise their professional judgement and how they felt that the increase in external constraint was reducing their time and energy to respond to children's individual interests and needs. In consequence of both the stress resulting from a declining sense of professional fulfilment and the absolute increase in workload, teachers were typically concerned about the present and pessimistic about the future. The data and analysis reported in Chapters 6 to 12 show an increase in the development of subject teaching, in conceptions of knowledge as established and in the influence of external constraint. Teachers were, however, very unwilling to give up many aspects of their roles, especially those related to commitment to pupils, which were associated with extended professionalism. This was, in itself, a major cause of their extensive workloads.

Our study showed that teachers' moral and personal commitments to the education of young children remained strong, despite the pressures on them. This underlines their very high order of expressive commitment to teaching. However, many teachers left the profession if they could, or said they would like to. Some others adopted more instrumental positions and began to minimize their personal and emotional commitment.

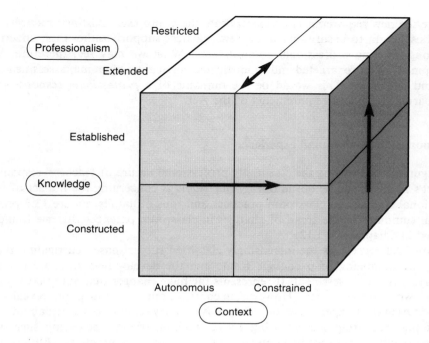

Figure 13.2 *Changing dimensions of teacher professionalism.*

Primary school teachers in England have tended to have an extended conception of their role. As we have seen, we found them to be concerned about the children in their class in social, emotional and physical terms, as well as intellectually. They were concerned about parents, the school, its role in the community and the nature of national education policy.

Many of the teachers in our study had derived a great deal of personal fulfilment from teaching over the years and their value commitment to an extended professional role was a moral one. Commitment to an extended role still existed among teachers with a strong sense of professionalism, but demoralization was leading to some retrenchment.

Some teachers feared that pupils' values, especially their level of commitment to school, might also become more instrumental because of the fragmentation and over-load of the National Curriculum, the necessary changes in classroom routines and the categoric labelling of national assessment procedures. We found little evidence of this so far, although our judgement is that teacher fears are well founded and that the lack of evidence is in fact, in major part, a measure of their commitment and expertise in pre-empting such developments.

Is it our conclusion that schools are being forced to revert to the elementary school tradition, with its emphasis on established knowledge, external constraint and a restricted professional role, as the various facets of the developmental tradition come under attack? Our evidence suggests a more complex answer, for, while many teachers may be forced to adopt new practices, this, in itself, will not necessarily change their values. It seems to be the case that the exercise of coercive power has challenged some teachers to explore their professional repertoire in order to find ways in which they can mediate the new requirements or incorporate them into their existing practices. They have thus sought to ensure that these new practices support, rather than undermine, their long-standing professional commitments. What we may see, therefore, is the development of more targeted and sophisticated curriculum planning, assessment practices and pedagogy. This would be the outcome of a *professional* response to the more barren, technicist requirements of the Act.

Classroom change and pupil experience

The argument concerning the essentially professional nature of teachers' responses to the Act's requirements is borne out by our findings concerning the impact of recent educational changes on classroom practices and thus on pupils. Figure 13.3 provides a visual summary of the trend of changes in classroom practices that we found and reported in Chapters 7 to 12.

Figure 13.3 represents the increasingly classified subject-based curriculum that we found, the tightening of pedagogic frame and the development of more overt and categoric forms of assessment. It represents the huge changes that have taken place in teachers' work in recent years. However, in contrast, our data from pupils revealed deep continuities in their experiences and perspectives. They remain concerned about having fun, doing interesting things, being active, making friends, achieving success and avoiding trouble – even at the young age of the children in our study. Pupil concerns about schools were much as they have always been.

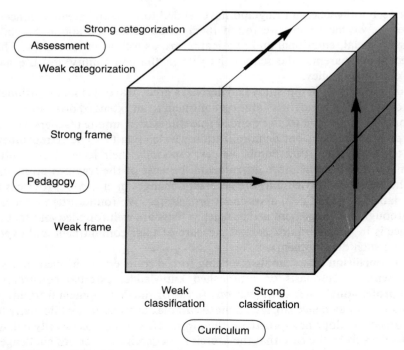

Figure 13.3 *Changing dimensions of curriculum, pedagogy and assessment.*

There are at least two possible reasons for this. First, it is the case that pupils have always had to respond to teacher control in classrooms. Thus, in itself, constraint is not new to pupils – in one sense, it is what being a 'pupil' is all about. Second, and much more significantly in the context of this study, pupils have arguably not experienced change on anything like the scale that teachers have, because of the supreme efforts of teachers to protect children from what they have seen as the worst effects of the changes in education policy. Among the illustrations of this are teachers' concern for maintaining positive classroom relationships and teachers' determination to protect the self-esteem of children during assessment procedures.

It is unfortunate, though again not new, that our data showed that such very young pupils seemed not to value highly their work associated with the core curriculum, but this is far from inevitable. The development of teachers' subject knowledge could well assist them in providing work that will engage pupils' interests more fully. To the extent that this happens, it will provide illustrative evidence of another main finding of our study, namely that the imposition of the Act's requirements has prompted some positive developments in teachers' professional skills. In this respect one might identify curriculum planning, clarity in aims and the development of a teaching repertoire and of assessment skills. Ironically, as developments continue through the 1990s, these skills may well be used by teachers to pursue their long-standing educational values. They may thus mobilize particular kinds of professional power to resist the coercive requirements of policy-makers. Some have done this already, by finding ways to use the procedures they are required to follow for very different ends from those originally intended by the Government. Thus procedures rooted in a very different set of educational values have been hijacked by the incorporation of a professional discourse that is still unambiguously rooted in constructivist, rather than established, views of knowledge and collegial, rather than competitive, practice.

It has been said that, while the major theme of the 1970s was 'equality of opportunity', the major concern of the 1980s was 'quality' – hence the emphasis on educational performance. However, although we have chosen not to report them in this overcrowded book, there are already indications of processes of social differentiation occurring as a result of the National Curriculum and assessment procedures in the classrooms we studied. At this stage it is too early to be sure of the emerging patterns, but these will receive a full analysis as the longitudinal aspect of this study evolves.

13.5 CONCLUSION

The picture we are left with is certainly unfinished and is perhaps rather confused. It reveals change and resistance, commitment and demoralization, decreasing autonomy but some developments in professional skills. Is it possible to make any sense out of these apparently contradictory findings?

Certainly there is currently a broad consensus in English primary schools on the structural benefits of having a national curriculum. It is seen as providing for progression and continuity and, with careful design, it is seen as a potential source of coherence. Organizational benefits for teacher training and supply, continuous professional development, curriculum development, parental participation, teacher accountability and national monitoring of educational standards are accepted.

Unfortunately, though, the introduction of the National Curriculum into England was seriously compromised because of the ways in which professionally committed teachers were alienated. As our data have shown, the Education Reform Act brought enormous changes for teachers. However, rather than providing a legislative framework through which they could offer and fulfil their professional commitment, the reforms introduced constraint and regulation into almost every area of teachers' work. Yet it seems most unlikely that education standards can rise without the wholehearted commitment of teachers, working to support pupils' learning.

Having said that, it is also clear that professional commitment has not yet been entirely dissipated. Ironically, collegiality has developed within many schools as a response to the reforms. Unprecedented levels of cooperation are often manifest in schools, between schools and between teacher associations, but these have often been used to defend the quality of the education service against government policies rather than to work in partnership with government towards shared goals.

Our final conclusion must be one that records, with sadness, the many lost opportunities of this period of change. The amount of legislative time, of financial resources, of public debate and of teacher energy devoted to the innovations was unprecedented. Yet so much was destructive or wasted because of the ideological clash between the Government and teachers. Nor are the struggles surrounding the implementation of the Education Reform Act and its supplementary legislation yet over; this is certainly a time in which history is being made.

Appendix

Systematic Observation: Definition of Categories

TEACHER OBSERVATION

1 Teacher activity

Coded at each ten-second interval. The code relates to what is happening at the 'bleep', not to a summary of the previous ten-seconds.

I   Instruction: Teacher is involved with child/children directly on a curriculum activity (excluding hearing reading, encouraging and assessment, as defined below). This includes explaining a task and watching/listening to children doing a task. It does not include managing the task.

C   Control: Control/discipline relating to children's behaviour, e.g. 'This room is getting noisy', 'Sit down Marilyn', 'Andrew!'. It does not include non-disciplinary directions, e.g. 'Stop what you are doing and listen to me'.

D   Direction: Management of curriculum task activity, e.g. 'Blue group go to the library', 'Put your things away now', 'When you've finished you can colour it in'.

A   Assessment: Explicit assessment, such as marking or correcting work, recording attainment or reviewing work with a pupil as an assessment activity.

E   Encouragement: Positive praise, support or encouragement, e.g. 'That's really good', 'You have all worked really well today'. It does not include routine feedback, e.g. 'Yes, that's right' which is coded I.

N   Negative: Negative feedback and comment on curriculum activity, e.g. 'That's no good at all', 'Why didn't you do it the way I told you?'. It does not include routine feedback, 'There are two h's in chrysanthemum'.

R   Hearing children read: This refers to 'reading to teacher' as a one-to-one activity.

O   Other: Including teacher talking to adult, teacher not involved with class and non-curriculum activities such as class administration. (NB class administration is not included in planned observation but may occur unexpectedly.)

2   Teacher interaction

Coded every ten seconds. The code relates to what is happening at the bleep. It is the teacher's interaction that is coded. Interaction includes verbal interaction (speaking and listening) and also other forms of interaction, such as touch, gesture and writing on the blackboard with the class watching.

O   Alone means not interacting. Children may be physically present.

TC   Teacher interaction with the whole class. It is coded whenever the teacher is working with all the children who are present in the room, even if some children from the class are missing. *But* if over half the children are out of the room, one of the group codes should be used. This code encompasses a range of settings, e.g. story time or discussions on class carpeted areas, as well as more direct instruction.

A   Interaction with any other adult.

G   With individual girl: One-to-one interaction with a single female pupil.

B   With individual boy: One-to-one interaction with a single male pupil.

X   With group of boys: Simultaneous interaction with more than one male pupil.

Y   With group of girls: Simultaneous interaction with more than one female pupil.

M   With a mixed group: Simultaneous interaction with a mixed group of pupils.

Note: A group is defined as two or more children but less than the whole class as defined above. For the teacher to be coded as interacting with a group, the children do not necessarily have to be working together.

3   Pedagogic context

This summarizes the teaching context *of the teacher* over the six minutes of observation. MAIN gives the overall summary of the teaching context and only one code should be used. PART is coded for any other teaching activity that took place and multiple codes may be used. Sometimes, if teaching is very varied or evenly balanced there may be no main context.

CLASS INTERACTION is defined as for TC above.

INDIVIDUAL WORK is when pupils are working individually on tasks. These may be the same tasks as other children.

COOPERATIVE GROUP WORK is when the teacher is working with a group of children who are also working cooperatively between themselves.

GROUP WORK WITH TEACHER is when the teacher is working with a group of children who are not otherwise working together (although they may be sitting together and doing similar tasks).

OTHER if none of the above contexts apply details are noted.

4   Curriculum context

This summarizes the curriculum content with which the teacher has been engaged in the preceding six minutes. MAIN gives the principal curriculum area, largely in terms of National Curriculum categories, and is normally coded once. PART refers to any other aspect of the curriculum that has been present. Sometimes, if the content is highly integrated with no subject category dominating, there may be no main code. Sometimes, if there has been a shift in the content the teacher is engaged with, there may be more than one main code. Clarification may be sought from the teacher if required.

CHILD OBSERVATION

1 Teacher activity

Coded as for teacher activity above.

2 Child interaction

Coded every ten seconds. The code refers to interactions of the target child at the bleep. Interactions may be verbal (both speaking and listening) or by touch or gesture.

O   Alone: The child is not interacting.

TC   With teacher in whole class: The child is part of the teacher's class audience (teacher whole-class interaction as defined above).

TO   With teacher one-to-one: The child is the focus of the teacher's individual attention on a one-to-one basis (although other children may be listening).

TG   With teacher in group: The child is part of a group with which the teacher is interacting (group as defined above).

AO   With another adult one-to-one: Any interaction with an adult other than the teacher.

G   With individual girl: One-to-one interaction with a female pupil.

B   With individual boy: One-to-one interaction with a male pupil.

X   With a group of boys: Simultaneous interaction with more than one male pupil.

Y   With a group of girls: Simultaneous interaction with more than one female pupils.

M   With a mixed group: Simultaneous interaction with a mixed group of pupils.

Note: If a child is notionally part of a class or group with the teacher but is actually interacting with one or more other children then the actual interaction should be coded.

3 Child activity

Coded every ten seconds. The code refers to the target child's activity at the bleep.

TE   Task engagement in curriculum task (excluding reading to teacher and being formally assessed). This includes listening to the teacher when the teacher would be coded as I.

TM   Task management activity associated with a curriculum task, e.g. moving around the classroom, fetching or arranging books or materials, moving desks and equipment, getting out or sharpening pencils, listening to the teacher when the content of the teacher's activity would be coded as D rather than I.

D   Distracted: Includes behaviour that is not task-focused, messing around, talking to other children about something other than work, day-dreaming, etc.

B   Both distracted and task management.

A   Assessment: Child being explicitly assessed by his or her own or another teacher. Assessment as defined for teacher activity.

W   Waiting for teacher: Usually either as part of a queue or with hand up.

X   Waiting (other): As above for another adult.

O   Out of room/sight.

R   Reading to teacher: Reading to the teacher as a one-to-one reading activity.

4   Pedagogic context

Summary of pedagogic situation of the target child for the six minutes of observation. MAIN is the overall summary of the child's teaching context and is coded once. PART refers to any other teaching context that occurred and may have multiple codes. Sometimes, if the teaching context is very varied or evenly balanced, there may be no main context. Categories are defined as in the teacher observation schedule. It is the context, not the actual activity, that is coded. If the child is part of a class lesson but has actually been interacting with other children, CLASS TEACHING is still coded. If the child is part of a cooperative group but has not contributed, COOP GROUP is still coded.

5   Curriculum context

This provides a summary of the curriculum content of the activities in which the target child was engaged. MAIN gives the principal curriculum context, mainly in terms of National Curriculum areas. PART refers to any other aspect of the curriculum that was present in the work being observed. Normally there will only be one code for MAIN and there may be several for PART. If the content is highly integrated, with no subject dominating, there may be no MAIN context. Occasionally, if the focus of a child's work has changed during the period of observation, there may be more than one MAIN code.

Bibliography

Abbott, D., with Broadfoot, P., Croll, P., Osborn, M. and Pollard, A. (1994) Some sink, some float: National Curriculum assessment and accountability. *British Educational Research Journal*, **29**(2), 155-74.

Acker, S. (1990) Teachers' culture in an English primary school; continuity and change. *British Journal of Sociology of Education*, **11**(3), 257-74.

Ahlberg, A. (1984) *Please, Mrs Butler*. Harmondsworth: Puffin Books.

Ahlberg, J. and Ahlberg, A. (1988) *Starting School*. Harmondsworth: Puffin Books.

Alexander, R. J. (1984) *Primary Teaching*. London: Holt, Rinehart & Winston.

Alexander, R. J. (1992) *Policy and Practice in Primary Education*. London: Routledge.

Alexander, R. J., Craft, M. and Lynch, J. (eds) (1984) *Change in Teacher Education*. London: Holt, Rinehart & Winston.

Alexander, R. J., Willcocks, J. and Kimber, K. M. (1989) *Changing Primary Practice*. London: Falmer.

Alexander, R., Rose, J. and Woodhead, C. (1992) Curriculum organisation and classroom practice in primary schools: a discussion paper. London: Department of Education and Science.

Apple, M. (1986) *Teachers and Texts: A Political Economy of Class and Gender Relations in Education*. London: Routledge.

Armstrong, M. (1981) *Closely Observed Children*. London: Readers and Writers.

Arnold, M. (1889) *Reports on Elementary Schools 1852-1882*. London: Macmillan.

Ashton, P., Kneen, P., Davies, F. and Holley, B. J. (1975) *The Aims of Primary Education: A Study of Teachers' Opinions*. London: Macmillan Education.

Auld, R. (1976) *William Tyndale Junior and Infant Schools Public Inquiry*. London: ILEA.

Ball, S. J. (1990) *Politics and Policy Making in Education: Explorations in Policy*. London: Routledge.

Banham, J. (1990) Competing in the 1990s. Unpublished speech to the Kent Management Development Programme by the Director General of the Confederation of British Industry.

Barker-Lunn, L. J. C. (1970) *Streaming in the Primary School*. Slough: NFER.

Barton, L. and Lawn, M. (1980/1) Back inside the whale: a curriculum case study. *Interchange*, **11**(4).

Bassey, M. (1978) *Practical Classroom Organization*. London: Ward Lock Educational.

Bennett, S. N. (1976) *Teaching Styles and Pupil Progress*. London: Open Books.

Bennett, S. and Dunne, E. (1992) *Managing Classroom Groups*. Hemel Hempstead: Simon & Schuster.

Bennett, S. N. and Kell, J. A. (1989) *A Good Start? Four Year Olds in Infant Schools.* Oxford: Blackwell Education.

Bennett, N., Andreae, J., Hegarty, P. and Wade, B. (1980) *Open Plan Schools: Teaching, Curriculum, Design.* Windsor: NFER.

Bennett, S. N., Desforges, C., Cockburn, A. and Wilkinson, B. (1984) *The Quality of Pupil Learning Experiences.* London: Lawrence Erlbaum Associates.

Bennett, S. N., Wragg, E. C., Carré, C. G. and Carter, D. S. G. (1992) A longitudinal study of primary teachers' perceived competence in, and concerns about, National Curriculum implementation. *Research Papers in Education*, **7**(1), 53–78.

Berlak, H. and Berlak, A. (1981) *Dilemmas of Schooling.* London: Methuen.

Bernstein, B. (1971) On the classification and framing of educational knowledge. In M. F. D. Young (ed.), *Knowledge and Control.* London: Collier-Macmillan.

Bernstein, B. (1975) *Class, Codes and Control*, Vol. 3: *Towards a Theory of Educational Transmission.* London: Routledge & Kegan Paul.

Bernstein, B. (1990) *The Structure of Pedagogic Discourse.* London: Routledge & Kegan Paul.

Blyth, W. A. L. (1965) *English Primary Education.* London: Routledge & Kegan Paul.

Blyth, W. A. L. (1984) *Development, Curriculum and Experience in Primary Education.* London: Croom Helm.

Board of Education (1931) *Report of the Consultative Committee on the Primary School* (the Hadow Report). London: HMSO.

Bowe, R. and Ball, S., with Gold, A. (1992) *Reforming Education and Changing Schools.* London: Routledge.

Broadfoot, P. (1990) Research on teachers: towards a comparative methodology. *Comparative Education*, **26**(3), 165–9.

Broadfoot, P. and Osborn, M. (1988) What professional responsibility means to teachers: national contexts and classroom contexts. *British Journal of Sociology of Education*, **9**(3), 265–87.

Broadfoot, P. and Osborn, M., with Gilly, M. and Brücher, A. (1993) *Perceptions of Teaching: Primary School Teachers in England and France.* London: Cassell.

Broadfoot, P., Osborn, M., Gilly, M. and Paillet, A. (1987) Teachers' conceptions of their professional responsibility. *Comparative Education*, **23**(3), 287–301.

Broadfoot, P., Osborn, M. and Pollard, A. (1993) Primary teachers and policy change: a comparative study. Proposal to ESRC for funding (R00023 4673). Mimeo, University of Bristol/University of the West of England, Bristol.

Brophy, J. E. and Evertson, C. M. (1976) *Learning from Teaching.* Boston: Allyn & Bacon.

Callaghan, J. (1976) Towards a national debate. *Education*, **148**(17), 332–3.

Campbell, R. J. and Neill, S. R. St J. (1992) *Teacher Time and Curriculum Manageability at Key Stage 1.* London: AMMA.

Campbell, R. J., Evans, L., Neill, S. R. St J. and Packwood, A. (1991) *The Use and Management of Infant Teachers' Time: Some Policy Issues.* Warwick: University of Warwick Policy Analysis Unit.

Central Advisory Council for Education (England) (CACE) (1967) *Children and Their Primary Schools (The Plowden Report).* London: HMSO.

Clarke, K. (1991) *Primary Education – A Statement: DES News.* London: Department of Education and Science.

Council on Education (1846) *Minutes of the Committee of Council on Education.* London: Council on Education.

Cox, C. B. and Boyson, R. (eds) (1975) *Black Paper 1975.* London: Dent.

Cox, C. B. and Boyson, R. (eds) (1977) *Black Paper 1977.* London: Temple Smith.

Cox, C. B. and Dyson, A. E. (eds) (1969) *Fight For Education: A Black Paper.* London: Critical Quarterly Society.

Croll, P. (1986) *Systematic Classroom Observation.* London: Falmer Press.

Croll, P. and Moses, D. (1988) Teaching methods and time on task in junior classrooms. *Educational Research*, **30**(2), 90–7.

Croll, P. and Moses, D. (1990) Perspectives on the National Curriculum in primary and secondary schools. *Educational Studies*, **16**(1), 187–98.

Cullingford, C. (1990) *The Nature of Learning*. London: Cassell.

Dale, R., Esland, G., Fergusson, R. and MacDonald, M. (1981) *Education and the State*, Vol. 2: *Politics, Patriarchy and Practice*. Lewes: Falmer Press.

Davies, B. (1982) *Life in the Classroom and Playground*. London: Routledge & Kegan Paul.

Densmore, K. (1987) Professionalism, proletarianization and teachers' work. In T. Popkewitz (ed.), *Critical Studies in Teacher Education*. Lewes: Falmer Press.

Dent, H.C. (1970) *1870–1970: Century of Growth in English Education*. London: Longman.

Department for Education/Welsh Office (1993) *The Initial Training of Primary School Teachers: New Criteria for Course Approval*. Draft Circular. London: DFE.

Department of Education and Science (1977) *Curriculum 11–16*. London: HMSO.

Department of Education and Science (1978) *Primary Education in England: A Survey by HMI*. London: HMSO.

Department of Education and Science (1980) *A View of the Curriculum*. London: HMSO.

Department of Education and Science (1981) *The School Curriculum*. London: HMSO.

Department of Education and Science (1982) *Education 5–9*. London: HMSO.

Department of Education and Science (1984) *English from 5 to 16*, Curriculum Matters Series. London: HMSO.

Department of Education and Science (1985a) *The Curriculum from 5 to 16*, Curriculum Matters Series. London: HMSO.

Department of Education and Science (1985b) *Education Observed 3: Good Teachers*. London: HMSO.

Department of Education and Science (1985c) *Better Schools: A Summary*. London: HMSO.

Department of Education and Science (1987) *Report of the Task Group on Assessment and Testing*. London: HMSO.

Department of Education and Science (1988) *Task Group on Assessment and Testing: Three Supplementary Reports*. London: DES.

Department of Education and Science (1989) *Survey of 1000 classes of 5–7 year olds*. London: HMSO.

Department of Education and Science (1991a) *Aspects of Primary Education in France*. London: HMSO.

Department of Education and Science (1991b) *Assessment, Recording and Reporting: A Report by HM Inspectorate on the First Year, 1989–90*. London: HMSO.

Department of Education and Science (1991c) *Testing 7 Year Olds in 1991: Results of the National Curriculum Assessments in England*. London: HMSO.

Department of Education and Science (1992) *Assessment, Recording and Reporting: A Report by HM Inspectorate on the Second Year*. London: HMSO.

Eccles, D. (1960) Speech to the House of Commons in the debate on the Report of the Crowther Commission, 21 March.

Egan, K. (1989) *Primary Understanding*. London: Routledge.

Etzioni, A. (1966) *A Comparative Analysis of Complex Organizations*. New York: Free Press of Glencoe.

Evans, K. (1975) *The Development and Structure of the English School System*. London: Hodder & Stoughton.

Filer, A. (1994) Contexts of assessment in a primary classroom. Unpublished PhD thesis, University of the West of England, Bristol.

Forster, W.E. (1869) In *Hansard*, CXCIV, 16 February.

Fraser, J. (1861) In evidence to the Newcastle Commission, *Report of the Commissioners into the State of Popular Education in England*, Volume 1. London: Eyre & Spottiswoode for HMSO.

Froome, S. (1974) Back on the right track. *Education 3–13*, **2**(1), 13–16.

Fullan, M. (1982) *The Meaning of Educational Change*. New York: Teachers College Press.

Fullan, M. (1991) *The New Meaning of Educational Change*. London: Cassell.

Gage, N. and Berliner, D. (1988) *Educational Psychology*. Boston: Houghton Mifflin.

Galton, M. (1987) An ORACLE chronicle: a decade of classroom research. In S. Delamont (ed.), *The Primary School Teacher*. Lewes: Falmer Press.

Galton, M., Simon, B. and Croll, P. (1980) *Inside the Primary Classroom*. London: Routledge & Kegan Paul.

Gathorne-Hardy, J. (1977) *The Public School Phenomenon*. London: Hodder & Stoughton.

Goodnow, J. and Burns, A. (1985) *Home and School: A Child's Eye View*. Sydney: Allen & Unwin.

Grant, M. (1989) *GCSE in Practice: Managing Assessment Innovation*. Windsor: NFER–Nelson.

Handy, C. and Aitken, R. (1986) *Understanding Schools as Organisations*. Harmondsworth: Penguin.

Hargreaves, A. (1989) *Curriculum and Assessment Reform*. Milton Keynes: Open University Press.

Hargreaves, A. (1992) Time and teachers' work: an analysis of the intensification thesis. *Teachers College Record*, **94**(1), 87–108.

Hargreaves, D. (1988) Educational research and the implications of the 1988 Educational Reform Act. Lecture given to the BERA annual conference, University of East Anglia.

Hargreaves, D. and Hopkins, D. (1991) *The Empowered School: The Management and Practice of Development Planning*. London: Cassell.

Haviland, J. (1988) *Take Care, Mr Baker!* London: Fourth Estate.

Hillgate Group (1986) *Whose Schools? A Radical Manifesto*. London: Hillgate Group.

Holmes, E. (1911) *What Is and What Might Be*. London: Constable.

Holmes, E. (1914) *In Defence of What Might Be*. London: Constable.

Hoyle, E. (1974) Professionality, professionalism and control in teaching. *London Educational Review*, **3**(2), 15–17.

Hughes, M., Wikely, F. and Nash, T. (1990) Parents and the National Curriculum: an interim report. Mimeo, University of Exeter.

Hughes, M., Wikely, F. and Nash, T. (1991) Parents and SATs: A second interim report. Mimeo, University of Exeter.

Hurt, J.S. (1979) *Elementary Schooling and the Working Classes 1800–1918*. London: Routledge & Kegan Paul.

Jackson, P.W. (1968) *Life in Classrooms*. New York: Holt, Rinehart & Winston.

James, H. and Connor, C. (1993) Are reliability and validity achievable in National Curriculum assessment? Some observations on moderation at Key Stage 1 in 1992. *Curriculum Journal*, **4**(1), 5–19.

Jones, G. and Hayes, D. (1991) Primary headteachers and ERA: two years on. *School Organization*, **11**(2), 211–21.

Karweit, N. (1984) Time on task reconsidered. *Education Leadership*, **41**, 32–5.

King, R. (1978) *All Things Bright and Beautiful? A Sociological Study of Infants' Classrooms*. Chichester: Wiley.

King, R. (1989) *The Best of Primary Education? A Sociological Study of Junior and Middle Schools*. London: Falmer.

Kogan, M. (1978) *The Politics of Educational Change*. London: Fontana.

Lang, P. (ed.) (1988) *Thinking about Personal and Social Education in the Primary School*. Oxford: Blackwell.

Lawn, M. (1987) The spur and the bridle: changing the mode of curriculum control. *Journal of Curriculum Studies*, **19**(3), 227–36.

Lawn, M. (1988) Skill in schoolwork: work relations in the primary school. In J. Ozga (ed.), *Schoolwork: Approaches to the Labour Process of Teaching*. Milton Keynes: Open University Press.

Lawn, M. and Ozga, J. (1981) The educational worker: a reassessment of teachers. In M. Walker and L. Barton (eds), *Schools, Teachers and Learning*. London: Falmer.

Lawton, D. (1989) *Education, Culture and the National Curriculum*. London: Hodder & Stoughton.

Lewis, A. (1991) *Primary Special Needs and the National Curriculum*. London: Routledge.

Lewis, A. (1993) Views of schooling held by children attending schools for pupils with moderate learning difficulties (MLD). Mimeo, University of Warwick.

Lortie, D.C. (1975) *Schoolteacher*. London: Routledge & Kegan Paul.

Lukes, S. (1974) *A Radical View of Power*. London: Macmillan.

MacCallum, B., McAlister, S., Brown, M. and Gipps, C. (1993) Teacher assessment at Key Stage 1. *Research Papers in Education*, **18**(3), 305–27.

Makins, V. (1969) Child's eye view of teacher. *Times Educational Supplement*, 28 September.

Mason, C.M. (1954) *An Essay towards a Philosophy of Education*. London: J.M. Dent.

Mavrommatis, I. (1993) Assessment in Greek primary classrooms. Mimeo, University of Bristol.

Meyer, J.W., Kamens, D.H. and Benavot, A. (1992) *School Knowledge for the Masses: World Models of National Primary Curricular Categories in the Twentieth Century*. London: Falmer.

Mills, C.W. (1959) *The Sociological Imagination*. Harmondsworth: Penguin Books.

Ministry of Education (1888) *Report of the Royal Commission on the Elementary Education Acts* (the Cross Report). London: HMSO.

Montessori, M. (1919) *The Montessori Method*. London: Heinemann.

Mortimore, P. and Mortimore, J. (1991) *The Primary Head*. London: Paul Chapman Publishing.

Mortimore, P., Sammons, P., Stoll, L., Lewis, D. and Ecob, R. (1986) *Report of the Junior School Project*. London: Inner London Education Authority.

Mortimore, P., Sammons, P., Stoll, L., Lewis, D. and Ecob, R. (1988) *School Matters: The Junior Years*. Wells: Open Books.

Muschamp, Y. (1993) Target setting with young children. In A. Pollard and J. Bourne (eds), *Teaching and Learning in Primary Schools*. London: Routledge.

National Curriculum Council (NCC) (1991) *Report on Monitoring the Implementation of the National Curriculum Core Subjects: 1989–90*. York: National Curriculum Council.

National Curriculum Council (NCC) (1993) *The National Curriculum at Key Stages 1 and 2*. York: National Curriculum Council.

National Primary Centre, South West (NPC-SW) (1991) *Survey of Teacher Opinion on Assessment*. Bristol: National Primary Centre.

National Union of Teachers (NUT) (1991) *Report of the Survey on Key Stage 1 SATs*. London: National Union of Teachers.

Newcastle Commission (1861) *Report of the Commissioners into the State of Popular Education in England*. London: Eyre & Spottiswoode for HMSO.

Nias, J. (1989) *Primary Teachers Talking*. London: Routledge.

Nias, J., Southworth, G. and Yeomans, R. (1989) *Staff Relationships in the Primary School: A Study of Organizational Cultures*. London: Cassell.

Nias, J., Southworth, G. and Campbell, C. (1992) *Whole School Curriculum Development in the Primary School*. Lewes: Falmer.

Office for Standards in Education (OFSTED) (1993) *Curriculum Organisation and Classroom Practice in Primary Schools*. London: DFE.

Osborn, M. and Broadfoot, P. (1990) Some international comparisons of teachers' classroom practice. *Times Educational Supplement*, 9 November.

Osborn, M. and Broadfoot, P. (1993) Becoming and being a teacher: the influence of the national context. *European Journal of Education*, **28**(1), 105–16.

Packwood, A. (1992) The implications of the National Curriculum for pre- and in-service teacher education. *Teacher Development*, February, 47–53.

Piaget, J. (1926) *The Language and Thought of the Child*. New York: Basic Books.

Piaget, J. (1950) *The Psychology of Intelligence*. London: Routledge & Kegan Paul.

Pollard, A. (1985) *The Social World of the Primary School*. London: Cassell.

Pollard, A. (1987) Primary school teachers and their colleagues. In S. Delamont (ed.), *The Primary School Teacher*. Lewes: Falmer Press.

Pollard, A. (1988) Rule frame and relationship. In P. Lang (ed.), *Thinking about Personal and Social Education in Primary Schools*. Oxford: Blackwell.

Pollard, A. (1990) Towards a sociology of learning in primary schools. *British Journal of Sociology of Education*, **11**(3), 241–56.

Pollard, A. (1992) Teachers' responses to the reshaping of primary education. In M. Arnot and L. Barton (eds), *Voicing Concerns: Sociological Perspective on Contemporary Education Reforms*. Wallingford: Triangle.

Pollard, A., with Osborn, M., Abbott, D., Broadfoot, P. and Croll, P. (1992) Balancing priorities: children and curriculum in the nineties. In R. J. Campbell (ed.), *Breadth and Balance in the Primary Curriculum*. London: Falmer Press.

Pollard, A. and Tann, S. (1987) *Reflective Teaching in the Primary School*. London: Cassell (2nd edn 1993).

Pollard, A. with Filer, A. (forthcoming) *Learning and Identity in a Primary School*. London: Cassell.

Poppleton, P. and Riseborough, G. (1990) Teaching in the mid-1980s: the centrality of work in secondary teachers' lives. *British Educational Research Journal*, **16**(2), 105–24.

Richards, C. (1984) *The Study of Primary Education: A Source Book*, Volume 1. Lewes: Falmer Press.

Rousseau, J. J. (1911) *Emile*. London: Dent.

Rowland, S. (1984) *The Enquiring Classroom*. London: Falmer Press.

Rowland, S. (1987) An interpretive model of teaching and learning. In A. Pollard (ed.) *Children and Their Primary Schools*. London: Falmer Press.

School Examinations and Assessment Council (SEAC) (1991a) *Handbook of Guidance for the SAT*. London: HMSO.

School Examinations and Assessment Council (SEAC) (1991b) *Key Stage 1 Pilot 1990: A Report from the Evaluation and Monitoring Unit*. London: HMSO.

School Examinations and Assessment Council (SEAC) (1991c) *The Pilot Study of Standard Assessment Tasks for Key Stage 1: A Report for the NFER/BGC Consortium*. London: HMSO.

Selleck, R. J. W. (1972) *English Primary Education and the Progressives 1914–1939*. London: Routledge & Kegan Paul.

Sexton, S. (1987) *Our Schools: A Radical Policy*. Warlington: Institute of Economic Affairs.

Sharp, R. and Green, A. (1975) *Education and Social Control*. London: Routledge & Kegan Paul.

Sharpe, K. (1992) Educational homogeneity in French primary education: a double case study. *British Journal of Sociology of Education*, **13**(3), 329–48.

Shorrocks, D., Daniels, S., Frobisher, L., Nelson, N., Waterson, A. and Bell, J. (1992) *The Evaluation of the National Curriculum at Key Stage 1: Final Report*. Leeds: University of Leeds.

Simon, B. (1985) *Does Education Matter?* London: Lawrence & Wishart.

Simon, B. (1989) *Bending the Rules: The Baker 'Reform' of Education*. London: Lawrence & Wishart.

Silver, H. (1980) *Education and the Social Condition*. London: Methuen.

Soar, R. (1977) An integration of findings from four studies of teacher effectiveness. In G. Borich and K. Fenton (eds), *The Appraisal of Teaching: Concepts and Process*. Reading, MA: Addison-Wesley.

Southgate, V., Arnold, H. and Johnson, S. (1975) *Extending Beginning Reading*. London: Heinemann Educational Books for the Schools Council.

Stallings, J. (1980) Allocated academic learning time revisited, or beyond time on task. *Educational Research*, **8**(11), 11–16.

Stenhouse, L. (1975) *An Introduction to Curriculum Research and Development*. London: Heinemann.

Stone, C. (1993) Topic work in the context of the National Curriculum. *Journal of Teacher Development*, **2**(1), 27–38.

Tharp, R. and Gallimore, R. (1988) *Rousing Minds to Life*. Cambridge: Cambridge University Press.

Tizard, B., Blatchford, P., Burke, J., Farquhar, C. and Plewis, I. (1988) *Young Children at School in the Inner City*. London: Lawrence Erlbaum.

Torrance, H. (1991) Evaluating SATs: the 1991 pilot. *Cambridge Journal of Education*, **21**(2), 129–40.

Vygotsky, L. S. (1962) *Thought and Language*. Cambridge, MA: Massachusetts Institute of Technology.

Vygotsky, L. S. (1978) *Mind in Society: The Development of Higher Psychological Processes* Cambridge, MA: Harvard University Press.

Wallace, M. (1991) Coping with multiple innovations in schools: an exploratory study. *School Organization*, **11**(2), 187–209.

Waller, W. (1932) *The Sociology of Teaching*. New York: Russell & Russell.

Warren-Little, J. (1987) Teachers as colleagues. In V. Richardson-Koehler (ed.), *Educators Handbook: A Research Perspective*. London: Longmans.

Whitty, G. (1989) The New Right and the National Curriculum: state control or market forces? *Journal of Education Policy* **4**(4), 329–41.

Woods, P. (1987) Becoming a junior: pupil development following transfer from infants. In A. Pollard (ed.), *Children and Their Primary Schools*. Lewes: Falmer Press.

Woods, P. (1988) Managing the primary teacher's role. In S. Delamont (ed.), *The Primary School Teacher*. Lewes: Falmer Press.

Wragg, E.C., Bennett, S.N. and Carré, C.G. (1989) Primary teachers and the National Curriculum. *Research Papers in Education*, **4**(3), 17–37.

Name Index

Subject Index